INDIA
A Political Economy of Stagnation

India
A Political Economy
of
Stagnation

Prem Shankar Jha

BOMBAY
OXFORD UNIVERSITY PRESS
DELHI CALCUTTA MADRAS
1980

Oxford University Press

OXFORD   LONDON   GLASGOW
NEW YORK   TORONTO   MELBOURNE   WELLINGTON
NAIROBI   DAR ES SALAAM   CAPE TOWN
KUALA LUMPUR   SINGAPORE   HONG KONG   TOKYO
DELHI   BOMBAY   CALCUTTA   MADRAS   KARACHI

Photoset by Spads Photosetting Industries (P) Ltd., Bombay
Printed by Raj Bandhu Industrial Company, New Delhi-110 064
and published by R. Dayal, Oxford University Press
2/11 Ansari Road, Daryaganj, New Delhi-110002

To Usha
in fond memory

Preface

This book sets out to examine the causes of the onset of economic stagnation in 1966 after fifteen years of seemingly healthy growth. By the penultimate year of the third five-year plan (1964-65) it seemed that India was well on the way to achieving an economic 'take-off'. Yet only two years later the momentum of growth had been broken, for nearly all the key economic indicators were moving inexorably downwards. In attempting to explain this turnabout in the country's fortunes, I have taken issue not only with the explanations put forward by the Government from time to time, but also some of those espoused by professional economists.

Without denying the importance of purely economic factors, it is my contention that these do not provide a sufficient explanation for the virtual reversal of growth trends, particularly in the secondary (i.e. industrial) sector of the economy, after 1966, and the onset of a stagnation which has not been broken even by two spurts in agricultural production under the spur of the green revolution. The theme of this book is that the decisive cause of economic stagnation after 1966 is political and not economic. It is the rise to dominance of an intermediate class or stratum consisting of market-oriented peasant proprietors, small manufacturers, traders and other self-employed groups, which benefited from economic stagnation and had a vested interest in its perpetuation. The growing political power of this class was reflected in the steady reinforcement of economic controls on all industrial activity in the country until these applied a severe brake to the growth of output and employment in the organized sector. (It is for instance against the law in India for a company with excess productive capacity to increase its output, even if there is an acute shortage of its products and the government is having to import these in order to bridge the gap between demand and supply). The large manufacturer in particular has to struggle through a forest of red tape to increase his production, and the instinctive reaction of the government to any request from him for an industrial licence is one of deep suspicion.

I have deliberately said above that the rise of the intermediate class was reflected in the *reinforcement* of a regime of economic controls, and not the *imposition* of controls, because it is my belief that historically the controls came first. Licensing and price control laws were very much in evidence during the Second World War and were never wholly lifted after it ended. They were reimposed, and their scope was widened, during the first Plan. The foreign exchange crisis during the first years of the second Plan (1956–61) saw the rapid imposition of a host of fresh import controls, as well as higher tariffs and excise duties.

The genesis of economic controls lay therefore in the government reactions to specific crises. But their imposition changed the pattern of income generation in society and with it the distribution of wealth. For instance those who had managed to import a large variety of consumer durables before the ban on such imports came in force in 1957, made huge profits on their resale. The Second World War had given rise to huge blackmarket profits, and the continuation of a variety of price controls throughout the 'forties and 'fifties swelled these profits. The entire period therefore saw an accumulation of trading or commercial capital. The government's failure to supplement the ban on the import of non-essential consumer goods in 1957 with a complementary ban on their domestic manufacture enabled the erstwhile importers to become manufacturers overnight using their contacts with their principals abroad to obtain machinery, know-how and brand names. The conversion of commercial into industrial capital was thus almost fatally easy, and the urban intermediate class of traders and small manufacturers was vastly reinforced.

Since this class had benefited from economic controls it tried, not unnaturally, to perpetuate and even strengthen the regime of shortages. The ways in which growing income and wealth, i.e. economic power were converted into political power are described in Chapters 5 and 6.

The existence of an intermediate class, or to be more precise, several intermediate classes, has been recognized in Marxist sociology, not least by Marx himself. Indeed Marx went even further and recognized that they had a vested interest in preventing the development of capitalism, i.e. in preventing what we would today call economic growth. In the Communist manifesto he made the prescient remark that the peasant, the artisan, the trader and the small manufacturer aim at nothing less than 'holding back the wheel of history'.

But Marx did not follow up this insight because he clearly believed that the advance of capitalism, with the concentration of capital into larger and larger manufacturing units with a higher 'organic composition of capital', could not be prevented. The intermediate strata were therefore doomed. They were essentially transitional classes whose study was not particularly rewarding to a sociologist who, in the tradition of Rousseau, was primarily interested in discovering the conditions in which man would attain freedom from alienation. As such, Marx concentrated on the last stage of capitalism and the transition to socialism, and neglected the early stages of the capitalist transformation.

Marx's insight was almost completely lost in the work of his followers, until resurrected by the Polish economist M. Kalecki in the late 'fifties. This book owes a great deal to Kalecki's treatment of intermediate regimes and the first application of his thesis to India by Dr K.N. Raj.

The intermediate class that I have defined above and in Chapters 5 and 6 is not necessarily a transitional class. Nor is it the new petty bourgeoisie' of late capitalism that has been extensively discussed by modern Marxist sociologists. It is truly the nascent bourgeoisie of early capitalism, but in countries that have started late on the capitalist road, it occupies an intermediate position between implanted 'late' capitalist formations i.e. professionally managed concerns often imposed on the underdeveloped countries by colonial rulers, and the truly transitional and doomed intermediate strata of artisans, tenant-farmers and others who are the left-overs of feudal or pre-capitalist formations.

The chief value of this book lies in the attempt it makes to trace the effects of economic development on the distribution of political power and the result of shifts in the latter on the future pattern of economic development. It is thus a true political-economy, in the sense of trying to incorporate political and economic *variables* in a single overall model of development.

Purely economic explanations of the pattern of development in a country, in terms of material balances and Harrod-Domar type relationships are either forced to ignore human motivations, or worse still to make simplistic assumptions about them. In the final analysis therefore they fail to illuminate the process of social change. In fairness it must be pointed out that most liberal growth-economists today are aware of the above limitations and seek to bring political and social factors explicitly into the picture. But these are usually treated as *parameters* of an economic model (e.g. the interconnection between the Japanese family system and the pattern of industrial relations in that country, or the limitations imposed by a democratic system on a government's capacity to take hard decisions) rather than variables in a single politico-economic model of change.

While the incorporation of political power as an explicit variable in the model of Indian economic development is the principal merit of this book, I am aware of the fact that the analysis itself could be more exhaustive. Research in this field has been hampered partly by the absence of any significant prior work along these lines. For instance nearly all orthodox analyses of the Indian political scene have so far focussed on caste and creed, not class. Marxist analyses have been even less helpful, for they have by and large been hamstrung by their adherence to imported notions of class and in particular to a six or eight-fold classification of society into various factions of the bourgeoisie, the proletariat and the peasantry. Although such a 'functional' and descriptive classification is present in Marx's writings, it is a part of his polemic and not of his exposition of historical materialism. In his analysis of social change, Marx recognized explicitly that the concept of class could be used as a tool for analysing social change only if society was viewed as consisting of two mutually opposed classes, arrayed against each other across a central line of conflict. A six or eight-fold classification is useless as an analytical tool, for it obscures instead of revealing the fundamental lines of conflict in society.

As a result I have had to rely mostly on information collected by other authors with quite different hypotheses in mind, and often of a purely incidental nature. A 'sifting' exercise of this type is not unrewarding, for it often enables one to highlight implications that the authors were not aware of and to underline the significance of what may have seemed to them to be of secondary

importance. But it is no substitute for field work directly aimed at
validating or qualifying the hypotheses with which one has started.
As such, a great deal of what I have said in the middle chapters of
this book concerning the rise of the intermediate class needs to be
treated as a set of promising hypotheses rather than as settled
conclusions. If this book inspires further research on these lines,
it will have served a large part of its purpose.

This book also bears the imprint of its origin, as the work of a
journalist rather than an academic economist. The difference is
visible in the absence of exhaustive references to the works of
other academics who have written on the various issues that I
have touched upon. Nor have I explicitly referred to all the articles
and books that I have read, for I have fallen into the bad habit,
common to all journalists who have to write against deadlines,
of not keeping an accurate record of my reading.

But against this disadvantage I have enjoyed an unparalleled
access to primary sources of information. It is the attempt to make
sense of the immense volume of information which has flowed in
daily for over twelve years on all aspects of social change in India,
that has given birth to this book. The economic chapters in particular which form the base of my analysis, are founded entirely on
primary sources of information—newspaper reports and the official
statistics published by the government. I am aware that others
have travelled parts of the same road and that some have come to
somewhat different conclusions. If I have not mentioned their
works explicitly, it is only because the nature of my work has prevented me from keeping as closely in touch with the writings of
academics and professional economists as I would have liked.

Although the political analysis of the book has been brought
forward till March 1978, the main focus remains the years from
1966 to 1976. These were the years when the forces of stagnation
were most clearly visible in the economy. Since 1976 two major
changes have taken place, which have partially obscured the working of the politico-economic model described in this book. These
are the second spurt in agricultural production and the sharp rise
foreign exchange remittances to India by Indians working abroad.
The first has led to an increase in the consumption of fertilisers of
25 per cent per year in the last three years (after a four-year stagna-

tion) a rise in the output of cereals from a previous peak of 108 million tonnes (1970–71) to 130 million tonnes (1978–79) and a glut of some principal cash crops like cotton and sugar-cane. The second has ended the perennial shortage of foreign exchange which had given birth in the late 'fifties to the regime of production and import controls which started the rapid rise of the intermediate class.

Thus in many important ways, the economic situation has returned to what it was during the first Plan (1951–56). The two major structural constraints to growth which have dominated development strategy since 1956, namely shortages of foodgrains and cash crops and of foreign exchange have eased. With this the purely economic forces which helped the intermediate class attain dominance have weakened. This shift is noticeable in small but significant policy changes, most of which occurred in 1978, after the final draft of this book had already been written. There was a major liberalization of the import of industrial raw materials and semi-manufactures in April 1978. This was accompanied by some liberalization in the import of capital goods, in as much as Indian companies were permitted to float international tenders for obtaining capital goods, subject only to scrutiny by a committee of secretaries to the economic departments of the government.

In the rural areas also, the availability of large buffer stocks of foodgrains and of generally easy supply conditions has given the Janata government the courage to push ahead with the programmes designed to create productive employment and to mitigate the under-employment of the rural poor, despite the fact that all of these may not immediately yield an increase in output commensurate with the rise in consumption. These include small-farmer development programmes, food-for-work schemes (which consumed a million tonnes of grains in 1978–79) and a variety of irrigation, dairying, handloom, handicraft and agro-industrial enterprise development schemes. Together there can be little doubt that these are making an appreciable dent on rural unemployment and under-employment. At 3 million hectares a year the rate of spread of irrigation is almost double of what it was during the fourth and fifth Plans and is generating around 120 million man-days of extra work in agriculture every year, (apart from the direct employment

created by the schemes themselves). Above all, the easy availability
of food and raw materials has helped to keep prices almost completely stable between October 1974 and March 1979. Since inflation has been the prime mode of transfer of real incomes to the
intermediate class from the other strata of society, its absence has
blunted, albeit only marginally, the edge of social conflict in the
towns, even as the programmes of rural employment have done so
in the villages.

But these recent changes do not invalidate the thesis presented
in this book. The intensity of class conflict may have lessened, but
the class configuration of society has not changed. The relative
rate of impoverishment of the strata falling outside the intermediate
class may have slowed down but the dominance of this class has
not been shaken and is manifested daily in dozens of government actions, many of which have been touched upon in Chapter 8.
Most important of all, the parasitic nature of the intermediate
class, which fattens on economic stagnation, has not altered. The
equilibrium in the Indian polity therefore remains an unstable
one, which can easily be tipped over towards self-reinforcing
economic decline and growing political anarchy by a return of the
conditions of scarcity which plagued the economy between 1957
and 1975. But the fact that the polity is in unstable equilibrium is by
itself no cause for dismay. Instability is implicit in the very attempt
to achieve rapid economic growth. Indeed any country that attempts
to do this within the framework of a stable political system is
aiming at the near-impossible. For economic development cannot
fail to unleash vastly powerful new forces in society, forces
which cannot be easily accommodated, and whose rise is in any
case bound to be resisted by the existing political order. What
is important for us is to understand the nature of these forces
and to see how best they can be accommodated and when necessary
curbed so as to create the maximum of good with the minimum
of disruption. That is what this book makes a modest attempt to do.

One final point needs to be made. Few readers will miss the fact
that I have employed Marxist sociological concepts in the middle
chapters of the book to analyse the causes of stagnation, while
in the concluding chapters where I outline an alternative strategy
of growth, I am advocating what are broadly speaking Gandhian

prescriptions. It may be tempting to dismiss this apparent contradiction as the product of muddled thinking or a clumsy attempt to marry dispassionate social analysis with Utopian social reform.

Such a conclusion would be a trifle hasty. It is my belief that the contradiction between Gandhi and Marx is more apparent than real. The incompatibility is deduced from the fact that Marx considered the development of capitalism inevitable and looked to the completion of the process to liberate man from the chains of bondage to the capitalist system. Gandhi by contrast believed that industrialization and the advance of capitalism was not inevitable and could be, (indeed *had* to be) prevented or minimized, at least in India where there were already too many hands and too little work. But it must be remembered that Gandhi and Marx, as philosophers, shared a common goal—the freeing of man so as to enable him to achieve his fullest potential as a human being. Having accepted the inevitability of industrialization Marx looked to automation and the emergence of a classless society to minimize the time a worker had to spend in the soulless task of production, and maximize the leisure he needed to explore his own creativity. By contrast Gandhi believed that man expressed himself most directly *through* his work and opposed all those developments which would take variety, spontaneity and creativity out of it.

The passage of time has weakened the validity of Marx's assumptions, while strengthening those of Gandhi's. Indeed one can go so far as to say that Gandhi's prescriptions are different from Marx's precisely because he lived three quarters of a century later and saw the end of the Industrial road more clearly. Marx believed that the whole world would eventually become industrialized and expected the large-scale export of capital from the advanced countries to achieve this transformation. Time has shown that while the capitalist system has engulfed virtually the whole world it has not led to industrialization in the nations of "periphery", i.e. the so-called less developed countries. Gandhi's concern over the de-industrialization of traditional economies, through the destruction of artisanal industry, was shared in India by Palme-Dutt, a leading contemporary communist and the thesis of de-industrialization has become one of the central pivots of the neo Marxist literature on economic

development. Finally, Gandhi's implied advocacy of a two-sector
model of industrial growth with the minimization of the modern
industrial sector (it is doubtful whether he ever seriously envisaged
the complete eradication of modern industry) found its closest
parallel in Mao's China.

The hypotheses explored in this book have taken a long time to
mature. It is therefore impossible for me to thank all those who
have contributed to this process over the years through discussions,
suggestions for further reading and occasional insights. I would
however like to single out Vijay Joshi and Gopal Krishan of Oxford,
Rajni Kothari of the Centre for the Study of Developing Societies,
New Delhi, Gilbert Etienne of the Graduate Institute for International Studies, Geneva, and Maya Chadda of William Paterson
College, New Jersey for reading my first draft and offering a number of invaluable suggestions. My debt to Smt. Chadda in particular
for reading the subsequent drafts and offering constructive com-
ments is hard to repay.

CONTENTS

Part I

Part II

Part III

CONTENTS

PART I

1 / End of a Dream

TWENTY-EIGHT YEARS AGO, when India first embarked on its experiment in democratic planning, the policy makers had no doubt about where they wanted it to go. Their goals were to increase consumption, improve housing, make the population literate and the country self-reliant.

They also entertained few doubts about how these goals would be achieved. Industrialization, more specifically investment in heavy industry, would lay the base for future increases in productivity, and the fruits of 150 years of science and technology which were unavailable to the nations of the west when they embarked on industrialization, would help the poor nations to bridge the gap between them and the rich nations.

In the last ten years this dream has turned into a nightmare. From planning confidently for a better tomorrow, the country and its government have been reduced to fighting frantically to hold on to the few gains they have made so far. And as succeeding five year Plans have been cut, first to the 'core' and then to the 'hard' core, it has become more and more evident that even this battle is being lost.

The present government is putting most if not all, of the blame for this on the fuel crisis and the worldwide inflation of the 'seventies. In much the same way, previous Congress regimes had blamed the country's economic misfortunes on wars, first with China and then with Pakistan, the suspension of American aid in 1965 and the droughts of 1965, 1966 and 1972. Implicit in this view of economic development is the belief that the current difficulties are merely transitory. This is based on a faith that the interplay of economic forces tends naturally to cause a rise in production and income and that all that a government needs to do is to remove the obstacles to this natural process.

Thus in the official litany, health, education and even agricultural programmes are not abandoned when a five-year plan is cut to the core, but only 'postponed' till the return of better times. If in the meantime impoverishment, disease and unemployment increase because of the remorseless growth of population, this is no cause for alarm because the faster rate of growth which will become possible once the 'sinews of the economy' have been built, will mop up the backlog.

The time has come, however, to question these cosy assumptions. The postponement of welfare and employment-oriented investment is not a new development. It began as far back as during the second Plan, when the government first defined the 'core' sector. Since then the axe has fallen, regularly on social, educational and welfare expenditures. Even agriculture has not escaped unscathed.

Partly because of this, after a quarter century of effort, the goals the country set for itself seem actually to have receded from view. The production of foodgrains has almost doubled but the average man eats no more than he did in 1951. Fewer people, on the whole, die of malaria, typhoid, cholera and small pox, but many more children have to do without milk. The area under crops of all kinds has increased but the forests have dwindled and each year the rains carry away more and more precious topsoil to the sea.

Industry has grown fast, but urban slums have grown even faster. The number of people with degrees has increased, but the number of people without jobs, has grown more rapidly. Twenty-five years ago, the country had enough food but no machines; now it has a technical base and the skills to build most of its own machines but has to import food and fertilizers.

Paradoxically, these failures have gone hand in hand with a progressive refinement of planning techniques and elaboration of planning models. The first five-year Plan (1951–52 to 1955–56) was little more than a collective of ongoing projects and its projections were derived from a simple application of the Harrod-Domar growth model. Yet in terms of achievements it was by far the most successful plan this country has ever implemented. Aided by good rains, the country exceeded the target for food production, and exceeded or attained nearly all the targets set for other areas of the economy.

The refinement of planning techniques developed with the second Plan. The economy was split into more and more sectors with detailed input and output calculations being made for each. The targets for the fifth Plan (1974–75 to 1978–79) were calculated on the basis of a 66-sector input-output model. For the sixth, the Planning Commission elaborated this further and constructed an 89-sector model. But the success of any planning exercise must ultimately be judged by its results for the economy. By this test, each succeeding Plan after the first one, has been more and more of a resounding failure.

Table 1.1
Targets and achievements in successive Plans

	I Plan	II Plan	III Plan	IV Plan (Prov.)
1. *Increase in Net income*				
(a) Target	10–11%	25%	34%	28%
(b) Actual	18%	21.5%	13.5%[1] (19.6%)	13%
2. *Investment (% of 1) (2)*				
(a) Target	6.75%	11%	14–15%	16–17%[3]
(b) Actual	7.3%	12.5%	13.4%	10.8%
3. *Foodgrains*				
(a) Target	17%	15%	32%	30%
(b) Actual	20%	18%	−12%[1]	9%[5]
4. *Industrial Production*				
(a) Target	—	64%[2]	70%	57%
(b) Actual	35%	40%[4]	64%	9.5%

1 The comparison is invalid because of a drought in 1965. A better index is the growth from 1960–61 to 1964–65, figures for which are given in brackets.
2 Of factory establishments (II Five Year Plan, p. 69)
3 17–18% in III Plan draft and 13.8% in IV Plan.
4 III Plan, p. 39.
5. Taking 107 million tonnes the best that can be achieved (1970-71 was 107.8 million tonnes under the present circumstances. This is rather optimistic estimate. The average yield of 1970-71 to 1973-74 was around 104 million tonnes.

Official spokesmen and a number of economists have sought to explain the paradox in one or more of three ways:
(1) That the statistics on which the plans are constructed, have been either inadequate or faulty;

(2) That the policy measures which were a precondition to the success of the plans were never carried out;

(3) That setbacks occurred which upset all the calculations of the planners but which could not possibly have been foreseen by them.

There is some truth in all of these explanations, but neither singly nor together can they explain the systematic divergence of targets from achievements which has characterized the third and fourth Plans and the three intervening years of the Plan 'holiday' and the first year of the fifth Plan when the investment in real terms instead of going up by 40 per cent, as envisaged by the planners has fallen to about 80 per cent, of what it was during 1972–73, the penultimate year of the fourth Plan.[1]

The first contention is the easiest to dispose of: inaccurate statistics can bias individual targets, resulting in overproduction in some sectors and underproduction in others. But they will not lead to a systematic divergence between targets and achievements in general aggregates like national income, net investment, or the index of industrial production, unless all the biases happen to operate *in the same direction*. This is a very tall assumption to make even for one plan period, let alone two or three. If statistical inaccuracies do not bias calculations in one direction only, underproduction in some sectors resulting from over-optimistic input-output assumptions should be offset wholly or partly by overproduction resulting from unduly pessimistic assumptions for other sectors of the economy. Thus the lack of accurate data is an argument against excessive elaboration in planning. It cannot serve as an excuse for the repeated failure to attain even the broader targets.

In one sense the second explanation is a tautology. Since the five-year plans were not conjured up out of thin air, there must have been a set of policy measures which, if vigorously implemented, would have made it possible to attain the targets set out in them. But what were those measures, and could they have been implemented within the framework of a federal democracy?

The second, third and successive plans have been based on three broad premises; that the government would enact land reforms to remove institutional hurdles to greater productivity;

that in the heavy industrial sector, there would be enough skilled labour and managerial expertise to ensure that projects were completed on time and within the budgeted sums of money, and finally, that the government would impose austerity on the people and self-restraint on itself to first generate the maximum of investible resources and then to make sure these were not frittered away in non-developmental spending.

The first two assumptions were quite unrealistic. The government's attempt to enact land reforms was not only frustrated by the dominant farm lobby but actually perverted to enable landowners to increase their holdings at the expense of tenants and sharecroppers. What is more, the government soon found out that it was unrealistic to expect industries embodying sophisticated technologies transplanted from rich to poor nations to work well from the very start. As it turned out, nearly every major industrial project in the public sector took on an average two years longer and cost 40 per cent more to set up than the planners had anticipated. Then when the factories were ready the government found that the country had neither the managers nor the skilled workmen to run them efficiently.

While the advocates of a capital-intensive strategy of growth have blamed the government for its failure to take the policy decisions needed to make it succeed, the government itself has put most of the blame for the miserable performance of the economy since 1966 on a string of unforeseen setbacks. These include the Sino-Indian war of 1962 and the resulting increase in defence expenditures, the Indo-Pak war of 1965 and the suspension of aid which followed it, the two droughts of 1965 and 1966, the American aid which followed it, the two droughts of 1965 and 1966, the Bangladesh crisis of 1971 and the drought of 1972.

These blows did undoubtedly hurt the economy. But they cannot by any means be considered decisive. To begin with, it is true that after the Sino-Indian war, the expenditure on defence trebled in four years—from around Rs 300 crores in 1962 to over Rs 900 crores in 1966. But this did not lead to a decline in the rate of investment. Indeed, this reached its peak of 13.4 per cent of the national income in 1965–66, the very year of the first great drought and the Indo-Pak war. In absolute terms also, gross capital formation at constant prices rose steadily from around Rs 2500 crores in 1960–61 to Rs 3200 crores in 1965–66 (in 1960–61 prices). Nor was there any slackening in the rate of growth of industrial output—which averaged more than 9 per cent a year during the third Plan.

And just as these misfortunes did not dampen the growth of investment and industrial production, the unforeseen boon of five good harvests in a row, coinciding with the wheat revolution (1967 to 1971) did not arrest the steady decline in investment and savings and the stagnation of industry and employment, which began in 1966–67.

A starting point in understanding what has gone wrong after 1965–66 is provided by a close study of the income, production and employment statistics of the last twenty-five years. These show unambiguously that in 1966, the fortunes of the economy changed alarmingly for the worse. In fact the year 1966–67 marks a decisive turning point when a healthy if modest economic growth turned into a prolonged economic decline.

This reversal of trends is most clearly visible in industrial production. The following tables make this only too clear.

Table 1.2
Growth of Industrial Production

Industrial Production	1950–51	1965–66	1972–73
1. General index (1956=100)	73(1951)	203(1965)	256(1973)
2. Finished steel (million tons)	1.10	4.50	5.10
3. Cement (million tons)	2.70	10.80	15.50
4. Textiles (million yards)	4,618.00	7,440.00	7,924.00
5. Sugar (million tons)	1.10	3.50	3.90
6. Paper ('000 tons)	114.00	558.00	733.00
7. Power generation (billion volts)	4.20	33.00	63.60

Thus while the production of steel, cement, and paper all went up by around 12 per cent a year in the first fifteen years, it went up by a mere 1.4 per cent, 5 per cent, and 4 per cent respectively in the next seven. For sugar, the figures are 10 per cent and 1.5 per cent; for textiles, 3.5 per cent and 0.5 per cent; and for power generation approximately 18 per cent and 10 per cent. Not surprisingly, the general index of industrial production rose by nine per cent a year in the first 14 years of planning, but only three per cent a year in the next eight (these figures are close approximation).

Agriculture

The trends in agricultural production are less clearcut partly because of the vagaries of the monsoon, and partly because of the major technological breakthrough that gave birth to the wheat revolution. Even so, there has been a marked decline in the rate of growth in the second decade of planned development in comparison to the first. Whereas agricultural production went up by 46 per cent between 1950-51 and 1959-61, it rose by only 28 per cent in the next ten years. Similarly, the production of food-grains rose at a compound annual rate of 3.3 per cent between 1949-50 and 1959-60 and 2.64 per cent between 1959-60 and 1969-70. Indeed if one separates the figures for wheat from the rest, the decline is even more dramatic, as Table 1.3 shows clearly:

Table 1.3
Rate of Growth of Output of
Selected Crops*

	1949-50 to 1959-60	*1959-60 to 1969-70*
Rice	3.30	1.80
Maize	4.30	3.52
Jowar	2.80	-0.73
Bajra	3.20	5.39
Pulses	3.10	0.48
Oilseeds	3.40	1.80
Sugarcane	4.00	1.67
Cotton	4.90	0.75
Jute	2.70	0.60
Wheat		

* Draft Fifth Five-Year Plan, Government of India, Planning Commission, Vol. II, Chapter 1, Annexure III, p. 48.

In the above table, on the one hand, bajra and maize show relatively good rates of growth because production has benefited from the introduction of new seed varieties, while on the other hand the decline in the growth of jute products is partly because of a shrinkage in the acreage under jute in the 1960's. This has taken place because while competition from synthetics in world markets has held jute prices in check, the domestic price of rice— its main competitor—has soared.

But the remaining figures, all tell the same story. There has been a sharp decline in the rate of growth of output, to levels below what is needed to keep pace with the rise in population in the 'sixties (2.3 per cent per year). As a result, per capita production (gross of all foodgrains except wheat, maize and bajra, particularly those of pulses, edible oils and cotton) has declined during the 1960's. The following table illustrates the extent of decline:

Table 1.4
Production per capita of
main consumer goods

Commodity	Per Capita (gross) Production		
	1951	*1965*	*1972*
Cereals (kg)	124	140	146
Pulses (kg)	21.2	22.5	17.4
	1950-51	*1965-66*	*1971-72*
Sugar (kg)	3.0	5.1	6.7
Edible oils (kg) including vanaspati	3.2	4.4	4.0
Textiles (metres) (cotton & manmade)	14.4	16.8	14.1

National Income

On the face of it the growth of national income does not show any marked change between the first and second decades of planning. While it grew by 45 per cent between 1950–51 and 1960–61 it increased by a further 42 per cent between 1960–61 and 1970–71. But this is partly because, as the figures cited so far show, the real break occurred in 1965–66. The fact is that the national income grew by 20 per cent in four years between 1960–61 and 1964–65 (a year of good monsoon).

But this is not the whole story. The apparent constancy of the growth rate over the two decades hides a serious weakening of the structure of the economy. Most of the growth in the second decade has taken place in the service industries—transport, communications, trade, banking, insurance, rents on real estate, public administration, defence and other services. The share of this tertiary sector in national income has risen from 28·7 per cent in 1960–61 to 35·4 per cent in 1974–75, while that of industry, construction, public utilities and agriculture has declined correspondingly from 71·3 per cent to 64·6 per cent.

It is a symptom of this shift that while employment in mining and organized industry has grown by 48 per cent between 1961 and 1975, in organized trade and commerce, transport and communication it has grown by 61 per cent, while employment in the services sector has increased by 87 per cent. This raises the question once again of the appropriateness of GNP estimates as an index of economic growth in a poor country. The gross national product, by aggregating the value of everything that can command a price in the market in terms of a common denominator—money—completely obliterates the distinction between material goods and services of various kinds. As many economists have pointed out, this is hardly legitimate even in the case of advanced economies where an increase in GNP through a rise in the earnings of musicians may on balance be preferable to one resulting from a rise in the production of crude oil and its conversion into petrochemicals (on the grounds that the first is non-polluting and reflects an increase in spiritual welfare while the second exhausts the earths' dwindling stock of oil and further spoils the environment). But in the poor nations the distinction needs to be made for the very opposite reasons. A man who has already met all his basic needs of food, clothing, shelter and employment may welcome the opening of a new store next to his home, even if he has to pay more than when he made his purchases at a supermarket several miles away. The increase in distribution costs may reflect a genuine rise in his welfare. But the choice means nothing to someone who does not have enough money to meet his basic needs at any shop whether nearby or far away. The rise in distribution costs can then hardly be termed an improvement in welfare.

There is thus an urgent need at the very least, to supplement national income figures for poor countries with estimates of its net material product (the concept used by the USSR and the east European countries) which do not take a large part of the tertiary sector into account.

Employment

If the picture painted by the indices of current output is alarming it grows immeasurably darker, when one sketches in the trends in the key indicators of economic growth—employment, savings and investment.

Total non-agricultural employment in the organized sector rose from 12.09 million in 1961 to 15.46 million in 1966— a rise of 28 per cent. In the next seven years, however, it grew from 16.19 million in 1966 (the discrepancy is caused by the adoption of a more comprehensive definition of the organized sector) to 18.82 million, an increase of only 16 per cent.

But these figures fail to tell the whole story. For of these, 7.05 million in 1961, and 11.88 million in 1973 were government servants, of whom, in turn, only around 0.77 million in 1961 and 2.58 million in 1973 were employed in productive enterprises run by the Central and state governments. The rest were salaried employees ranging from railwaymen at one end of the scale to an army of *chaprasis* (peons) at the other.

Since many jobs have been created in the bureaucracy in response to political rather than economic compulsions, the rate of growth of employment is a poor index of the rate of growth of productive employment in the economy. A better index is the growth of employment in the organized private sector, and here the trend is truly disturbing. While employment in the private organized sector grew from 5.04 million to 6.81 million—a rise of 33 per cent—during the third five-year Plan, in the subsequent eight years (1966-67 to 1974-75) it declined fractionally to 6.80 million. Even after adding the 500,000 or so workers in industries nationalized during this period, the rise in employment is only marginal. No other developing country can boast of so dismal a performance! In fact since private entrepreneurs are not wholly insensitive to the rising tide of misery and joblessness around them, and have also created sinecures for the children, widows and relatives of their employees, in addition to employing engineering graduates and diploma holders as apprentices under various government acts, the real growth of employment here is probably even smaller than these figures suggest.

Savings and Investment

In so far as the data available is accurate, the estimates of net domestic savings and aggregate net investment showed parallel increases to a peak in 1965-66, followed by a sharp decline till 1969-70. Thereafter both savings and investment rallied for three years, only to decline once again in the last year of the fourth Plan (1973–74) and the first year of the fifth.

However, the data are themselves subject to such wide variations that these conclusions need to be carefully hedged with qualifications.

The table below gives the different estimates for these two indicators, as prepared by various organizations at various times to illustrate just how wide is the variance between them:

Table 1.5
Estimates of Net Domestic Capital Formation as a Ratio of National Income

	1968-69	69-70	70-71	71-72	72-73	73-74	74-75
1. RBI Currency & Finance Report 1971-72	8.2	8.6	9.4	10.0	—	—	—
2 RBI Currency & Finance Report 1973–74	8.4	8.5	10.1	11.4	11.0	10.0	—
3 RBI Currency & Finance Report 1974–75	—	—	—	—	12.6	12.1	11.8
4 CSO White Paper on National Income 1976	—	11.5	11.8	11.4	13.2	12.2	11.8
5 Planning Commission —Mid-Term Appraisal of 4th Plan	8.4	8.4	8.3	—	—	—	—

The variations in the figures given are a result not only of conceptual changes but also the frequent revision of data that has ostensibly been collected on the same basis, for the same years. Thus the difference between RBI figures given in the Currency and Finance Reports of 1971–72 and 1973–74 and the Planning Commission estimates result to a large extent from the exclusion of depreciation reserves in the former and their inclusion in the latter. (See RBI Currency & Finance Report of 1971–72, p. 9). Similar conceptual differences underlie the wide gap between the CSO's estimates and those of the RBI. But the differences between the RBI's own estimates and between the CSO's estimates in its national income estimates published in 1973 and 1975 (1973 not given here) are the result of unexplained and perhaps arbitrary changes in the data. A close look at the disaggregated statistics of savings and capital formation given by the Central Statistical Office (National Accounts and Statistics 1960–61 to 1972–73 disaggregated tables shows that the change is mainly in the savings and capital formation in the household sector. This is a residual sector comprising individuals, non-government, non-corporate enterprises in agriculture, trade and industry, non-profit making organizations like charitable trusts, etc. Furthermore, household savings are subdivided into those in the form of financial assets, which are easy to calculate accurately, but make up about one third of the total, and those in the form of physical assets, which make up two thirds of household savings and almost half of the aggregate net savings in the country. Since this item includes dubious categories like house construction, and since almost the whole of this saving is in practice taking place in the rural areas, the estimates are little better than informed guesses. In the CSO's disaggregated tables, the estimates of net domestic capital formation by households went up by Rs 1,006 crores in 1966–67, without any explanatory footnote. Subsequent enquiries by the writer and others have not elicited any satisfactory explanation. This increase caused the ratio of net savings to national income to rise to 15.4 per cent in 1966–67 and effectively masked the full extent of the decline in savings and capital formation which may have taken place in subsequent years.

In this welter of conflicting data only broad trends can therefore be discerned. These are given in the table below:

Table 1.6
Estimates of Net Domestic Savings (at current prices) as a Percentage of National Incomes

Sector	'50–51	'65–66	'68–69	'69–70	'70–71	'71–72	'72–73	'73–74
1. Public	—	3.2	2.0	2.2	2.2	2.0	1.9	1.7
2. Private	—	0.4	0.2	0.4	0.6	0.5	0.3	0.3
3. Household	—	7.5	6.2	5.9	7.3	8.9	8.8	8.0
4. Total	5.0	11.1	8.4	8.5	10.1	11.4	11.0	10.0
5. Net inflow of foreign reserves	NA	2.3	1.3	0.8	1.2	1.5	0.8	0.8
6. Agg. Net Investment (4 & 5)	4.9	13.4	9.7	9.3	11.3	12.9	11.8	10.8

Sources: 1950–51 Third Plan Draft, Planning Commission

1965–66 Mid-Term Appraisal of Fourth Plan Planning Commission pp. 36–37

1966–67 to 1973–74 RBI Currency & Finance Reports.

The above data shows that both saving and investment rose from around 5 per cent in 1950–51 to a peak of 11.4 and 13.8 per cent respectively in 1965–66 and since then have stagnated with two phases of decline between 1966 and 1969 and from 1972–73 to 1974–75. However, if one takes into account the fact that a much larger part of the post 1967 savings is in the household sector, these figures indicate that the ratio of investment in productive activities and in the organized sector, to the national income, has almost certainly declined. Alternately even if this investment is taking place, it is in areas and by individuals over whom the government has little control. This is probably the reason why (accepting the latest CSO data as an improvement over the earlier figures) the rate of growth of the economy has slackened after 1965–66 even though the ratio of savings and investment to national income has not changed by very much.

Unambiguous Pattern

The behaviour of each of the above indicators since 1965–66 is alarming enough. But taken together they paint a truly bleak picture. The three basic facts which emerge are (a) industrial and agricultural output are growing, but at a snail's pace; (b) productive employment has ceased to grow; and (c) savings and investment are actually declining both as a proportion of national income and in crucial areas (such as the public sector) in absolute terms also. The pattern is unmistakable: just as a man first saves (or borrows someone else's savings), then sets up a factory, then employs workers and finally turns out a product, in a nation also saving precedes investment, the two precede the generation of employment, and all three must take place before there is an addition to the national product. Thus if savings and investment decline continuously, sooner or later employment and national product will also begin to fall. Indeed the decline may be about to set in. Since 1971–72, there has been virtually no rise in agricultural output, and only the barest increase in industrial production.

Even this took place mainly in 1972–73 when, thanks to an excellent cotton crop the previous year and the difficulties of the Bangladesh jute industry, the production of both cotton and jute textiles shot up. What is more, there is good reason to suspect that the weightage given to these two traditional industries in compiling the index of industrial production is excessive because it has not been revised since 1960–61. What is more, since 1974, employment has begun to decline perceptibly. The private organized sector employed 40,000 fewer people on March 31, 1974 than it had twelve months before. In late 1974 came a major recession in the building industry which may have thrown up to half a million people out of work although mainly in the unorganized sector. Since then the economy has slipped steadily into the valley of recession.

If the present trends are allowed to continue, there is reason to fear that the next three or four years may witness a decline in industrial production, and in the output of those sectors of the agricultural economy which have switched to higher-risk, capitalist farming.

The precise point at which this happens will be when the net capital formation in the economy become negative, i.e., when annual (gross) investment is no longer sufficient to maintain the capital stock, and replace the machinery that wears out. This may happen long before the net rate of investment actually becomes zero, because under the current accounting procedures net investment includes the provision made by companies towards depreciation, less the amount actually spent during the current year on replacing worn-out machinery. However, replacement costs tend to rise over any period of time, and do so very rapidly under inflationary conditions. Thus although a part of the depreciation reserve is being counted as net investment *today*, in reality, even the whole of it if put away year after year, may not suffice to meet the replacement cost of a plant ten years from now.

In this sense a number of industries in the country have already attained a negative rate of capital accumulation. In the steel industry, while the gross investment per tonne of steel of the Tata Iron & Steel Company, the oldest plant in the country, was Rs 1,180 in 1962, in the three Hindustan Steel plants (stage 1), set up in the late '50s and '60s it was Rs 1,900 per tonne and in Bokaro, set up a decade later it is expected to be around Rs 4,100 per tonne. Since steel prices even today remain pegged more or less to the lowest of those capital costs, not a single steel plant is generating enough depreciation and reserve funds to meet the cost of replacing its worn out equipment. HSL, for instance, has eaten steadily into its capital in all years but one, of its existence. As replacement costs mount its losses will also mount.

The estimates of capital formation published by the CSO confirm this impression. While the gross fixed capital formation by private corporate non-financial companies and by the Central government either directly or through non-departmental commercial undertakings rose by about 31 per cent between 1969–70 and 1972–73, the index of wholesale prices of machinery and transport equipment, and of intermediate products rose by 28 per cent and 45 per cent respectively in four years between 1969 and March 1973. What is worse, they rose even more sharply by another 33 per cent and 45 per cent respectively in the twelve months which followed. Since the eventual replacement cost of worn-out machinery will reflect this steep rise in prices, the rate of capital accumulation (net capital formation) is being squeezed both by the decline in real gross capital formation and the rise in replacement costs.

The pattern which has been traced out in the preceding paragraphs shows unmistakably that what India is experiencing is not economic growth but economic decline. This is difficult to grasp as much for linguistic as for emotional reasons. The whole lexicon of economic transformation is so impregnated with what Gunnar Myrdal has described as the 'bias towards optimism', that it is difficult even to find words to describe a long-term decline in the level of economic activity.

To talk of 'developing countries' regressing is self-contradictory and to talk of a downward 'growth path' is to border on absurdity. Yet, as Myrdal has shown there is not a shred of justification for this optimism. Economies do not just grow. They have to be *put* on a growth path and then *kept* there. The first needs not one but an interlocking group of policy decisions. The second requires a continuous monitoring of trends and the application of corrective measures whenever the economy tends to stray off the assigned growth path.

By the same token, once an economy begins to slide back towards poverty and stagnation, it becomes twice as hard to wrench it back onto a growth path again.

NOTES

1 For total Plan outlays see the Tables giving Five Year Plan outlays in Vol. II of the Reserve Bank of India's Currency & Finance Reports 1975–76, 1976–77, 1977–78 etc. Total Plan expenditure rose from Rs 3727 crores in 1972–73 to Rs 4188 crores in 1973–74, or 11.5% but the price rise in this period was 30 per cent. In 1974–75, Plan investment rose to Rs 5039 crores or about 22 per cent, but apart from the fact that prices rose again by around nine per cent, the 1975–76 figures are for gross capital formation which includes replacement of machinery and expenditure in residential and administrative premises. These account for about Rs 500 crores of the nominal increase.

2 / Agriculture

THE ONE AREA in which the long term economic decline has not been as clearly marked as elsewhere, is agriculture. Although the growth of agricultural output did slow down in the 1960's as compared to the 1950's, the decline was not as marked as in industry and the overall index of agricultural production concealed mixed trends, with the rate of growth of output of wheat and bajra (a millet) showing a sharp increase, over the previous decade. Since four-fifths of the country's population lives on agriculture, this should give some cause for comfort. But a close look at recent trends shows that the spurt in production resulting from the introduction of high yielding wheat, maize and bajra seeds in 1966–68 is almost over. As a result agricultural production is once stuck on a plateau. The highest output of foodgrains, of 107.8 million tonnes, was attained in 1970–71. Production has stayed below this level ever since.[1]

There is even now a good deal of reluctance to recognize that the so-called green revolution has lost its momentum. The Fifth Plan draft, issued as recently as in 1974, assumes blithely that the output of foodgrains will rise from 114 million tonnes in 1973–74 (the actual production that year was around 104 million tonnes) to 140 million tonnes by 1978–79. Of this increase around one-quarter is to come from the spread of multiple cropping and the balance from higher yields per acre, mainly through an extension of the green revolution to new areas and further increases in yields in the areas to which it has already come. Yet even as long ago as in 1972, it had already become clear that the green revolution had run out of steam.

The first major indication that the agricultural boom was over came when there was a mysterious and entirely unexpected fall in the output of foodgrains in 1971–72. Until as late as June 1972, Mr A.P. Shinde, the Central Minister of State for Food and Agriculture had been predicting an output of around 110 million tonnes of foodgrains. In fact the Central government received the first reports a few weeks later, that it was no more than 105–106 million tonnes, with utter disbelief.

It was soon forced to concede that the output of foodgrains had declined in 1971–72 by around 1.6 per cent despite a fairly good monsoon and, if its claims were to be accepted, a sharp increase in the area under the high-yielding seed varieties, and in the consumption of fertilizers. But revised statistics showed later that the fall had been of the order of 4 per cent. Hard pressed officials in New Delhi, preoccupied with the fight against the Maharashtra drought, preferred to put all the blame for the setback in 1971 on the weather. They received powerful support from the Agricultural Prices Commission, a body of experts set up by the government to advise it on the procurement and pricing policies for each crop. The APC pointed out that the monsoon had not been as good in 1971 as in 1970. For instance, of the increase in food-grains production of nearly eight million tonnes in 1970–71, over the previous year, Rajasthan alone had contributed four million tonnes, composed mainly of coarse grains which are grown on unirrigated land, while Uttar Pradesh had contributed another two million tonnes. In 1971–72, by contrast, the output of these two states alone had declined by almost four million tonnes.

However, this explanation left a number of questions unanswered. While some fall in the 1971–72 *kharif* (winter) harvest was to have been expected this should have been made up in part by the *rabi* (spring) crop, for which as the APC had pointed out, weather conditions had turned out to be exceptionally favourable. This was not all. In 1971–72, Punjab and Haryana took to growing *kharif* rice in a big way and their output increased by at least a million tonnes. Together therefore, these two developments should have more or less neutralized the adverse impact of the weather on the 1971–72 *kharif* harvest.

If so, what happened to the expected increase in output from the extension of the area under the high-yielding varieties? What, in particular, was the fate of the 'big push' to increase the cultivation of high-yielding paddy as a *rabi* or summer crop in the Ganga valley? Quite obviously weather alone was not the key to the riddle.

The other possibility, which New Delhi was understandably reluctant to face, was that the so-called green revolution had lost its momentum. As little as a year earlier such a view would have been a heresy. The bumper harvests of 1970–71 had induced an all-pervasive euphoria. A rice revolution was being confidently forecast and many people were predicting that the country would be producing 45 million tonnes of wheat by 1980. But even then, there was disturbing evidence that all was not well with the green revolution.

To begin with, there were unmistakable signs in the statistics collected by the Agricultural Prices Commission that the output of wheat was increasing by smaller and smaller amounts every year in Punjab, Haryana, and to a somewhat less marked extent in Uttar Pradesh. The decline in the rate of growth set in around 1968–69 in Punjab, and 1969–70 in Haryana. If the overall growth of wheat output in the country did not also decline it was only because the spread of the high-yielding varieties to new states kept one jump ahead of the decline in growth rate in each state.

By itself this would not have been too alarming. Indeed a trend towards diminishing returns is normal after the first effects of a major technological breakthrough have been absorbed by the economy. But the declining trend was not the result of a fall in the return on each additional dose of input. It was caused by a fall in the rate of growth of the application of inputs, notably of fertilizers.

Initially the ministry of agriculture was extremely reticent on this subject but in the face of mounting evidence it was forced to concede that not only was the demand for fertilizer growing far more slowly than the government had anticipated, but even the lower growth curve had tended to flatten out in the previous four years. Figures given to parliament by Mr Shinde in May 1971 showed that the consumption of fertilizers had risen by no more than 6 per cent in 1970–71 as against 15 per cent in 1969–1970. The government felt sufficiently alarmed to set up a high powered committee to enquire into the causes of the fall.

The committee's finding was quite unambiguous. Between 1969 and 1972, the consumption of fertilizers had grown by 15 per cent a year as against 40 per cent in the previous three years. But it was curiously myopic when it came to looking for the causes. There seemed to be a virtual unanimity of views that this was caused by various bottlenecks in supply. For instance it emphasized the lack of adequate credit facilities to enable the poorer farmers to buy fertilizers and the government's inability to move the fertilizer to the consumption centres in time to benefit the crops. It also suggested that farmers were not buying more fertilizers because they were not sure of getting water from the canals and state tube wells when they needed it.

Other explanations included the power famine in Punjab and Haryana, the high price of fertilizers, and the failure of the rice revolution to get under way. The last in turn, was attributed to the poor grain quality of the high-yielding varieties and their susceptibility to pests and water logging which made them unsuitable for planting in the *kharif* season.

This preoccupation with technical problems and bottlenecks in the supply of inputs prevented the experts from asking a number of questions that were even then obvious to laymen. For instance, it was not only in the consumption of fertilizers but also of power that the eastern and southern states were lagging behind Punjab and Haryana. Indeed many rural electrification projects were running at a loss in the eastern region because of lack of consumers. At the same time, there was a power famine in Punjab and Haryana even though the per capita availability of electricity in these states was far higher than in the east and south.

The failure to ask such a basic question gives rise to the suspicion that in 1972 (and for that matter even today) most scientists, agronomists and policy makers were wearing the wrong pair of spectacles. It was not the inadequate supply of power or fertilizer, in Punjab and Haryana that ought to have been worrying them, but the lack of *demand* for these inputs elsewhere in the country. Some of the other questions they should have been investigating were why had the spread of the high-yielding varieties ground to a virtual halt in Kerala? Why was the output of rice stagnating in Andhra, formerly the rice bowl of the country? Why did increases in the output of wheat begin to level off in Uttar Pradesh when only 32 per cent of the area under the crop was sown with the high-yielding varieties (1970–71) whereas in Punjab and Haryana this did not happen until over 65 per cent and 53 per cent had been brought under the new seeds respectively?

Nor were the various excuses for the failure of the rice revolution altogether convincing. They explained the reluctance of most farmers in the rice growing areas to take to high-yielding varieties in the *kharif* season, but not their failure to do so in the *rabi* and summer seasons. Indeed, once again it was the farmers of Haryana and Punjab who took eagerly to growing summer rice, while those of Bihar and Bengal lagged behind in growing a second crop. In 1972, the area under paddy in Punjab and Haryana alone was as great as the acreage under summer paddy in the rest of the country.

Table 2.1
Annual Output of Cereals
(Selected states, in million tonnes)

	Rice		Wheat		
	Andhra	Kerala	Punjab	Haryana	U.P.
1966–67	4.85	1.08	2.49	1.05	4.2
1967–68	4.67	1.12	3.35	1.47	5.8
1968–69	4.34	1.40	4.52	1.52	6.09
1969–70	4.70	1.21	4.80	2.12	6.31
1970–71	4.79	1.30	5.15	2.34	7.69
1971–72	4.71	1.35	5.62	2.40	7.55
1972–73	4.26	1.38	5.27	2.23	7.52
1973–74	5.35	1.35	5.26	1.81	6.01

Source: Compiled from reports of the Agricultural Prices Commission 1969–70 to 1974–75.

After 1972, the food situation grew steadily more precarious and it became increasingly clear that the wheat revolution was coming to a halt. The output of wheat touched a peak of 26.4 million tonnes in 1972 declined to 24.7 million tonnes in 1973 and much more sharply to 22 million tonnes in 1974. (In 1975, the wheat growing areas received the best winter rains in many a year, but the wheat crop only went up to 24.2 million tonnes).[2]

The government attributed the fall in 1974 to a decline of around 2.5 per cent in sown area, a shortage of fertilizers, severe frost in December and January and the subsequent failure of the winter rains. But these factors cannot explain the entire decline, let alone the failure to maintain the rising trend in production witnessed during the previous seven years.

The break in the wheat revolution might not have mattered so much if it had coincided with the long awaited breakthrough in the rice growing areas. But although the output of rice had been increasing at the rate of 3.5 per cent a year it was becoming more and more clear that technological, climatic and other factors precluded any repetition of the experience with wheat, at least in the immediate future.

Indeed there was reason to fear that even the present modest rate of growth would not be easy to maintain. Most of the increase in the output of paddy in the 'seventies had come from higher yields in a few selected areas such as the Thanjavur district of Tamil Nadu and the West Godavari district of Andhra Pradesh, and from paddy cultivation in areas where the crop was not grown before, such as Punjab and Haryana. But there is reason to believe that the same forces that halted the wheat revolution were also at work in many of these areas.

The causes were both technological and economic. In 1975 there was a good deal of talk about the dangers posed by rust, a plant disease that brings down wheat yields drastically, and the deteriorating quality of wheat seed. But these had little or no impact on crop yields. Rust, in particular, had made an appearance only in two small areas. But the government maintained a studied silence about the real threat that hung over the wheat revolution. This was the steady deterioration of the soil in the areas which had so far been the granaries of the country.

Soil management has indeed become the major preoccupation of agricultural scientists, particularly of those attached to the Punjab Agricultural University. Their experience has shown that whereas in the first four years of the wheat revolution, the soil in Punjab required mainly nitrogen, in the next four years it was the dosage of phosphatic fertilizers that has had to be increased progressively.

What is more, in several tests they also found that the soil was being increasingly drained of micronutrients like zinc, sulphur and iron. All in all, the scientists at the PAU have found that under the intensive rice-wheat cropping pattern currently in vogue in Punjab and Haryana the soil now needs double the quantity of nutrients to obtain the same per acre yields as eight years ago! It hardly needs to be stressed that what is happening in Punjab and Haryana is bound to take place sooner or later in other areas where high-yielding varieties and chemical fertilizers have come into use.

While technological factors thus required the farmer to invest more in inputs to get the same yield as before, economic considerations were compelling him to reduce his dosage of inputs. While the nation wanted the farmer to maximize the yield per acre of land under the plough, the farmer was more interested in maximizing his profit per acre by ensuring that the cost he incurred in using an extra dose of inputs was equalled or exceeded by his return from selling the extra output he obtained.

Unfortunately, crop response data collected from all over India by the Indian Agricultural Research Institute show that faced with the sharp increase in the cost of inputs in 1973 and 1974, the farmer was maximizing his profits by reducing the amounts that he used. For instance, with nitrogen costing Rs 4.35 per kg in 1974 as against Rs 2.10 two years earlier, and phosphorus costing Rs 4.60 as against Rs 2.30, the economically optimum dose of fertilizers had declined from 120 kg per hectare in 1972, to a mere 55 kg per hectare in 1974. This decline meant a loss of output of ten quintals of wheat per hectare. Similar statistics had also been collected in Thanjavur from paddy growers.

The government could make it profitable for farmers to get the maximum yield from their fields either by subsidizing the sale of fertilizers or by raising the support price of wheat to a level higher than that prevailing now in the market. But during the severe inflation of 1973–74, both were in any case ruled out by their strong inflationary impact of subsidies on an economy that was already suffering from chronic shortages and an excess of monetary demand.

The inescapable conclusion was that Punjab, Haryana and western U.P. had done what they can for the country and it would be idle to expect much more of them. The surplus needed to feed the towns, finance development and raise the standard of living had to come from other areas.

The government knew this, but by 1975 it was clear that its strategy of spreading the high-yielding varieties programme to new areas and to the small and marginal farmers had run into difficulties.

The truth is that a plentiful supply of inputs is not enough to ensure the spread of the high-yielding varieties. The farmer must be in a position to take advantage of them. For this he must have a large enough holding in a single plot to make it worth his while to sink a tube-well and he must cultivate the land himself.

These conditions are fulfilled over a large part of the net sown area in Punjab, Haryana and western U.P. In 1961-62 the average farm according to the National Sample Survey, was of 7.1 hectares in the Amritsar and Ferozepur districts of Punjab, and 4.17 to 6.46 hectares in western U.P. In 1969, Ladejinsky noted that in spite of the sharp increase in population, three out of four operational holdings in Punjab were still of more than 7.5 acres.[3]

What is more, as a consequence of the first round of land reforms in the 'fifties, the number of tenants in undivided Punjab declined from around half a million to no more than 80,000. Similarly, most of western U.P. lies outside the talukadari areas of the state (in which absentee landlordism in still common) and has a thriving tradition of peasant proprietorship.

Finally, all three states launched vigorous drives to consolidate land holdings, and the process was virtually completed in 1969.

The picture could not be more different in Bihar and Bengal. A large part of the land is still owned by absentee landlords, few tenants enjoy security of tenure, and the pressure of population on the land is almost unbearable. A decade ago, the average size of a farm in north Bihar and West Bengal was no more than 1.85 and 1.23 hectares respectively. Not only are they smaller now, but virtually no attempt has been made to consolidate individual holdings in the intervening years. By 1966 Bihar, for instance, consolidated no more than 89,000 hectares out of a total of 11 million! It is thus common to find a farmer with 20 acres of fertile, irrigable land chained to poverty by the fact that it is split into half a dozen tiny pieces, often scattered over two or three villages.

Institutional factors thus conspire against a growth in yields per acre; the peasant who tills the land for an absentee landowner and can be evicted at a moment's notice, has no incentive to improve it. The absentee landowner has no desire to do so either, and the few peasant proprietors who own enough land to make it worthwhile to sink a tube-well, often cannot because their holdings are fragmented.

As a result, the green revolution has only touched the surface of rural society. How few are the farmers who have benefited from it may be seen from the studies of the IADP districts carried out by Francine Frankel in 1967–70.[4] For instance, in the West Godavari district only one in every seven landowners has more than 10 acres. With most of the larger holdings concentrated in the less fertile upland areas, the consolidation of holdings far from complete, and much of the land held by non-cultivating owners, it is doubtful if even half of those who own large holdings are in a position to switch to the high-yielding varieties. The picture differs only in detail in Kerala, Bengal, Bihar and Tamil Nadu.

Poorer farmers and tenants have been able to switch to the new seed varieties only in areas where irrigation from government sources has brought the cost of doing so within their reach. However, without effective protection against eviction, tenants have been forced to surrender most of the extra yield from the land to the landlord. Miss Frankel noted that in the canal irrigated areas of West Godavari, the rent had increased by about one bag (2 maunds) per acre every year since 1963–64 and stood at 11 bags, which is 60 to 70 per cent of the average *kharif* crop in the Delta areas of the district, in 1968–69.

Thus the notion that there are substantial new areas which have yet to adopt the new seed varieties is false. The new wheat varieties, for instance, are now to be found in every wheat-growing state in the country. This is also true of the new rice varieties. However, there is evidence to show that in each area, nearly all those who are in a position to take early advantage of the package programme have already done so. Not surprisingly, their number is largest in Punjab and declines progressively as one moves to Haryana, western U.P. and Bihar, the other traditional wheat growing states. The number of farmers who have taken to wheat production in Bengal and Madhya Pradesh is very small indeed. The story is not much different in the case of rice. Outside Tamil

Nadu and a few districts of Andhra only a handful of farmers have taken to the new rice varieties in each district. While institutional factors have severely limited the number of farmers who can switch to capital intensive farming using the new high-yielding seeds, the sky-rocketing cost of inputs in the last three years has increased the working capital and therefore the financial risk involved in changing over to the new technology, further reduced the number of farmers in each district who are willing to make the change. For instance, diesel oil and fertilizers cost more than twice as much now as they did three years ago, and spare parts for pumps, tractors and so on, cost three times as much or more.

Even if the state governments show far greater zeal than they have so far in consolidating land holdings, sinking and running state-owned tube wells and arranging easy credit for the small farmers, not more than ten per cent of the farmers, owning perhaps a third of the land in the irrigable areas, will be able to switch over to the new technology. This is because there are obvious limits to the ability of a country that is starved of capital to adopt a technology which in the final analysis is highly capital intensive.

The high-yielding varieties programme cannot therefore be relied on to ensure a sustained growth of agricultural output in the future. For this the government will have to supplement it with an intermediate technology, which aims at more modest increases in the yield per acre, but spread over very much larger areas of the country.

But as yet it has made no attempt to develop such an alternative strategy in a systematic manner.

Dwindling Marketable Surpluses

The renewed stagnation of agriculture does not merely spell growing poverty and unemployment for the rural poor, but also threatens to strangle the future growth of industry. With a rising population, as the output of food stagnates the amount of grain coming to the urban markets shrinks from year to year and severely limits the amount that the government can invest during any particular year, without triggering off the wage-price spiral of inflation.

Indian planners are familiar with this constraint on development.

It has been very much in evidence ever since the partition of British India in 1947, when the new state of Pakistan inherited one-fifth of the population of the sub-continent, but one quarter of its food supply. The resulting shortage of food in India was worsened by the need to grow cash crops on land that was previously devoted to growing food. While nine-tenths of the acreage under jute and perhaps three-quarters of that under cotton in undivided India went to Pakistan, nearly all the jute and cotton mills remained in India. To supply them with raw materials it became necessary to convert paddy lands in Bihar, Bengal and Assam to jute and land growing foodgrains and oilseeds in western India to cotton. Thus in 1951, when the country embarked on planned development, the per capita production of foodgrains was a meagre 145 kg, among the lowest in the world.

Most farmers keep back the foodgrains they need for their own consumption and sell only the balance in the market. Such a low per capita production therefore meant a correspondingly small marketable surplus of grain. The government's immediate response to the problem posed by partition was to continue with the food rationing system imposed during the war and to give top priority in the first Plan to bringing more land under the plough. The emphasis on extending the area under cultivation continued during the second Plan with the result that the total cultivated area rose from 115 million hectares in 1951 to 139.4 million in 1972. Combined with some increase in yields per acre particularly in Tamil Nadu, and a small increase in cropping intensity, this led to a reasonably sharp rise in food output from around 55 million tonnes in 1951 to 82 million tonnes by 1961 and a rise in the per capita production of foodgrains to nearly 170 kg per head in that year.

The rise in production ensured an adequate supply of grain to the urban markets at reasonable prices and reduced the government's task during the 'fifties to running a skeletal rationing system to ensure subsidized grain for the urban poor. The situation began to change in the early 'sixties when the output of food stagnated on a plateau of 80-85 million tonnes for four years. The supply of grain to the urban areas failed to keep pace with demand. Open market prices rose and more and more urban consumers turned from the free market to the ration shops. With a rising demand from the public distribution system, the government was forced to spend more and more of its time and effort in ensuring that a minimum amount of grain did reach the urban market. It sought to do this by procuring as much as possible from the farmers and by importing the balance of the foodgrains needed to meet the minimum needs of the growing urban population and of the workers on its development projects.

The following table indicates the amounts imported in successive years since the mid 'fifties.

Table 2.2
Shares of Imports in the Total Net Availability of Foodgrains 1956–1974*

Year	Imports	Net availability of foodgrains·	% of imports to net availability
1956	1.44	62.65	2.3
1961	3.50	75.69	4.6
1962	3.64	76.09	4.8
1963	4.56	74.84	6.1
1964	6.27	78.10	8.0
1965	7.46	84.57	8.8
1966	10.36	73.48	14.1
1967	8.67	73.87	11.7
1968	5.69	86.80	6.6
1969	3.87	85.62	4.5
1970	3.63	89.49	4.1
1971	2.05	94.31	2.2
1972	0.45	96.21	0.5
1973	3.61	88.98	4.1
1974	4.78	95.91	5.0

* *Source:* Government of India, Economic Survey, 1974-75, Table 1.9, p. 69.

As it shows, the proportion of imports to the total volume of grain available in the country grew steadily during the second and third Plans, reaching a peak of 14 and 11.7 per cent during the drought years of 1965–66 and 1966–67. In these years, imports which amounted to 19 million tonnes were more than double of what the government managed to procure domestically (8.47 million tonnes). It is no coincidence that the fifteen years of the first three plans are precisely the ones in which the Indian economy grew at a comfortable pace. The per capita production of foodgrains climbed till it reached a peak in 1960-61 of 82.3 million tonnes. Although it then stayed unchanged till 1964–65, the resulting decline in the marketable surplus was offset by ever larger imports from abroad. Thus the per capita net availability of foodgrains in the economy continued to grow (although more slowly) till the penultimate end of the third Plan.

By the same token it is not surprising that the troubles of the economy began in 1966, when the worst drought of the century caused food production to drop from 89 million tonnes to 72 million tonnes. Even massive imports did not succeed in preventing a sharp drop in the per capita availability of foodgrains particularly in the cities.

The wheat revolution of 1968-72 only managed to restore the overall level of food availability in 1971–72 to what it had been seven years earlier. But since it was concentrated in a few areas, notably Punjab, Haryana, western U. P. and the canal-irrigated areas of Rajasthan, it created large local surpluses and sharp local drops in prices. This enabled the government to mop up a large part of the extra produce for sale through its ration shops.

Since the days of the British, the government has followed very different procurement policies for wheat and rice, the two principal cereal crops. In the case of rice, since the grain has to be hulled and milled before it can be consumed, the bulk of the marketable surplus passes through the hands of a few thousand rice mills in the country before entering the market. Since policing a few thousand rice mills is easier than policing five million reasonably well-to-do farmers living in a quarter of a million or more villages, the state governments have traditionally fixed quotas for the rice millers of the proportion of the total grain that they must surrender to them at the fixed procurement price, before selling the balance in the open market at far higher prices.

Theoretically the governments should be able to extract more rice from the millers simply by raising the levy ratio. But in practice there are severe limits to how far they can do this. Too high a levy has encouraged millers to conceal a part of the grain that passes through their hands and also forced them to reduce the price they offer to the farmers. This has encouraged the growth of a cottage industry in hulling rice, which is impossible to police.

Even so, when the marketable surplus has fallen in poor harvest years the state governments have been able to raise the levy ratio somewhat and thus maintain some degree of stability in the amount of rice procured from year to year.

But since the mid 'sixties, the mainstay of the government's public distribution system has been the rapidly growing wheat harvests of the northern states. Since unlike paddy, wheat does not have to go through any processing before being ground into flour for consumption, there is no convenient bottleneck, such as the rice mills, at which to concentrate the procurement effort.

As a result, until 1972, the government depended on pre-emptive purchases of wheat in the *mandis* (rural grain markets) at a fixed procurement price. Under this system it identified districts and even entire states like Punjab, which had a sizable surplus of wheat, threw a cordon around them, to prevent the grain from moving out and forced prices to fall drastically as the new crop arrived in the market. It then bought all that the farmers were prepared to sell at the prevailing procurement price.

The weakness of this system was that firstly the cordon thrown around the surplus districts was never very tight, and secondly that the richer farmers, who owned most of the marketable surplus were precisely the ones who could afford to sit out the government's 'blockade'. As a result, preemptive procurement only forced grain out of the poorer farmers, who needed money to meet urgent commitments. Since the poor farmers usually have relatively little to sell, the government was able to procure very little in years when the market price of wheat was well above the procurement price. Indeed in 1966, just before the green revolution gained momentum, government agencies were able to procure only 1.9 per cent of the total crop of 10.5 million tonnes. Two years later when the first of the big wheat harvests came into the market, they were able to buy as much as 13.7 per cent. In 1971 the procurement rose to a peak of 21.4 per cent of the total crop and even in 1972, the last year of the old system, it was as high as 19 per cent.[5]

The key to the success of the preemptive system of procurement after 1967-68 was the fact that for three years and eight months, beginning in April 1968 the price which the private trader was prepared to pay for the common varieties of wheat was lower than the procurement price. Thus in 1970 and 1971 the Food Corporation was able to buy over 90 per cent of the total market arrivals of these varieties. In fact 1971 proved to be the only year since independence in which the government was able to meet the whole of the needs of the public distribution system by domestic procurement alone. (It has been able to do so once again in 1976 because market prices have crashed once again.)

In these years the government was able to pay relatively high procurement prices to the farmers and yet keep down the issue price of wheat in the ration shops only by importing three million tonnes or more of cheap American wheat every year and offsetting the loss it incurred on the sale of indigenous wheat with the profits made from the sale of imported wheat. For instance, in 1969 when the procurement price was Rs 76 per quintal after adding storage, handling and distribution costs the economic cost of the indigenous wheat to the Central government worked out to Rs 96 per quintal. As against this the economic cost of imported wheat was no more than Rs 64 per quintal. By mixing imported with local wheat in a ratio of 3 to 2, and selling the entire amount to the states at Rs 78 per quintal the Centre was able to nearly balance its losses (Rs 18 per quintal) on indigenous wheat against its profits (Rs 14 per quintal) on imported wheat. As a result, the subsidy on the sale of wheat through the ration shops amounted to less than Rs 10 crores in 1969.

But the picture changed dramatically in 1972-73. Foodgrains prices rose to dizzy heights all over the world and in the wake of widespread crop failure in 1972 the market price of wheat in this country, which had already begun to move upwards from January 1972 shot far above the procurement price of Rs 76 per quintal. Late in 1972, at the start of the *rabi* sowing season, the government found itself facing the prospect of a sharp decline in domestic procurement under the preemptive system, at the precise moment when massive purchases by the Russians and the Chinese had foreclosed the option of importing cheap food from the USA and Canada.

Convinced that the pre-emptive system would not meet the needs of the public distribution system, the government sought to safeguard its share of the total marketable surplus by introducing the monopoly procurement of wheat in April 1973. It did this by simply banning the private trader from the wholesale market and trying to corner the whole of the marketable surplus for its own ration shops. The system was as leaky as a sieve and gave birth to wheat smuggling from the producing to the consuming states and the villages to the towns on an unparalleled scale, but in a very limited sense it worked, for despite a decline in wheat harvest of 1.7 million tonnes from 26.4 million tonnes in 1972 to 24.7 million tonnes in 1973, 18.1 per cent of the total crop flowed into government godowns. This was only a shade below the proportion procured in the previous year. But the government was only able to protect its share of total harvest at the expense of driving the free market underground and forcing millions of consumers in the deficit states who could not afford the fancy prices demanded by the blackmarketeers to turn to the ration shops. Thus whatever advantages it may have derived from monopoly procurement were promptly nullified by a large increase in the demands made on the public distribution system. When it failed to meet these demands, food riots ensued in many parts of the country and prices rose by one per cent a week during the inter-harvest months of June to September.

In view of the failure of monopoly procurement the government decided in 1974 to abandon monopoly procurement and impose a 50 per cent levy on the wholesale traders in wheat. Under this system the traders were to sell half of all that they bought from the farmers to the government at the official procurement price selling the remainder in the free market at whatever it would fetch. There was also a 'gentleman's' agreement that they would aim at a fair rate of profit over their entire transactions and not charge exorbitant prices in the open market. This decision was prompted partly by extravagant promises of the wholesale traders to procure up to six million tonnes of grain on behalf of the government, and partly by the government's realization that by driving the free market underground it had vastly expanded its obligation to feed the people of the cities without in any way increasing its ability to meet it.

The fifty per cent levy on traders did not prove to be the panacea that the government was looking for. Procurement declined from 4.5 million tonnes in 1973 to 1.9 million tonnes last year. But the traders were not entirely to blame.

A close examination of production and procurement statistics of the last seven years shows that the sharpest rise in wheat production took place in 1968, the very first year of the green revolution, when the harvest was about 45 per cent more than that of the previous year. This massive increase caused the market price of the common varieties of wheat to fall below the procurement price, but *in spite of this* only 30 per cent of the increase in wheat production found its way into the government's hands.

In the next four years although market prices remained below procurement prices, the additional quantity that the government was able to procure was no more than 25 to 28 per cent of the annual increase in production. After attaining a peak output of 26.4 million tonnes in 1972 wheat production fell successively to 24.7 million tonnes in 1973 and then to 22 million tonnes in 1974. But procurement declined even more sharply—from 5 million tonnes in 1972 to 1.9 million tonnes last year. Thus, while nine-tenths of the decline in total production in the last two years has been reflected in a decline in procurement, less than one third of the increase in the previous five years came into the government's godowns.

On the face of it this asymmetry in ratios reinforces the suspicion that the farmer and the trader had conspired to hold back stocks from the government for sale in the open or the black market. But a close examination will indicate that this is at most a small part of the explanation.

If three quarters of the increase in production of wheat between 1968 and 1972 remained in the farmers' hands even when the government had virtually edged the private trader out of the market for the common wheat varieties it can only mean that this was

Table 2.3
Trends in Production and Procurement of
Wheat 1967-68—1973-74 *(in million tonnes)*

Marketing year (April-March) following harvest	Production	Increase in production over previous year/2 years	Procure-ment	Increase in procure-ment	Ratio of 5 to 3 in percentage
1	*2*	*3*	*4*	*5*	*6*
1967-68	11.393	—	0.893	—	—
1968-69	16.540	+ 5.147	2.298	+ 1.405	+ 27.3
1970-71	20.093	+ 3.553	3.192	+ 0.894	+ 25.1
1972-73	26.410	+ 6.317	5.006	+ 1.814	+ 28.7
1973-74	21.778	− 4.632	1.91	− 3.09	− 65
1974-75	24.28	+ 2.50	4.0	+ 2.09	+ 82

needed to feed the growing rural population, support a higher level of consumption and make barter payments for the variety of investments within the rural economy (such as the rebuilding of houses). Since the population has continued to grow and the consumption habits once acquired are not easily given up, it was only natural that when the output of wheat fell in 1973 and 1974 most of the decline was reflected in the sales to the government agencies, and not in the direct consumption of the rural sector.

This conclusion is reinforced by the trend in market arrivals between 1968–69, the first year when the bumper wheat crop arrived in the market and 1972–73, the year in which the output of wheat touched its peak, the ratio of market arrivals to total production in the three main wheat growing states, Punjab, Haryana and Uttar Pradesh, rose steadily from 25 to 36 per cent. But between 1972 and 1974, the market arrivals declined to 28 per cent and then to 22 per cent of the harvest. In absolute terms, while the total harvest declined by only 450,000 tonnes in these three states in 1973, the fall in market arrivals was of the order of 1.34

Table 2.4
Wheat Procurement
('000 tonnes)

| State | Marketing Year (April-March) | | |
	1971-72	1972-73	1973-74
Bihar	13	2	50
Gujarat	53	1	
Haryana	709	818	586
Jammu & Kashmir	16	27	18
Madhya Pradesh	50	66	191
Punjab	2,938	3,179	2,707
Rajasthan	154	46	147
Uttar Pradesh	1,145	843	816
All-India	5,101	5,006	4,531*

* Relates to the period April 1973 to mid-February 1974.
Source: Department of Food, Ministry of Agriculture.

million tonnes. Significantly, in 1974, although the harvest declined by 2.04 million tonnes the marketed surplus again fell by 1.38 million tonnes, the same amount in the previous year.

The dual significance of these figures should not be missed. Firstly, the steady decline in the proportion of the marketed surplus reinforces the conclusion that in these three states which enjoy a large surplus of foodgrains the increase in consumption of the villages is more or less unaffected by the nature of the harvest and that it is only after this need has been met that the farmer spares a thought to selling his grain in the market.

Secondly, the constancy of the decline in market arrivals in 1973 and 1974 under radically different systems of procurement proves fairly conclusively that the activities of the wholesale trader have affected the marketed arrivals and the amount procured, only peripherally. In both years he has had an equally strong incentive to enter into collusion with the farmer to withhold grain from the market, and in both years he risked incurring the same penalties. Thus if market arrivals were artificially depressed in 1973, because the trader paid the farmer to withhold grain so that he could smuggle it later to Bombay, Calcutta and other large cities, they should have been equally affected in 1974. Yet in 1974, the decline was exactly the same as in the previous year, and far less than the fall in the harvest. The most plausible reason for this is that if marketed surplus did not decline more sharply in 1974, as against the government's monopoly procurement price of Rs 76 per quintal in 1973, the traders were paying the farmers Rs 115–130 per quintal in 1974.

The main cause of the decline in procurement in 1973 and 1974 was therefore the fall in the proportion of grain brought to the market in the three states after 1972, resulting from the decline in the harvest of 4.4 million tonnes. The government's procurement policy only affected the division of the marketed surplus between the state agencies and private traders. Thus in 1973, under monopoly procurement it cornered over 95 per cent of market arrivals, while in 1974, its share fell to around 60 per cent.

It follows therefore that no change in the procurement system alone will solve the government's food distribution problem. For this what is needed is a sharp rise in marketed surplus which can come only from an increase in food production. Until this occurs, the scope for increasing the rate of industrialization or the creation of employment in the urban areas will remain limited.

NOTES

1 Production rose beyond this to 120 million tonnes only in 1975–76. But the entire rise was caused by an exceptional monsoon. This is shown by the fact that the level of fertilizer consumption remained unchanged.

2 Since 1976–77, there has been a second spurt in the green revolution. This is shown by the fact that fertilizer consumption which amounted to 2.8 million tonnes of nutrients in 1975–76, has gone up by 50 per cent in the next two years It is likely to come very near 5 million tonnes in 1978–79.

3 The results of two field trips to green revolution areas in Punjab and Bihar were published in the June and September (1969) issues of *Economic and Political Weekly*.

4 Francine Frankel, *The Green Revolution in India*, Princeton University Press, 1971.

5 See the Annual Rabi Reports of the Agricultural Prices Commission, Ministry of Food and Agriculture, particularly for the years 1968 to 1973. The commission presents its Rabi report in March.

3 / Inflation

THE DECLINE in the marketed surplus following the return of agricultural stagnation has undoubtedly acted as a brake on investment. Only this can explain the failure of the Central government to raise the rate of investment in the organized sector significantly during the fourth Plan. But the break has been applied not through a direct reduction in planned investment, but through inflation which has eroded the real value of investible resources.

Some official spokesmen have made half-hearted attempts to put the blame on 'worldwide inflation', but these do not merit serious consideration. With the combined value of India's exports and imports amounting to barely 10 per cent of its national income it is difficult even to conceive of the increase in world prices which would be needed to cause a 60 per cent rise in domestic prices in less than 30 months.

But there is no consensus among economists either. While most have tended to put the blame on the abnormal rise in the supply of money caused by indiscriminate deficit financing and a sharp increase in the net bank credit to the government, a smaller number have observed that it is futile to look for causes of inflation in a poor country which ignored the effect of changes in the supply of food. Both these explanations are correct, but neither tells the whole story.

While the primary cause of inflation in India is not the increase in supply of money, but the periodic failure of the monsoon—approximately once every four years in the last two decades—the price rise touched off by the fall in the marketed surplus of food has forced the government to resort to deficit financing to meet its commitments—notably its obligation to pay dearness allowances to offset the rise in cost of living to over 13 million government employees. However, the inter-relationship between the two is complicated by the operation of two additional factors. The first is the time-lag between the rise in prices caused by a poor harvest and the increase in deficit financing, and the further lag between this and the resulting increase in prices. The second is a change in the velocity of circulation of money in the economy, with changes in the output of foodgrains.

Increases in dearness allowance are granted when the average cost of living index for the previous twelve months crosses a certain threshold. One may assume that the increase in allowances comes at least six months after a poor harvest although in practice it is usually delayed somewhat more and given with retrospective effect. In normal circumstances, there should have been a time lag of a few weeks at least between the increase in government expenditure and a further rise in prices, but wholesalers and retailers have grown so used to the periodic increase of dearness allowance, that they treat the mere announcement that the DA threshold has been crossed as a signal for raising their prices. All in all therefore the time-lag between the primary rise in price caused by a crop failure and the secondary increase caused by rise in deficit financing is seldom more than 9 months. This time-lag is particularly unfortunate because the secondary rise comes just in time to nullify the deflationary effects of the arrival of the next year's *kharif* harvest.

The effect of changes in the velocity of circulation of money is to exaggerate the rise in prices after a poor monsoon out of all proportion to the decline in harvest. This is because it shows a marked tendency to go up after a poor harvest and to go down after a good one.[1] The reasons for this change are not entirely clear, but it is obviously connected with the dissaving that occurs after a poor monsoon and the saving that occurs after a good one. In the first case as poor farmers seek to turn their assets into cash, any given supply of money changes hands faster.

Dissaving takes not only the familiar form of selling cattle, implements and bits of land, but also the sale of gold ornaments. While no statistics are available on the annual sale and purchase of gold in the country for the simple reason that most transactions are clandestine, in all probability the distress sale of gold ornaments is sizable and exerts a strong influence on prices.

Since nearly all the gold that goes into making ornaments is smuggled into the country, distress sales probably lower gold prices in this country in relation to international prices and squeeze the profit margins of the smugglers. This leads to a decline in the inflow of smuggled gold, which has exactly the same inflationary effect as any other decline in imports.

Some indirect proof of this is furnished by the movement of average gold prices in the Bombay market. Thus, a poor monsoon in 1957 led to a decline in the rate of increase of gold prices in 1957–58 and 1958–59. More dramatically, the poor monsoon of 1962, coming as it did, on top of an indifferent one in 1961, undoubtedly contributed to the sharp fall in the gold price in 1962–63 and 1963–64. (By the same token, good monsoons in 1956, 1958, 1964 and 1969 were accompanied by spurts in gold prices in 1957, 1959, 1965 and 1970).[2]

Thus, after a poor harvest, the decline in agricultural production, the rise in the supply of money, rural dissaving and a probable decline in the inflow of smuggled gold—all conspire to raise prices by far more than the fall in agricultural production warrants.

However, all of these forces do not reverse themselves after a good monsoon. There is heavy saving in the rural areas and an increase in the inflow of gold which leads to a fall in the velocity of circulation of money and undoubtedly reinforces the deflationary effect of the rise in agricultural outputs. But the annual rise in the supply of money tends to work in the opposite direction. When this is small, there may still be a slight fall in the level of wholesale prices. Thus, for instance, the deflationary forces let loose by a 12 per cent increase in agricultural production in 1953-54 completely overwhelmed the inflationary effect of a two per cent increase in the supply of money, and caused a drop in prices of nearly 7 per cent in the succeeding year.[3]

But when there is a very large increase in money supply, as in recent years, it more than offsets the deflationary effect of a good harvest. This is what happened in the 1969–70 and 1970–71 when prices rose by around five per cent a year in spite of two successive bumper harvests. However, in 1971-72, and more spectacularly in 1972–73, the decline in the output of foodgrains once again conspired with the huge increase in the supply of money to push prices up by 14 and 26 per cent respectively.

One is tempted at this point to draw the conclusion that the economists who have been pressing for a cut in the supply of money are after all on the right track. A sharp reduction in the supply of money after a poor harvest will undoubtedly counter the inflationary pressures generated by the fall in food production. A reduction after a good harvest will at least allow full play to the deflationary pressures that it normally generates.

However, what is needed is not just a cut in money supply, but a cut in the money that is used to finance consumption. This is just what the government cannot bring about because it is committed to neutralizing the increase in cost of living for ninety-five per cent of its 13 million employees.

In earlier years, when the bureaucracy was much smaller, and the armed forces no more than half their present size, the government was able to meet the rise in their salary bill from the normal growth of its tax revenues. Today it is no longer able to do so. As a result, it is being forced to meet its growing commitments by making cuts in planned expenditure, and through deficit financing.

Whenever it has surfaced, this endemic inflation has touched off two vicious cycles of disruption, the first inexorably feeding demand and the second forcing down investment and thus preventing the satisfaction of that rising demand. At the cost of some over-simplification their operation can be outlined as follows: To take investment first, a rise in the cost of living forces the government to increase salaries and dearness allowances. This pre-empts Central and state revenues which would normally have gone into planned investment. The resulting drop in public investment induces a fall in investment in the private sector, for many of whose products the government is the main, and often the only buyer.

After a time-lag of three or four years, the overall drop in investment leads to widespread shortages. These induce the government to clamp down a wide variety of price controls, or to intensify those that already exist. Price controls then combine with rising costs to squeeze the profits of the manufacturers, and further discourage private investment. They also slow down the rate of growth of tax revenues accruing to the government from the private sector and profits and dividends coming from the public sector. This leads inevitably to a new round of cuts in investment in the public sector.

Taking the demand side of the picture, inflation causes an all-round increase in money wages, which intensifies the pressure of demand on prices and serves to spark off another round of wage increases. As this process gains momentum, the average housewife begins to lose faith in money and begins to hoard goods, the middle class salary earner with money in the bank sees his life's savings vanishing before his eyes and starts buying gold or real estate, and the retailer and wholesaler scent a kill and start cornering stocks of anything they can lay their hands on.

The scramble for goods gives birth to a black market and widens the gap between controlled and black market prices where one already exists. This leads to a diversion of more and more income out of legitimate channels of consumption, saving and investment into the parallel economy. Since the reluctance to hold cash is greater and the velocity of circulation of money probably even higher here than in the legitimate economy, the overall effect is to further push up the rate of inflation. If unchecked, the end product of this twofold process in hyper-inflation and economic collapse.

No one who has observed the functioning of the economy closely in the last 15 years will seriously deny that if conforms to the model described above.[4] Indeed most of this chapter is devoted to spelling out the operation of these cycles in detail. But here it is sufficient to say that not everyone realizes that these forces have actually been at work ever since partition which upset the precarious food balance of the sub-continent to the advantage of Pakistan and to the detriment of India.

Since then, inflation has been triggered every three or four years by the failure of the monsoons in one or another part of the country. The only safeguard against this danger was to build up huge buffer stocks of grain in the way that China has done. But the government could have built a food buffer only when the average availability of grain, taking the good years with the bad, was enough to feed the population. Since partition this has never been the case. Every increase in food production has been matched by a rise in population with the result that the per capita availability of grain in the 1970's was no higher than it was in 1953–54.

The twin cycles of disruption did not manifest themselves before 1965 only because of a chain of fortuitous circumstances.

During the first Plan period inflation itself was kept at bay by a succession of good harvests that led to a sharp increase in agricultural production, and the recession in commodity prices after the Korean war.

Inflation began to poison the roots of the economy during the second Plan. But for almost ten years the government was able to draw on the country's vast unused potential for taxation to meet a galloping wage bill and maintain a rising tempo of investment. It was also helped in this by fairly large foreign loans, while a food buffer of sorts was provided by increasing imports of wheat from the USA under PL 480.

The forces of disruption came into the open only after the droughts of 1965 and 1966. By ill luck these coincided with the removal of all the cushions on which the economy had been resting so far. In that same year the government exhausted the country's taxable capacity.[5] The war with Pakistan led to stoppage of U.S. aid for industry, and even the 10–11 million tonnes of food imports only made good two thirds of the deficit caused by the failure of the monsoon. The result was unprecedented inflation, and in order to pay its rising salary bill, the government was forced to declare a plan holiday. The recession which this triggered and the widespread shortages which followed are still with us.

The temporary re-emergence of food surpluses after 1967, as a result of the wheat revolution and continuing imports from the U.S. helped to keep prices in check for the next four years. But with the wheat revolution petering out, with only a trickle of foreign aid and little hope of raising more real resources through taxation, the forces that have been pushing up demand while pushing down investment, have asserted themselves once more. Between 1972 and 1974, they conspired to bring the economy very near the brink of collapse.

The Parallel Economy

The rise in effective demand on the one hand and the shortages resulting from the decline in investment have given birth to a flourishing black market in the country which over the years, has developed its own institutions for earning, saving and investing money. In its institutionalized form the black market has come to be known as the 'parallel economy', a term that has passed long ago from the realm of economic jargon into the lexicon of everyday usage. Yet very few people in the country, except those who actually operate in it, know exactly what it is or how it functions.

Although economists have been talking of the parallel economy for well over a decade, the first major official probe into its working was made by a committee it set up to examine the country's direct taxation system, which came to be known by the name of its chairman, Justice K.N. Wanchoo. The Wanchoo Committee submitted two reports, the first in December 1970 on the problem of 'black' money, i.e., the parallel economy, which urged the government in the strongest terms to demonetize all currency notes, and the second in March 1972, which in addition to giving a more exhaustive analysis of the parallel economy, also made detailed recommendations for reforming the direct tax system.

To those who have grown used to the noncommittal language of most government reports, the Wanchoo Committee's description of black money in its final report as a 'cancerous growth which is not checked, will surely lead to its (the economy's) ruination' may sound a little melodramatic. The Committee was probably stung into using such strong language by the cavalier treatment which the Central government had given to its interim recommendations, for New Delhi eventually accepted only one, and that too the least important, of its many proposals.

But with hindsight and a clearer conception of how the parallel economy functions it becomes clear that far from being melodramatic, the Wanchoo Committee had failed to appreciate its true malignancy. If anything, it actually underestimated the extent to which people were concealing their incomes, and its description of the insidious way in which the growth of black money was frustrating the government's economic policies, perverting public morality, and corroding the foundation of the economy was far from adequate.

The majority report of the Committee placed the concealment of income at Rs 700 crores in 1961–62 and Rs 1,400 crores in 1968-69. These estimates were based on a method devised by Nicholas Kaldor, the Cambridge economist who submitted a report on tax reforms to the Central government in 1957. Kaldor's method was to choose a base year for which the tax authorities had carried out

detailed income studies (in this case 1961-62) and first divide the
national income for that year into its salary and non-salary components. The proportion of non-salary income which was above
the exemption limit in each industry was then calculated on the
basis of the tax department's studies. The sum gave the assessable
non-salary income in the base year. The next step was to assume
that the whole of the salary income above the exemption limit was
being declared and apply the ratio between the declared salary
income and the assessable non-salary income in the base year
to salary incomes in successive years. This gave an estimate of the
assessable non-salary income in these years. The difference between
this and the non-salary income that was actually declared gave an
estimate of the amount that had slipped through the tax net.

This method had two drawbacks. First, the assumption that all
salary income was declared may have been more or less correct
in 1961-62 but was more questionable at the end of the decade,
when even large business concerns were paying a part of the salaries
and bonuses of their employees in unaccounted cash. Secondly,
the Wanchoo Committee applied the same ratio between assessable
and total non-salary incomes for later years as for 1961–62. Since
prices had risen sharply over the course of the decade, the proportion of non-salary incomes above the exemption limit had also
risen. On both counts, therefore, the Committee's estimates were
far too low.

The low estimates also made nonsense of the Committee's
own assertion that the 'parallel' economy was growing at a faster
pace than the legitimate one, for they gave a growth rate of just
over 10 per cent a year, as against the growth of national income
in money terms of 11 per cent a year during the 1960's. Had its estimates been correct, this would have meant that the government
had only to sit tight and do nothing, for the parallel economy to
fade away into insignificance with the passage of time.

A more realistic assessment of concealed incomes was given by
Dr D.K. Rangnekar, one of the members of the Committee, in his
minute of dissent. On the basis of data gathered by the National
Sample Survey, and a detailed breakdown of expenditure in 1961–
62 and 1968–69, he estimated that the income which slipped through
the tax net amounted to Rs 1,031 crores in 1961–62 and Rs 2,833

crores in 1968–69. These estimates showed that concealed income
had been growing at 13 per cent a year, or two per cent faster than
the national income, in current prices.

The Committee also failed to grasp clearly that black money was
not a 'stock' of cash, or of bullion and other assets purchased with
concealed earnings, but a 'flow' of black income. This confusion
was mirrored in its provision of not one but two definitions of the
concept. The majority implicitly accepted the second, that 'black
money denotes not only unaccounted currency which is either
hoarded or is in circulation outside disclosed trading channels,
but also its investment in gold, jewellery, and even precious stones
made secretly, and in land and buildings and business assets over
and above the amounts shown in the books.'

This definition shows clearly the confusion between stocks and
flows which bedevils all discussions of the parallel economy.
The harm is not being done by the cash, gold, precious stones,
real estate or concealed business assets that make up the *stock*
of "black" wealth, but by the *flow* of 'black' income with which these
assets are purchased. After each transaction, this 'black' income
flows on to finance other clandestine transactions that wreak havoc
in the economy, such as smuggling and the construction of luxury
apartments, Successive recipients hoard only a small part of this
income and use the rest to finance further clandestine deals. What
the Committee referred to in its definition was 'black' hoarding
which forms only a small fraction of the total 'black' income generated by each original act of concealment.

This failure to distinguish clearly between 'black' savings and
'black' incomes may be one reason why the Committee did not
try to trace the flow of the latter. It thus missed an excellent opportunity to cast some light on the working of the parallel economy.
As it is, the report devoted no more than three or four paragraphs
to the subject, and contented itself with making *a priori* generali-
zations.

Nonetheless, the picture which emerged from the report was
sombre indeed. Dr Rangnekar's estimate of concealed income for
1968-69 showed that one rupee in every ten earned every year in
the country was being concealed and was finding its way into the
parallel economy. Assuming as the Committee did that one third

of this sum should have come to the exchequer, the government was losing Rs 1,000 crores a year by way of tax revenues alone!

If this estimate sounds incredible, it is partly because the average citizen only becomes aware of the existence of black money when it surfaces in the legitimate market, in extravagant spending in restaurants and smart shops, in holidays at five-star hotels, on the race track, and in the purchase of luxurious apartments and furnishings. But this is only the tip of the iceberg.

Like the flow of national income, most of the black income continues to circulate inside the parallel economy in a closed circle. The man who sells an import licence at a premium may spend only a small part of his gains on lavish consumption. He may also not put the money in a bank for fear of drawing attention of the tax authorities. As a result, he is compelled to find other uses— for instance he may lend the money at a high rate of interest to some one else to finance smuggling or to purchase scarce materials in the black market. The recipient, needless to say, then finds himself in the same predicament. Indeed the worst aspect of transactions in black money is that they force the owners to look for illegal and usually harmful ways of putting it to use.

How money enters the parallel economy

The parallel economy receives its daily infusion of funds from tax evasion and the concealment of income earned from illegal activities like black marketing, smuggling and bootlegging. People conceal their incomes or a part of their output of goods and services to evade crippling high direct and indirect taxes or to get around the price controls which the government has clamped on a very large number of intermediate as well as final goods.

To take indirect taxes first, every hike in excise levies has increased the temptation for manufacturers to conceal a part of this output and to siphon it directly into the black market. Few entrepreneurs have been able to resist the temptation. As a result, the Central Excise (self-removal procedures) Review Committee (the Venkatappiah committee) found in 1974 that such evasion was almost universal in at least 21 of the 123 industries on which the government levies excise duties. Since thirty one industries contributed 90 per cent of the Central government's excise revenues this meant that evasion was common in practically every industry where the incidence of the levy was more than purely nominal. (The exceptions to this rule significantly are the industries in the public sector and those in which the bulk of the output is in the hands of a handful of very large Indian or foreign firms).

The indiscriminate use of indirect taxes has therefore caused a very large flow of funds into the parallel economy. But this is only one of its effects. Such duties also squeeze the producer's profit and tend to distort the pattern of investment. In India, high excise duties have been levied not only on luxury goods such as air conditioners, refrigerators, cars, petrol, cigarettes and alcohol but also on a bewildering variety of intermediate goods such as steel, cement, aluminium, fertilizers, chemicals, paper, nylon and rayon yarn, electric motors, power driven pumps and nuts, bolts and screws. Even sugar, soap and cotton textiles— by no means luxury goods—have not been spared. The imposts have thus discouraged investment in these industries and led directly to many of the critical shortages from which the economy is suffering today.

Nor has the government failed to push direct taxation beyond all rational limits. In the 'sixties it pushed up the marginal rate of personal income taxation to $97\frac{1}{2}$ per cent above an annual income of Rs 70,000. In subsequent years it also raised the rates of wealth tax steeply. Since at the same time the trebling of prices between 1961 and 1973, had lowered the tax ceiling by two-thirds, it is hardly surprising that taxpayers took refuge from these crippling levies in wholesale evasion. The growth of tax evasion was revealed clearly by decline in the ratio of income tax revenues to the national income.

In money terms the yield of the income tax quadrupled between 1960-61 and 1973-74. But since prices also trebled during the period, the real increase in the yield of the tax was only of the order of 35 per cent. Since the gross national product grew during this period by 52 per cent in real terms and since thanks to inflation its distribution became if anything more and not less top-heavy, the failure of income tax revenues to keep pace is indubitable proof of the rapid growth of evasion.

Tax evasion is only one, and arguably the less important generator of black money. The other is the all-pervasive system of price controls, which hedges the functioning of the economy. Price controls were first born out of shortages of essential goods caused by the Second World War, but were given a new and indefinite lease of life by the Industries (Development and Regulation) Act of 1951, and the Essential Commodities Act of 1955.

Under these acts the government has steadily extended price controls to cover a larger and larger number of commodities including steel, cement, drugs, fertilizers, non-ferrous metals, chemicals, tyres and tubes, coal, automobiles, cotton textiles, and practically every other industry in the core sector, as well as foodgrains, bread and butter, edible oils and other consumer goods.

However justified price controls may have been as a temporary measure in wartime, their prolonged use has done incalculable harm to the economy. Born of shortages, they have served only to create a flourishing black market, to siphon money in ever increasing quantities into the parallel economy, to deny profits to honest manufacturers, to discourage the expansion of production, and thus to intensify and perpetuate the very shortages which brought them into being.

All this has happened because while the government has found it relatively easy to make sure that the manufacturers, who are few in number, do not charge more than the price it has fixed for their products, it has not been able to exercise any kind of control on the prices charged by millions of traders all over the country.

Once he enters the black market, a retailer cannot possibly show the actual prices he charges in his account books. He therefore conceals the whole of his extra income. The enormous premium conferred on such concealment by the high rates of taxation only confirms him in his path for it swells the reward for his initial act of dishonesty out of all proportion to the risk that he runs.

In fact the black market is so highly organized today that even the risks attendant on flouting price controls have been largely eliminated. In every trade, a chain of intermediaries effectively separates the black marketing retailers from the premium paying consumer. The mushroom growth of a black market in bread and butter in Delhi in 1973–74 provides an excellent illustration of the way in which it functions. When in the face of rising flour prices the government refused to permit an increase in the price of bread, a point was soon reached when *chapathis* became more expensive than bread, causing a run on all the retail stores. Scenting a kill, the black marketeers moved in, and against the controlled price of 70 paise, began to offer authorized retailers 90 paise for a standard loaf. They then passed it from hand to hand until it was sold to the operators of industrial canteens in the neighbouring towns of Faridabad, Ghaziabad and Shahdara, for Re 1.25 per loaf. Much the same story was enacted with Amul butter. The black market in bread disappeared only when almost a year later, the government raised the controlled price of bread to Re 1.35 a loaf.

Until the onset of recession, which was heralded by a sharp fall in prices in October 1974, there was a flourishing black market in practically every scarce commodity. Steel rods of all dimensions could be had for Rs 2,800 per tonne, as against the controlled price of Rs 2,000 to Rs 2,200, cement for Rs 25 to Rs 30 a bag as against Rs 12, galvanized iron pipes at Rs 6 per foot of length, as against a little over Rs 2, and so on. Since most of the black profit was going to traders it was hardly surprising to find them reinvesting in the one enterprise with which they were already familiar—the cornering of still more stocks in order to make still more money in the black market.

While retailers have thrived on price controls, manufacturers have found their profit margins squeezed to the point where many of them no longer have the money to make good the depreciation of their capital stock. A study by the author of public sector plants in five key industries—steel, fertilizers, bulk drugs, ship building and oil refining—based on the prices and costs reigning in 1971–72 showed that not a single plant is capable of earning a ten per cent return on capital employed, even when working at full capacity.[6] Private sector plants in these fields are not much better off. The lack of investment in the core sector and the decay of the textiles industry are the direct result of the price controls.[7]

Price controls have also driven many entrepreneurs into concealing a part of their production and siphoning it into the black market. The manner in which private colliery owners used to divert lorryloads of coal to the black markets of Patna and Calcutta is now common knowledge. What is less well known is the fact that in several core sector industries, such as cement, entrepreneurs continue to apply for industrial licences only because they feel that they can count, if the worst comes to the worst, on diverting a part of their output into the parallel economy, in order to make ends meet.

The immense damage that price controls are doing is illustrated by the experience of three industries on which the government lifted such controls in 1974. These are the soap, vanaspati (hydrogenated vegetable oils for cooking) and the rubber tyres industries.

In 1972, the organized sector of the soap industry had attained an annual output of 270,000 tonnes but in 1973, when oil prices began to rise the industry found that it was no longer able to make a reasonable profit on the common varieties of soap, and began to cut back the output of those varieties. As a result the total production fell to 235,000 tonnes, in spite of a small price hike in July. In 1974, oil prices rose even faster than in the previous year, but the government stuck adamantly to the prices it had fixed in the previous year. As a result, the overall production fell sharply to a paltry 15,000 tonnes a month—an annual rate of only 180,000 tonnes.

Not surprisingly, the popular brands of soap became scarce, and a huge black market developed overnight. The most widely used varieties which were supposed to sell at 70 paise a cake, were only available at Re 1.50 and Rs 2.00. In all, spokesmen for the industry themselves estimated that the blackmarketeers were making no less than Rs 2.5 crores a month!

Ironically, even while this was happening the government was spending Rs 40 crores a year on imported tallow to keep down the cost of production of soap. Prior to 1971, mutton tallow was obtained from the U.S. under the PL480 aid programme. After the suspension of American aid, the government had to pay for it in free foreign exchange. Price control thus created an absurd situation in which the government found itself spending Rs 40 crores in foreign exchange in order to hand over Rs 30 crores of 'black' profits to dishonest traders and unscrupulous manufacturers.

Even this was not the whole story. In the late 'sixties and early 'seventies the leading firms in the soap industry developed the technology needed to make use of a variety of non-edible forest oils, obtained from *sal* and *neem* seeds, various types of grass seeds, rice bran and so on, thus releasing large quantities of edible oil for human consumption. However, they were prevented from using these techniques to the full because of the rising cost of even these types of oil. *Sal* oil for instance costs no less than Rs 8,500 a tonne in 1974.

The government's decision to lift price controls in September 1974 transformed the outlook for the industry. To begin with, soap production went back to the 1972 level of 270,000 tonnes. Secondly, increased availability and the removal of price controls wiped out the black market in soap, diverting Rs 30 crores of black incomes back into the legitimate economy. Better still, the soap manufacturers were at last able to use non-edible oils on a much larger scale than before. This made it possible for the government to stop importing mutton tallow.

Best of all, of the Rs 30 crores that came back into the legitimate economy, while approximately Rs 13 crores went to the Central government in the form of excise duties and corporate taxes and another Rs 4 to 5 crores went to the state governments as sales tax proceeds. At least two thirds of the remaining Rs 12 to 13 crores, went to the villagers and forest dwellers who collect the minor oil seeds and extract the oil. These are some of the poorest people in the country today.

The story of vanaspati closely parallels that of soap. The industry has an installed capacity of 1.2 million tonnes, but production has seldom risen above 600,000 tonnes a year, because of the steadily growing shortage of edible oils. To make good the shortage, as well as to keep prices down, the government has been importing increasing quantities of oil. Imports grew from 74,000 tonnes worth Rs 18 crores in 1969–70 to 103,000 tonnes worth Rs 28 crores in 1971–72. However, the sharp rise in the international price of oil in 1973 and 1974 closed this avenue for subsidizing the sale of vanaspati in the local market. As a result production fell continuously from around 50,000 tonnes a month in 1972 to a mere 13,000 tonnes in September 1974. The shortage inevitably gave rise to a black market, with vanaspati commanding a premium of

Rs 20 to Rs 22 per tin of 16.5 kg. Thus once again, the government has found itself spending precious foreign exchange to swell the profits of the blackmarketeers.

The lifting of price controls early in 1975 coincided with large market arrivals of edible oils, with the result that the actual market price in February 1975 was less than a rupee per kilogramme, above the old controlled price, but once again the black market had vanished. The freeing of vanaspati prices has also paved the way for the use of other edible oils, which were previously going waste.

Among those which can be put to better use are *kardi*, sunflower, sesame, soya bean and rice bran. While the use of the first three will depend to a large extent on increasing the acreage under those crops, if the rice bran that is now mostly being wasted or burnt by rice mills for fuel is processed immediately before it begins to ferment, it can yield around 500,000 tonnes of the very finest quality of edible oil.

In the same way, the nation's *neem* trees can yield 100,000 tonnes and its *sal* forests 650,000 tonnes of non-edible oil for soap and other industries. To make full use of this potential, will take not only time but also a great deal of careful organization at the village level and a judicious mixture of fiscal incentives and penalties. But none of these would have been of any use, so long as it remained unprofitable for the soap and vanaspati industries to use these oils.

The experience of the rubber tyre industry differs only in minor ways from that of soap and vanaspati. Here price controls have not led to a decline in production, but have completely strangled the growth of the industry. As a result although the fourth Plan had intended to raise the capacity of the industry to 8.5 million tyres the production has remained frozen at 5 million tyres for several years. The reason is that the tyre industry is highly capital intensive. A new plant with a capacity of 500,000 tyres a year will cost at least Rs 30 crores to set up today, as against Rs 8 crores twenty years ago. Since it is also a continuous process industry that works round the clock, the life of much of the machinery is not more than ten to fifteen years. As a result tyre companies have to set aside as much as 10 per cent of their turnover to meet the cost of depreciation and replacement.

At the prices which prevailed till May 1974, no firm was in a position to cover these costs let alone to build a reserve for expansion. Not surprisingly, only three new plants were under construction, although the government had issued more than a dozen letters of intent.

As a result, there was an acute shortage of truck tyres, made worse by the shortage of nylon and rayon cord. Until May 1974, when the government allowed a price increase of more than 50 per cent and reorganized their distribution, there was a thriving black market in truck tyres: a nylon tyre commanding a premium of Rs 500 to Rs 700 over the controlled price. And once again, as in the case of vanaspati and soap, the government was forced to meet a part of the growing shortage of tyres through imports.

In view of the economic recession which began towards the end of 1974, and the rise in petrol and diesel prices, the two price increases permitted by the government in 1974, which raised tyre prices from 25 to 60 per cent, did not lead to an immediate increase in the production of tyres. But they did make it possible for the industry to finance its own modernization and expansion to a much larger extent than before.

How money is spent in the parallel economy

Just as in the legitimate economy, the income that enters the parallel economy or is earned within it must either be consumed, invested or hoarded (i.e., used to satisfy the liquidity preference of the income earner). But as in a witches' sabbath, these simple actions take on a perverted significance and are extremely harmful to the economy. Thus, consumption becomes synonymous with ostentatious spending, and in cities like Bombay it takes place on a scale that would make a Park Avenue millionaire blush with shame. This is because firstly the mere fact that tax evasion, corruption, hoarding and black marketing are the main sources of 'black' income means that it is necessarily concentrated in a relatively small number of hands. In other words, income is far more unevenly distributed in the country than estimates based on tax returns and other data culled from the legitimate economy would suggest. The gap between the consumption of the rich and the poor is therefore correspondingly greater.

Extreme disparities of income are not peculiar to India, but are characteristic of all poor countries where they are often more pronounced than in the rich nations. But these disparities are mainly feudal and historical in origin. In this country before independence, apart from the princes and zamindars, the rich included the members of the civil services, the managerial cadres of Indian branches of foreign firms which reserved most of their top posts for their own nationals, lawyers and doctors, and a growing tribe of businessmen, many of whom had made huge profits in the black market during the Second World War.

On attaining independence the government took steps to eliminate some of the historical causes of income disparities by abolishing the zamindari system, depriving the princes of a part of their revenues, reducing the salaries of civil servants, and raising the rates of income taxation.

But the real task of levelling down, as far as the 'old rich' are concerned has been accomplished by a relentless inflation. Salaried employees at all levels have been squeezed in the nutcracker of rising prices and steeply progressive income taxation. Today even the top professional managers in private enterprise with nominal salaries of Rs 5,000 a month or more, seldom take home more than Rs 2,500 which is equivalent to barely Rs 700 in 1951. With their perquisites this is still sufficient to permit a comfortable life, but such incomes can hardly sustain the five-star hotels, the chic boutiques, the smart restaurants, and the market for smuggled goods, through which contraband worth Rs 500 crores passes every year.

The growing demand for such luxury consumption originated in an entirely different quarter—the class of self-employed 'new rich' that has been spawned by the government's economic policies.

It is precisely this class that has benefited the most from the government's economic policies and the inflation of the last ten years. The constraints placed on investment in large-scale industry by the government's licensing policies have encouraged investment in trade rather than industry, while the strong bias against larger investors and in favour of the so-called small-scale sector has given birth to a primitive capitalism which is simply not amenable to fiscal discipline.[8]

Unlike the salary earners, the self-employed can protect themselves against inflation by raising their prices while concealing a large part of their income. As a result inflation has led to a steady transfer of incomes from the poor to the rich, and with it a rapid growth in the demand for luxuries the bulk of which, including gold and precious stones, are provided by the smugglers. Indeed, so great are income disparities today, that while two out of five Indians still live on Rs 40 or less per month, on a single day during Divali 1974 as many as 35 persons bought pastries and cakes worth Rs 1,000 or more each from a single pastry shop in Bombay.

The catalogue of ostentatious spending does not end there. Foreign travel has become a useful avenue for spending one's concealed income aided by the government's thoughtful regulation permitting every Indian who can afford it to travel abroad once in every three years. Conversations with travel agents reveal that on an average every Indian who goes on a group tour abroad spends between Rs 20,000 and Rs 25,000 of which the fare accounts for no more than a third. The balance is spent in foreign exchange, obtained in a hundred complicated but thoroughly illegal ways. In spite of this colossal expense, and the difficulty of obtaining foreign exchange, throughout the summer months at least a thousand and quite possibly twice that number of Indians go abroad on pleasure trips alone.[9]

Finally, one has only to walk the streets of Bombay, Delhi, Calcutta or Madras and see the select boutiques, the smart stores, the busy restaurants and bars and the crowded five-star hotels, with their numerous bars and restaurants offering Indian and exotic cuisines, to see how the new rich spend their money. A meal in one of these hotels costs up to Rs 80–100 per person (and fifty per cent more with wine or drinks) and a table of four seldom spends less than Rs 400–500 for a meal. Few secondary school teachers in the country earn as much in a month!

Secondly, the fact that this income has been illegally obtained puts an enormous pressure on the owners to dispose of it in ways that will not attract the attention of the tax authorities. The easiest by far is to consume it. The most common form of consumption is the purchase of luxury flats, and the expenditure of literally lakhs of rupees on furnishing them. Once again, nowhere is this more apparent than in a large city like Bombay, where it is very nearly impossible to sell a flat without accepting some money 'under the table' or to buy one without paying 'on money' for it. Until late 1974, on an average 40 per cent of the sale price of a Bombay flat was paid in 'black' money. By 1979 this ratio had gone to 60 per cent.

Indeed the sale price of flats and the 'on' money being demanded by the owners is an infallible barometer to the state of the parallel economy. In fact an infallible index of the way inflation fostered the growth of the parallel economy was the rise in the price per square meter of floor space which was of the order of 100 to 120 per cent between January 1972 and October 1974. This was far in excess of the rise in prices. What is more, while even as late as in 1971, a man could buy a flat entirely with 'white' money, if he bought it in a building that was still under construction, a year later nearly all the builders in the city were asking for 30 per cent of the sale price 'in black.'

The other major area of conspicuous consumption is the purchase of consumer durables such as television sets, cameras, tape recorders, and nylon fabrics, a large part of which are smuggled into the country. Estimates of the volume of smuggling vary widely. A study team of the Finance ministry on foreign exchange leakages had concluded in 1972 that India lost Rs 240 crores in foreign exchange by way of smuggling and currency rackets, every year, but, it is common knowledge that this was a gross underestimate, designed to protect the various delinquent government departments. A more reliable estimate is obtained by applying the well known 10 per cent rule which assumes that smugglers enter into agreements with corrupt customs and police authorities to intercept 10 per cent of the total inflow of contraband. Since the annual haul even in the early 'seventies amounted to as much as Rs 40–50 crores it is a safe bet that the value of smuggled imports was in the range of Rs 400–500 crores a year, a quarter of the legitimate export earnings of the country!

People earning 'black' incomes tend also to hold a part of it in liquid form. They do this in the form of cash and increasingly in recent years as demands for a demonetization of the currency have multiplied, in the form of gold, gold ornaments, and jewellery, silver plates and vessels, and precious stones.

It is this hoard that most people refer to when they talk of black money. Yet few realize that these hoards account for only a very small part of the income generated in the parallel economy.

By far the larger part is in constant circulation either being consumed (and surfacing in that way into the legitimate economy) or 'invested'. But investment here is a very different thing from investment in the legitimate economy. It is true that some of it does go into the creation of productive assets. Many small entrepreneurs conceal their incomes in order to reinvest a large part of it back into their businesses. Again, some of this money goes by clandestine 'banking' channels into financing high risk ventures which the ordinary banks will not touch. Thus a mechanic wanting to open his own garage, or a cook his own modest wayside cafe on a major highway may get a loan in the parallel economy, even though he lacks the security and guarantee that an ordinary bank would demand.

But the bulk of the investment goes into financing smuggling and into cornering stocks of goods in short supply. This became evident during the inflation from 1971 to 1974, where the imposition of even the most stringent credit controls by the Reserve Bank of India failed to curb either speculative stockholding or the rise in prices, to any appreciable degree.

NOTES

1 For a detailed study of the relationship of changes in the output of foodgrains and the velocity of circulation of money see the article by S.R. Krishna Iyer, 'Monetary Resources, Agricultural Production, and Wholesale Prices', *Economic and Political Weekly*, December 19, 1970.

2 For a more careful study of this relationship see appendix to this chapter.

3 See Krishna Iyer *op. cit.*

4 The decline in prices after September 1974 was caused partly by a determined attempt to cut down purchasing power through a partial wage freeze. But mainly by a huge import surplus of Rs 100 crores a month. With the re-balancing of

the external account after February 1976 inflationary pressures conforming to the above model have reappeared.

5 For a more detailed treatment of this, see Chapter 4.

6 This was done by using break-even analysis on detailed profit and loss account data obtained from the Bureau of Public Enterprises Ministry of Finance, New Delhi.

7 In 1977 and 1978 when agricultural and industrial growth finally began to pick up again, the government was rapidly forced into importing large quantities of fertilizers, steel, cement, aluminium, non-ferrous metals and chemicals.

8 These assertions form the subject matter of Chapter 4 (defective economic laws).

9 In 1977, even this restriction was wholly withdrawn. Since then airline bookings out of India have trebled in 2 years.

PART II

4 / Causes of Economic Decline

The Turning Point

THE EVIDENCE presented in Chapter 1 shows unambiguously that the country's economic fortunes began to wane in 1965–66. Was this the result of any new development in the economy, or was it the first visible manifestation of forces which had been at work in the economy for sometime? The first possibility can be ruled out very quickly. The only important change that took place at about this time was one that should have boosted the rate of economic growth. This was the spread of the new, high-yielding, varieties of wheat in the northern wheat zone. In fact, the economic decline after 1966 took place in spite of the wheat revolution. The spectacular increases in the output of cereals between 1968 and 1973 only masked the growing weakness of the economy and prevented policy makers from recognizing the true gravity of the situation.

The reversal of economic trends in 1966 was a manifestation of deep rooted structural imbalances in the economy and of the rise of political forces which, at least in the short run, were inimical to economic growth. However, these forces may not have revealed themselves in such a dramatic reversal of fortunes had it not been for the jolt given to the economy by two successive droughts in 1965 and 1966. The production of foodgrains dropped from 89 million tonnes in 1964–65 to 72 million tonnes in 1965–66, and was only a shade higher, at 76 million tonnes, in 1966–67. The decline in the harvest conspired with the Indo-Pakistan war of September 1965 and the necessary, but ill-timed, devaluation of the rupee in June 1966, to push up the general price level by 32 per cent in two years. But inflation alone would not have caused a decline in savings and investment if the government had not, over the previous 15 years, created conditions in which every rise in prices forced a disproportionate increase in consumption expenditure by the Central and state governments, a decline in government savings out of current revenues and therefore a decline in investment in the public sector. It did this first by creating literally millions of sinecures in the Central, state and local government bodies, and then protecting more than nine-tenths of all Central and state government employees either wholly or partially against increases in the cost of living, by means of a dearness allowance pegged to the cost of living index.

While the national income grew by around 42 per cent between 1960–61 and 1972–73, employment in the government sector grew by 69 per cent to 11.8 million. Together with periodic increases in basic salaries and frequent upward revisions of the dearness allowance, this caused the salary bill of the Central and state governments to rise by 15 to 18 per cent a year throughout the 1960's and by even more in the 'seventies.

For the first fifteen years of planned development the government was able to meet this increase in its consumption expenditure and still increase its planned investment, by levying extra taxes. Its fiscal revenues rose as a result from around 6 per cent of the national income in 1951 to 14.1 per cent in 1965–66. But at this point, the government exhausted the taxable capacity of the nation. Taxpayers reacted to further increases in tax rates by concealing their incomes or by putting up their prices to cover the increase in indirect levies. As a result the ratio of tax revenues to national income declined to 13.2 per cent in 1968–69. Thereafter it began to rise once again under the spur of an unprecedented annual increase in tax rates, but even so, in 1973–74, it was still only 14.7 per cent of the national income.

The exhaustion of the nation's taxable capacity coincided with a 32 per cent price rise in 1965–66 and 1966–67. Unable to raise more real revenues at a faster rate than the rise in national income the government had to choose between reneging on its commitments to pay dearness allowances (or retrenching some of its employees) and cutting back investment drastically. It chose the politically easier but economically disastrous course of declaring a 'Plan holiday' in the beginning of 1967 and cut planned investment in real terms by no less than 30 per cent. So steep was the cut that the average annual investment in the public sector in *current prices* for the three years of the Plan holiday 1966–67 to 1968–69, of Rs 2.268 crores, was around Rs 100 crores less than the investment that took place in 1965–66

The cut in public investment was only the beginning of the slide backwards. The public sector provides the lion's share of the demand for the output of private industry. During the second and third Plans private entrepreneurs had invested heavily in the cement, chemicals, aluminium, copper, engineering and other heavy industries. These were dependent on the orders placed by the government which now accounted for about 60 per cent of the total investment in the country. On a rough estimate the government was buying half the cement, one third of the paper, and half or more of the steel, aluminium and copper produced in the country. As a result, a decline in its demand dealt a severe blow to the profitability of the private sector and caused a sharp decline in the utilization of productive capacity. Predictably the worst hit were the engineering industries: the railway wagon industry had built up a capacity of 40,000 wagons a year, but their main buyer, the railways cut its demand from 26,000 to 10,000 wagons a year. In the same way, the machine building and machine tools industries languished for orders. Even in current prices the total sale of machine tools in the country declined from Rs 54.16 crores in 1965–66, to Rs 5.42 crores in 1970–71, the second year of the fourth Plan. The government-owned Hindustan Machine Tools went plunging from a comfortable surplus in 1965–66 into a heavy deficit in 1967–68 and began to diversify production and look for export orders in order to keep afloat. The steel plants found themselves with a glut of steel, and the Mining and Allied Machinery Corporation, designed to produce coal mining equipment, found itself without a single order of any kind!

The government's announcement of a Plan holiday triggered off a spate of bankruptcies. A giant engineering plant like the Structural Engineering Works in Bombay, which had borrowed heavily in order to set up a new boiler plant in the confident expectation of new orders, simply ran out of working capital and went into liquidation. And even as late as in July 1971, two years after the fourth Plan had begun, a study of 335 industries by the Economic Times Research Bureau showed that two out of every five industries, mainly those producing machinery and structures were working at less than three-fifths of their rated capacities. Needless to say, the existence of this excess capacity acted as a severe brake on investment in the private sector also.

The government had confidently expected that good harvests in 1967–68 and the ensuing years would revive the demand for industrial goods and raise the rate of industrial growth and investment once again. But this expectation was belied. In the four years from 1968 to 1971 the industrial growth rate showed a declining trend going from 6.8 per cent in 1968 to 7.5 per cent, 5.1 per cent and 1.0 per cent in the succeeding three years.

The experience of these years showed conclusively that the agricultural sector is only partially integrated with the industrial and that a rise in income in the rural areas does not necessarily cause a rise in demand for industrial products. While no one has yet given a satisfactory explanation for this phenomenon, it is possible that a fairly large part of the increase in incomes goes into the purchase of land, cattle, ploughs, bullock carts and the purchase of gold (most of which is smuggled into this country and does not benefit domestic industry) as well as into other forms of saving. As a result it does not directly stimulate industrial output. This also reveals the extent to which industrialization has occurred in response to specifically urban demands and patterns of consumption.

The overall decline in investment and the slower growth in industrial output caused the government's tax revenues to grow more slowly. This is because customs duties, sales and excise levies and corporate taxes, which account for around 85 per cent of the total tax revenues of the Central and state governments, are directly proportional either to the total turnover of industry or to its gross profits. At the same time, the low level of capacity utilization in the public sector and its mounting losses in the period between 1966–67 and 1972–73, caused a fall in the government's non-tax revenues.

Thus the cut in planned investment which was intended to alleviate the immediate financial crisis actually worsened it, albeit after a time lag of one or two years, and completed the vicious circle that forced saving and investment relentlessly downwards for nine long years. Indeed in real terms the planned investment of Rs 4,500 crores in 1974–75, the first year of the fifth Plan is still marginally less than the Rs 2,400 crores invested in 1965–66, the last year of the third Plan. For six years after

1969–70 the government struggled to break the grip of this vicious circle by resorting to heavy deficit financing to shore up the rate of planned investment. The supply of money which had been rising on an average of 7 per cent during the years of the Plan holiday, rose by 11.5 per cent in 1970–71, 13.9 per cent in 1971–72 and 15.6 per cent in 1972–73. But this only served to strengthen inflationary pressures. The rise in prices which began in January 1972, and gained momentum after the drought in Maharashtra later in the year, dwarfed the increase that took place between June 1965 and October 1967, and once again crushed the government's drive to raise its own rate of saving by triggering the mechanism of the dearness allowance.

How far is the strategy of growth to blame?

The Plan holiday was triggered by drought, but drought in India is a recurring phenomenon. Why then did the government not take steps from the very start to protect its growth plans from the vagaries of the monsoons? To be more specific why did it not build a large buffer stock of foodgrains to guard against failures of the monsoon? (This was the principal recommendation of a Foodgrains Enquiry Committee set up a full ten years earlier!)

Alternatively, if the government did not wish to invest in a large permanent buffer of foodgrains, why did it make itself progressively more vulnerable to inflation by hiring more and more civil servants at a reckless pace, and then undertaking to protect their real income by means of automatic increases in the dearness allowance?

The most commonly accepted answer is that both problems arose from the undue emphasis that the government gave to the setting up of heavy industry, and its neglect of agriculture.[1] Heavy industry created far too few jobs, forcing the Central and State governments and even private concerns to create sinecures in order to accommodate the new entrants to the job market, and the neglect of agriculture was the direct cause of the failure to build a food buffer. Since this argument has considerable force, it is worth presenting in some detail.

To take the supply of food first: the government could have tempered inflation by operating a buffer stock of foodgrains only if their overall availability of food in the country, taking the good and bad harvest years together, had been sufficient to feed the population of the towns and the villages. But except in 1970–71, the amount of grain procured by the Central and state governments always fell short of the amount they sold through the ration shops at subsidized prices and the gap between the two had perforce to be filled by imports. Thus the basic condition for the operation of a successful buffer stock policy has never been fulfilled in India.

It may be argued that the gap between procurement and subsidized sales could have been filled by making use of sterner methods of procurement such as a compulsory levy on the better-off farmers. This is a question to which no definite answer can be given. However, two major constraints need to be remembered. Firstly, India began her development with perhaps the lowest per capita availability of foodgrains of any country in the world. In 1951, this was no more than 146 kg per head per year. The scope for extracting a larger surplus from the farmer, no matter by what means, was therefore very limited. Secondly, the amount of coercion that would have been needed in order to extract say another four million tonnes of grain a year from the farmers was most probably far beyond the capacity of any democratic government which had to renew its mandate from the electorate every five years.

In short, an increase in marketed surplus, whether procured by the government or brought to the towns by the traders, could only come from extra production. What is more, the increase in output had to outstrip the growth of population by a handsome margin in order to make this possible. In fact, this happened only in two short periods, the first of six years from 1953 to 1959, and the second of four years from 1967–68 to 1970–71.

If the country could not produce enough food to build a buffer stock could it not have exported other products to buy foodgrains, particularly as it already enjoyed an excellent market for its textiles, leather, tea, jute and, within quota limits, its coffee and sugar? Other exports could doubtless have been developed, such as long-grain rice. But this alternative was never seriously explored. The second Plan was framed in the shadow of the protracted decline in the prices of primary products which followed the end of the Korean war. The planners assumed therefore (and probably with reason) that India's exports would not rise significantly in the immediate future and that the country's growth strategy should therefore be oriented towards the attainment of self-reliance, defined not as the balancing of imports with exports, but as minimizing the absolute consumption of foreign exchange. Since the government had already decided that industrialization was the only feasible road to prosperity, the decision to build a heavy industrial base for the economy followed logically from its decision to attain the highest degree of self-reliance. In time the drive for self-reliance came to overshadow all the other avowed objectives of planned development.

As for the reckless expansion of the bureaucracy, the Central and state governments have not been entirely blind to its economic consequences. There is hardly a single budget speech in which the Union finance minister has not solemnly affirmed that the government will endeavour to curb the rise in non-development expenditures. If successive governments have failed to do so, it is because they have come under pressure to create jobs at any cost which they have found extremely difficult to resist within the framework of a functioning democracy.

Nor is this at all surprising, for with the population growing by an average of 10 million a year between 1956 and 1975, even if each income earner could look after a family of four, this meant that a responsible government needed to create at least two and a half million new jobs a year, just in order to prevent unemployment from increasing. In the face of such remorseless pressure, any realistic planning would have had to make the creation of productive employment on a sufficiently large scale its prime objective. This is just what the actual strategy of growth adopted by the government in 1956 failed to do. Beginning with the second five-year Plan, the government consciously adopted a capital-intensive strategy of development. This is shown less by the share of investment going to different sectors of the economy, than by the choice of projects and the choice between different technological alternatives for each project.

Sectoral allocations between the first and successive Plans do show a shift of emphasis away from agriculture towards industry. Thus whereas the government planned to spend 8.5 per cent of the resources raised for the first Plan on industry, it actually spent less than 5 per cent. At the same time, it planned to and actually spent 45 per cent of the funds on agriculture, irrigation and power projects, and 24 per cent on education, health, housing and other social services.

By contrast, the share of industry went up to over 23 per cent in the second Plan, 20 per cent in the third Plan, 23.3 per cent during the Plan holiday, and around 20 per cent in the fourth Plan. The corresponding share of agriculture, irrigation and power went down to 32 per cent in the second Plan, 35 per cent in the third, and rose to 41.6 per cent and 42 per cent during the Plan holiday and the fourth Plan.

However, these small shifts are not enough to account for the steady increase in the vulnerability of the economy to inflation or the slow pace of job creation in industry and agriculture. Far more important than the pattern of investment was the choice of projects in each area of investment. Practically all the money invested in the public sector, has gone into capital-intensive basic industries like steel, mining, oil and petro-chemicals, and heavy engineering and electricals. The projects conceived and executed by the state governments have differed only in scale from those taken up by the Central government. The low potential of these industries for employment generation may be judged from the fact that a fertilizer plant costing Rs 150 crores (in 1974) creates productive employment for at most 1,500 to 2,000 people, while an oil refinery costing Rs 60 crores can be run by just 500 people. In the same way the Bhilai steel plant and its captive mines which have, over the last twenty years, absorbed Rs 400 crores of fixed investment, employ only 47,000 persons.

The choice of technology also betrays a strong penchant for capital-intensive investment. In a study of the Bhakra-Nangal irrigation and power project, published in 1960, Dr K. N. Raj showed clearly that the location of the dam, its size and the very long distances over which both its water and power had to be carried (water to Rajasthan 400 miles away and power to Delhi 200 miles away) had made the entire project enormously expensive in terms of capital, and that had capital been valued at its social opportunity cost, which meant imputing a much higher accounting rate of interest, the government would have opted for a less ambitious project catering mainly to irrigation needs and relying on thermal stations to supply power to Delhi.[2]

The same insensitivity to the social price of capital is characteristic of nearly all the industrial projects executed by the government. To give a few examples: in no project did the government allow for the possible escalation of costs during the construction period. Nor at any time did the government take into account the delays which are inevitable in executing giant projects, and which correspondingly depress the present discounted value of the future stream of benefits to be expected from each project.

In practice most projects have cost up to 40 per cent more and taken two years longer to complete than was anticipated. If the Central and state governments had made realistic calculations of costs and benefits for at least the second and third generation of projects, it is doubtful if they would have been able to proceed so blithely with them.

The planners' insensitivity to the cost of capital is also revealed in the fact that they have changed the scope of many of the largest public sector projects repeatedly without waiting for the original project to be completed. This has often caused long and unnecessary delays as plans have had to be redrawn and factory layouts reorganized. Some of the projects that have suffered on account of such mid-stream changes are the Bokaro Steel plant, the Heavy Engineering Corporation, the Neyveli Lignite Corporation, Heavy Electricals (India) Limited, and the Khetri Copper Project of Hindustan Copper Limited. These have absorbed around Rs 2,600 crores of investment and account for more than one third of the total investment made by the Central government till 1974.

Needless to say, there is a vital difference between setting up a four million tonne steel plant costing Rs 2,000 crores in one go, and setting up a two million tonne plant costing half this sum and letting it expand to four million tonne by ploughing back the profits that it has itself generated. In theory the first should yield four million tonnes of steel sooner than the second, but as the experience of Bokaro has shown, both the processes often take the same amount of time, because of construction delays and a lack of demand for the full four million tonnes in the earlier years. (The construction of the four million tonne Bokaro plant which began in 1966 will be completed by about 1979 or 1980). However, the first locks up twice as much scarce capital and therefore each unit of investment generates at most half as many jobs as it could have in any given period of time.

The stress on capital-intensive industries in the public sector was paralleled by a corresponding shift in emphasis in the private sector. R.K. Hazari, who examined the pattern of private investment in the country, as revealed by the industrial licences issued by the Central government, concluded that between 1959 and 1966 there was a significant shift in investment away from consumer goods to basic and capital goods industries.[3]

The importance that the government attached to setting up heavy industry was a product of the closed strategy of economic planning adopted in 1956. The government justified this on the grounds that in order to minimize the quantity of foreign exchange required to obtain a given output of a final consumer good, the right course was to break into the production chain as far back as possible. For instance, if the aim is to obtain more food, the foreign exchange cost of importing a given quantity will be greater than the cost of importing fertilizer, to grow the food in India. However, importing fertilizers will in turn cost more than importing a fertilizer plant. And by the same reasoning, the foreign exchange cost of buying a single fertilizer plant is more than that of a heavy engineering plant that will build many fertilizer plants.

In other words a given investment of capital in heavy industries gives an expanded stream of future benefits in the form of consumer goods, the size of this stream depending on how far back in the production process one has gone. The drawback with this reasoning is that the further back one goes, the longer does one defer the enjoyment of the final benefits. Thus by importing fertilizers one can provide extra food within six months, but importing a fertilizer plant forces one to wait six years, and setting up a heavy engineering plant to build fertilizer plants puts back the final benefit by twelve years or more.

The choice of where to break into this production chain thus depends crucially on the government's ability to persuade people to postpone the satisfaction of their needs, in other words not to discount future benefits too heavily in relation to present ones.

The root cause of the failure of planning in India is that the rate at which the government has been prepared to discount the future in relation to the present has borne absolutely no relation to the rate at which the people have been prepared to do so. What is more, under a democratic system the government has lacked the means to coerce people into falling in line with its preferences.

Nor is it at all certain that an autocratic regime, whether of the left or the right would have done any better. With not enough cereals, oils, sugar and proteins in their daily diet, not to mention clothing and housing, there literally was no room for tightening the belt further. What the people wanted, and what they needed desperately was an immediate improvement in their living standards. What the government gave them in effect was a promise of better living standards at some indefinite date in the future. When the people grew impatient the government lacked the political will to force them to wait.

When put this bluntly, the above statements sound oversimplified, as indeed they are. The planners did not close their eyes to the need for attaining higher consumption standars. The perspective Plan for 20 years formulated alongside with the first Plan specifically mentioned that raising consumption was of paramount importance and that the rate of saving could be raised only by saving a part of of the rise in income not a part of existing incomes. In fact, the planners envisaged that only 20 per cent of the extra income generated during the first Plan would be saved, the balance going to raise consumption standards.

However, what the planners intended and what the government did were quite different. To begin with, the rate of growth of population turned out to be very nearly double of what they had anticipated, with the result that the per capita income rose throughout the 'fifties and 'sixties by not much more than one per cent a year. The scope for increasing the rate of saving was therefore correspondingly reduced. But in addition to this, as pointed out earlier, the government found that the capital-intensive projects it had undertaken took much longer to bear fruit than it had anticipated and cost a great deal more. The benefits were therefore correspondingly less and took longer in coming.

In these circumstances, it is hardly surprising that the patience of the people has worn thin. The pressure for an immediate improvement in living standards has taken two forms. The first is an urgent demand for jobs. The second is the demand by the organized sectors of the working class for better wages. Both are perfectly reasonable demands and the government has found both irresistible. The natural avenue for creating more jobs would have been industry. But with the bulk of the country's investible funds committed to highly capital-intensive projects generating relatively few jobs, the government was forced to meet this demand by creating more and more posts in the government services irrespective of whether these were necessary or not.

This is revealed clearly by the structure of the bureaucratic pyramid. Data collected by the Third Pay Commission for the Central government in 1969–70 showed that 97.2 per cent of the Central employees belonged to the Class III and Class IV services whereas only 2.8 per cent belonged to Classes I and II, whose members actually make the decisions. The Commission described Class III in very broad terms as 'skilled workers' (including stenographers and typists). But by any orthodox classification (in which skilled workers refers to those with conceptual, perceptual, manual and motor skills), a large proportion would be regarded as semi-skilled. In the same way, Class IV employees are mainly unskilled workers with a sprinkling of semi-skilled persons among them. In other words, at least two out of three people in the Central government are unskilled or semi-skilled—precisely those who, under a less capital-intensive pattern of development, would have been absorbed into industry and its supporting activities.

The wheel has thus turned a full circle. The capital-intensive strategy of growth which the government adopted in 1956, has given birth to conditions in which the funds needed to sustain further capital-intensive investment simply cannot be raised by fair means or foul. Today, the country is witnessing the pathetic spectacle of the heavy engineering industries to which it gave birth with so much pain soliciting orders frantically from foreign buyers because the Central and state governments, whose factories these were primarily intended to build, simply do not have the money to place new orders for machinery, and often (as in the case of the power generating equipment built by Bharat Heavy

Electricals) even to pay for what they have ordered. The country is thus to be denied all the downstream benefits of the very investment which it toiled so hard to make.

Objections to the economic argument

That the case against the capital-intensive development strategy adopted in 1956 has considerable weight cannot be denied. But it does not merit the sweeping condemnation that it has attracted in recent years from an entire generation of 'development' economists. The attack on capital-intensive models of growth has come from many quarters, notably from Professor Dudley Seers and the economists he drew to the University of Sussex in the United Kingdom, from the International Labour Office (which was heavily influenced by his thinking) and more recently from the World Bank which has been influenced by the ILO. An attack on capital-intensive strategies aiming at excessive self-reliance is also implicit in the very use of social cost-benefit analysis using world prices as indices of real costs and benefits. All these rival approaches to development stress in different ways, and for somewhat different reasons, the need to make the most of a country's given factor endowment, which in effect means to look for labour-intensive methods of production and to plan consciously to increase productive employment rather than merely the gross national product. This view is basically correct. Three decades of experience in the developing countries have shown that capital-intensive growth may give increases in product, but cannot solve the problems of poverty and unemployment. But in the specific case of India the role of this strategy in undermining the prospects of development can easily be overstated.

Turning first to the neglect of agriculture, it is true that since the second Plan, the share of agriculture, irrigation and flood control has hovered between 20 and 24 per cent of the total outlay between the second Plan as against 32.1 per cent in the first Plan. But while this indicates a relative decline in emphasis, it does not necessarily mean that these sectors have been starved of funds. For one thing, these figures do not take into account the investment in tube-wells and pump-sets installed in open wells by the farmers.[4] While this was negligible during the first Plan period, it was quite substantial during the Plan holiday and formed a major part of total investment in irrigation during the fourth Plan period. In the same way a much larger part of the outlays on power projects, as well as of the actual power generation in the country was designed to meet the needs of agriculture in the fourth Plan period. Again the amount spent on agriculture must not be related solely to the population it sustains, but to its capacity to absorb investment. As pointed out in Chapter 2, there are a host of institutional obstacles to making good use of investible resources in agriculture, such as the system of land tenure and the fragmentation of holdings. Where these have been overcome as in Punjab and western U.P. even very small investments have yielded very high returns indeed. On both counts therefore, a direct comparison of the sums invested in agriculture and industry would provide a misleading yardstick of the relative importance attached to these two sectors by the planners. A case can be made against the Central and state governments for their failure to remove the institutional hurdles to investment in agriculture. But the reasons for this neglect are political rather than economic, and form the subject of a later section of this book.

Again while delays in the setting up of new industrial plants and unanticipated increases in their cost and the choice of needless capital-intensive technological alternatives did slow down the growth of output and employment and add to inflationary pressures their role cannot be considered crucial to the failure of the development process in this country. Such errors have been made in every country, whether advanced or underdeveloped, and continue to be made even today. Indeed perhaps no country has been as guilty of overplanning as the Soviet Union. Bukharin and others warned repeatedly, in the late '20s, against the tendency among planners to 'put up todays factories with tomorrows bricks,' i.e., against tying up the available resources of the country in too many incomplete projects. Thus unless they reinforce other anti-growth forces, such mistakes are more likely to cause slowdown of growth rather than a reversal of growth.

Most important of all, while the argument that the slow growth of employment in capital-intensive industry, forced the government to create sinecures in the bureaucracy, is also broadly true, it too needs to be heavily qualified. It does not need great insight to see that creating new posts in the bureaucracy is an inordinately expensive way of providing employment. Every such job adds to consumption in the economy, and produces nothing tangible that will feed the employee in future years. By contrast, when money is invested in productive enterprises, although it may create far fewer jobs to start with, once the enterprises start operating, the sale of their products will pay for the future upkeep of their employees, and even provide a surplus for expansion. In India studies carried out by the Reserve Bank of India showed that the investment cost per job in the first three Plans was fairly constant at Rs 14–15,000 (in 1969–70 prices). In the same year, the average emoluments of each employee in the Central government was in the neighbourhood of Rs 5,000 a year. But the employee has to be paid a similar if not larger sum for a total of 30 years (his average working life). Thus the investment per job in the bureaucracy works out to at least Rs 1,50,000 spread over 30 years.

To put it another way, every decision made by the government *not* to hire an extra clerk or peon in the government, will create an extra job in industry, agriculture, trade or transport, within three years, and ten extra jobs at least in thirty years. While these precise calculations may not have been available to the Central and state governments before 1967 (the year of the Reserve Bank study) it will be naive to assume that the Central and state governments and the Planning Commission were not aware, however dimly, of the implications of increasing government *consumption* as against government *investment*.

Thus, the blame for mounting unemployment and for the drying up of public sector investment cannot be laid solely, or even principally, on the growth strategy enshrined in the five-year Plans. Hindsight permits us to see that the capital-intensive strategy adopted in 1956 was not the one best suited to the country. But a second best growth strategy should have yielded slow or lopsided growth. It should not have prevented economic growth altogether. The heavy investment strategy failed because the government chose to make it fail, and adopted policies which ensured that this would happen. Chief among them was the reckless creation of *sinecures* in the bureaucracy. In the thirty years since India gained her independence, if the rate of recruitment into the bureaucracy had been kept down to half of what it was between 1961 and 1975, the government would now have employed less than 10 million instead of over 13 million persons (excluding the armed forces), and would have been able to create an additional fifteen million productive jobs mostly in the organized sector of the economy. It is worth examining what this would have meant in concrete terms. To begin with, nearly all the more than ten million persons who are now on the live register of job seekers in the cities and a large part of those who have given up looking for jobs (such as educated women) would have been gainfully employed. What is more, the surpluses generated by this investment would have swelled the government's tax revenues, increased the flow of public and private investment and created still more jobs, and India would have been long past the point of economic take-off. If instead it is on the path of decline, it is not because it adopted a capital-intensive growth strategy, but because of the deliberate decisions of the political leaders to use resources amounting to one sixth of the national income, raised as tax and non-tax revenues, to increase consumption rather than investment and thus make a mockery of their own avowed economic goals.

Anti-growth bias of economic laws

The spectacle of a government ostensibly committed to a particular strategy of economic growth, enshrined in a succession of five-year Plans, nevertheless contriving to take decisions which emasculate that very strategy is not manifested in its employment policies alone. A close look at its use of the principal weapons of economic policy reveals the same anomaly in virtually every area of decision-making.

The prime objective of the government's five-year Plans has been to build the infrastructure of the economy and set up a core of heavy industries which will produce both the mother machines as well as the basic and intermediate materials which are needed to set up industries in the future.

The first industrial policy resolution of 1948 listed only three industries as the exclusive preserve of the state, namely, armaments, atomic energy, and the railways, while reserving its exclusive right to develop six others, namely coal, iron and steel, aircraft manufacture, shipbuilding, telephone and telegraph equipment, and minerals including oil. In these latter industries the government guaranteed existing private concerns ten years of freedom from a takeover.

The area of state participation in industry was greatly widened by the second industrial policy resolution of 1956, which prepared two schedules, the first consisting of 17 industries whose development would be the exclusive preserve of the state, and the second of twelve industries in which the state would take the lead in the creation of productive capacity, but would also allow the private sector to do so, if it wished.

The two lists consisted almost entirely of capital and intermediate goods. Nearly all the remaining industries. which were reserved for the private sector, produced consumer goods.

Add to these two schedules the railways, major irrigation and power in the public sector, and road transport, minor irrigation and most important of all agriculture, in the private sector, and the picture is complete. The state systematically took up not only basic and infrastructure industries,. but also made a point of entering the most capital-intensive sectors of the economy. For making use of the productive capacity that it intended creating in these major areas, and also for generating employment, it relied on the private sector and the vast farming community of the country to make the complementary investment that was needed.

If the supply of essential consumer goods has not risen, if employment generation, which was in any case slow, has come to a halt, at least in the organized sector, if trained engineers and scientists are leaving the country for want of work and if the machine-building industries are short of orders, the reasons must be sought not only, or even primarily, in the government's own preoccupation with capital-intensive investment, but equally in the failure of the private sector (urban and rural) to take advantage of the facilities that have been created to produce more of these goods. This is the crux of the failure of Indian planning.

One reason for the private sector's failure has already been discussed. The diversion of a larger and larger share of its current revenues into salaries for the bureaucracy has left less and less for investment. In desperation the government has resorted to deficit financing and borrowing heavily from the banking system. This has pre-empted resources that could and should have gone into private investment.

But this is not a full explanation. The government's scramble for resources may have made it more difficult for the private sector to raise fresh capital from institutional sources. It does not explain why firms have failed to generate resources internally after 1966, when during the first three Plans when they were able to match the public sector in investment, almost rupee for rupee, mainly by reinvesting their own profits.

It can be argued that the decline in the real level of public investment has caused an even sharper decline in the output of the capital goods industries set up in the private sector during the second and third Plans. But since the fall in planned investment affected mainly the engineering industries in the private sector, it cannot explain the all-round decline in private investment and the very slow growth of output that has taken place during the last decade, and particularly after 1971.

Nor can one put the blame for the fall in investment on the decline in consumption resulting from the decline in investment. For the decline in investment has been matched by a corresponding rise in government consumption expenditure, which has risen by 18 to 20 per cent a year. Thus the overall demand for consumer goods and the pull of this demand on the producer goods industries should have actually increased production instead of causing it to to decline. This pull undoubtedly exists, and is the main cause of the endemic inflation which has so nearly wrecked the economy. The reason for the failure of industry, and to a lesser extent of agriculture, to respond to the stimulus of demand by raising investment and productive capacity, must therefore be sought elsewhere.

The prime cause is the creation over the last 25 years of an entire edifice of economic legislation which has systematically discouraged investment in productive activities, and weighted the scales in favour of low-priority over high-priority investment.

Industrial Licensing

To take the government's industrial licensing policies first, the Industries (Development and Regulation) Act of 1956 which sought to give concrete shape to the second industrial policy resolution decreed that licences would only be needed for an investment of Rs 25 lakhs or more. This was raised in stages to Rs 2 crores in 1974. In a major modification of the 1956 Act, in February 1970, the government further exempted investment which involved an expenditure of less than Rs 10 lakhs of foreign exchange from the licensing formalities. The ostensible purpose of this exemption was to save the ministries from being buried under the paper work. (Indeed in spite of the exemption this was so voluminous that the licensing committee, which met once a fortnight to look at the fully processed applications, was able to spend no more than four minutes on each application!). But it also had the not altogether unintended effect of creating a formidable bias against large and medium scale investment, and in favour of small scale investment. The reason, as several committees have pointed out, is that while the acceptance or rejection of applications took as little as four minutes, their processing by the various departments and concerned state governments took an average of 400 days! For the applicant, just applying for a licence involves a mountain of paper work. Each application has to be submitted in 15 copies. This entails literally thousands of pages of typing. This forces the applicants to maintain an enormous staff of clerks and a battery of lobbyists to chase the application from desk to desk in New Delhi. All this has added enormously to their costs. On top of this, the long delays in granting applications, delays that are invariably longer for larger projects involving complex technologies, has tended to invalidate the cost and return calculations on which these applications were based. Not only have these hurdles made entrepreneurs fight shy of large-scale investment, but on many occasions to abandon projects for which they have already been given licences.

In the years of the second and third Plans, when the industrial economy of the country was booming, these obstacles did not dampen the enthusiasm of the private entrepreneur. The number of licences issued average 800–1,100 a year during the later years of the second and the earlier years of the third Plan. There was also a gradual shift in the pattern of private investment away from consumer goods industries towards the producer and intermediate goods.

But in succeeding years in spite of the fact that industry was in the grip of recession, the government strengthened the bias against large investment progressively, by creating a number of additional hurdles to investment by the larger industrial houses. These included banning further increases in capacity in some sectors of the economy notably consumer goods and requiring them to prove that the investment they were contemplating would not lead either to the emergence of a monopoly in that product, or further add to the 'concentration of economic power' in their hands. Since the procedure for doing this was complicated and involved having to appear before the Monopolies and Restrictive Trade Practices Commission (set up in 1970 under an act of the same name) this not only meant additional delays but also made it difficult for the larger companies to expand production in the industries with which they were already familiar. To continue to grow they had to enter new industries, which many understandably were reluctant to do. Most important of all, the government introduced legislation giving the right to convert long-term loans by public bodies into equity shares, thus threatening the owners with virtual loss of control.

While placing new hurdles in the path of large scale industries, the government made things progressively easier for those wishing to open small enterprises. Apart from progressively raising the exemption limit for licensing, it also specifically reserved 128 industries for small entrepreneurs alone.[5] In addition, since 1970, it has systematically given credit at low rates of interest and allocated scarce raw materials on a priority basis to the small scale sector of industry.

All in all therefore, the government's industrial licensing policy has intentionally made small scale investment far more attractive than large scale investment. But, unintentionally, it has also made investment in trade far more attractive than any form of investment in industry. A large industrial concern may take two years to get a licence, a small entrepreneur may be able to complete the necessary formalities in three months. A trader has only to locate a shop. He can get his licence from the municipal authorities in a few days. What is more, in an economy of shortages, trade is far less risky than industry.

This bias has had an entirely predictable effect on investment in the country. Firstly it has encouraged investment in trade, which adds nothing to the net material product rather than industry. This is the chief reason why employment grew by 50 per cent in trade and transport during the 1960's as against only 20 per cent or less in organized industry. Secondly, it has discouraged investment in large scale industry and particularly in the capital and intermediate goods industries, the so-called 'core' sector of the economy, where the minimum size of investment is large, whose management is complicated and in which, therefore, only the largest and best established firms in the country can normally be expected to invest. Thus the industrial licensing policies of the government have had exactly the opposite of the desired effect, which was to channel investment into the 'core' sector.

Tariff Policies

The government's tariff policies have reinforced the effect of its licensing policies in discouraging investment in the core sector. Even today imported capital goods attract the lowest tariffs. Until 31st March 1973, the duty was a mere 27 per cent. It has since been raised to 42 per cent on their c.i.f. value. Intermediate goods have attracted somewhat higher duties from 40 per cent to 100 per cent, but there is a total ban on the import of manufactured consumer goods. Since the government has not prevented entrepreneurs in the country from making these goods, the effect of its policies has been to confer next to no protection on the manufacturers of capital goods, while giving infinite protection to those making consumer goods. As a result, entrepreneurs can hardly be blamed for preferring to invest in the production of consumer durables, baby and canned foods, cosmetics and so on, than in steel, chemicals or engineering goods.

This is not the end of the story: by imposing lower tariffs on imported capital goods, but much higher ones on the imported alloys, steels and components, needed to make them, the government more or less made sure that the prices charged by indigenous manufacturers would never be lower than those of imported capital goods. It thus gave entrepreneurs a powerful motive to enlarge the import content of their applications for new investment, and then to use lobbying, influence and outright bribery in New Delhi to get these requirements accepted by the government. Not surprisingly, R. K. Hazari found that between 1959 and 1964, 60 per cent of the capital cost of new investment projects was incurred in foreign exchange.

Finally, almost as if to make sure that the effect of low tariffs in discouraging investment in the capital goods industries would not somehow be blocked, the government linked prices of the engineering goods, fertilizers and other petroleum derivatives produced in the public sector (this meant the bulk of the total output) to the 'landed' cost or import parity prices of these products. The landed cost formula which was applied to the products of heavy engineering units, stipulated that the public enterprises could charge at most 10 per cent more than the c.i.f. price, plus customs duty and internal transport. Import parity pricing, applied till the rise in crude oil prices in 1973 to all petroleum products and fertilizers stipulated that the domestic producer would charge exactly what it would cost to get the product from abroad. Worst of all, till 1972 when import prices were low, domestic producers got no relief from import duties on machinery, raw materials and components, but when international prices rose by four and five times respectively between 1972 and 1974, import parity pricing was promptly discontinued on the grounds that it would push up the domestic prices structure. This argument did not however inhibit the government from nearly trebling the prices of petrol, diesel and kerosene, by raising excise duties

All in all therefore the government's tariff and allied price policies have encouraged the growth of low-priority industries, and discouraged the expansion of high priority industries. It is worth noting that the fact that the bulk of the latter are in the public sector while the bulk of the former are privately owned, has not made the slightest difference. The tariff policies have thus helped to frustrate not one, but both of the major avowed objectives of the government: to foster self-reliance by building the industrial base of the economy, and to promote socialism by ensuring that the public sector grows more rapidly than the private sector.

Price Controls

Landed cost and import parity pricing are only one facet of the all pervasive price controls in the economy. In actual fact, the government has taken upon itself the task of administering the prices of as many as eighty major commodities. These have immeasurably reinforced the drift of capital away from large to small scale industry and from industry to trade.

Over the years, the government has imposed stringent and often unrealistic price controls on such vital commodities as steel, cement, aluminium, copper, zinc, coal, ships, fertilizers, bulk drugs, chemicals, and ferro alloys. By contrast, refrigerators, air-conditioners, pop-up toasters, blenders and cooking ranges, radios and record players, superior varieties of cotton textiles, luxury soaps and detergents, cosmetics, cigarettes, alcohol, readymade garments, restaurants, hotels and a wide range of formulated (as against bulk) drugs are subject to no price controls whatsoever.

Since costs have been rising continuously over the last two decades, profits have dwindled steadily in industries that are subject to price controls, to the point where no entrepreneur in his senses wants to invest in them any longer. What is more, many of the existing enterprises in these industries are finding themselves without the funds either to replace worn out machinery, or to further expand their production facilities.

But it is not only the core sector that has been affected. Price controls have also been imposed on essential consumer goods, such as soap, vanaspati (hydrogenated vegetable oils), rubber tyres, coarser qualities of cotton textiles, and a number of other essential consumer goods. The inhibiting effect these have had on investment, and the way in which they have encouraged the growth of a black market and increased the flow of funds into the parallel economy has already been described. Needless to say, exactly the same thing has happened in every other industry that has been subjected to these controls.

Price controls have also reinforced the bias in favour of small scale enterprise. For instance, till 1977 20 per cent of the output of large cotton textile mills amounting to around 800 million metres had to be of coarse cloth. Indeed in 1975, the textile mills have been losing 80 paise a metre on such cloth. They were expected to make up their losses by charging correspondingly higher prices for the finer textiles, and on those which use synthetic fibres. However, no such requirement to produce coarse cloth has been imposed on the powerloom industry in the small scale sector, which is free to produce whatever will fetch the highest price in the market. Since there are now 200,000 looms in the small scale sector (just as many as in the mills) the latter have found their profits squeezed by their statutory obligation to produce controlled cloth at one end and the stiff competition being offered by powerloom operators at the other end of the product range. Small wonder that more and more entrepreneurs have eaten into their depreciation funds, or pulled these out of the textiles industry altogether, and allowed their mills to go sick. The government has already been forced to take over 106 such sick mills in the country. At least another hundred, if not more, out of the·remaining 500-odd mills are also sick although still in private hands.

By now it should come as no surprise to the readers that while most of the products in the core sector are subject to price controls, hardly any of the 128 industries which the government has reserved for the small-scale sector suffer from this handicap. Thus in industry after industry while the final product (say an automobile) was subject to price controls, the components that are produced by small scale ancillary units were not.

Excise Duties

The harm being done by the government's pricing and tariff policies has been compounded by its scheme of excise duties. No one will deny that such taxes can play an important role in discouraging the consumption of goods in short supply. There is everything to be said for taxing luxury consumption heavily in order to mop up some of the purchasing power in the hands of the rich. But these have not been the only or even the major aims of the government in levying these duties.

For one thing, it has not merely taxed luxury consumption, but also a wide variety of essential intermediate goods. Indeed, the excise duties on steel, cement, aluminium and other industrial raw materials have been more severe than those on many consumer durables, such as domestic electrical appliances, motor cycles, scooters, and so on. In fact, of the 21 industries in which the central excise (self-removal procedures) committee headed by Mr Venkatappiah, found tax evasion to be most widespread, 16 were producing intermediate goods of one kind or another. This list did not include basic commodities like steel and aluminium whose production is either concentrated in the public sector or in so few private hands that there simply is no scope for tax evasion.

For another its main aim has not been to discourage the consumption of either scarce commodities or luxury goods, but simply to collect more and more money for the public exchequer. Its motives are revealed clearly by the fact that it has imposed both price controls and excise levies on the same products—thus effecting a direct transfer of profits from the manufacturers to the exchequer. In the process, it has not merely discouraged further investment in key industries but since it has been unable to control its own non-productive expenditures, has actually diverted funds that could have gone into investment into consumption instead. Apart from discouraging investment in the core sector, the pattern of excise duties has also favoured the small scale sector. The cotton textiles industry once again furnishes an excellent example of this tilt.

In the case of the large textile mills, the government levies excise duties on every metre of cloth produced. This duty is about four times higher on cloth using fine and superfine yarn, as on inferior cloth. By contrast the powerloom industry has to pay a single fixed excise duty *per loom*. In other words, while the incidence of the excise duty rises for the mills with every improvement in the quality of cloth, it actually declines for the powerlooms. Add to this the obligation on large mills to produce coarse cloth for sale at controlled prices and one has an excise duty-cum-controls structure which is designed to force the mills to produce poorer grades of cloth, on which there is little or no profit while encouraging the powerloom industry to produce fine and superfine cloth, and scoop the cream off the top of the market.

However, even without such built-in advantages, small scale industry has invariably paid less excise duties than the large enterprises, because with no divorce of ownership from management, they have always found it easier to evade excise duties (and for that matter price controls) than large widely held joint stock companies. Indeed, this was one of the more important but less publicized findings of the Venkatappiah committee.[5]

Thus all the four major instruments of government policy—its industrial licencing, fiscal, tariff and price policies—reinforce each other in diverting investment firstly from more to less important industries, then from large scale to small scale enterprises and lastly from industry into trade.

A large industrial concern today has to cut its way through the red tape of the industrial licensing policy, and pay high rates of interest on its fixed and working capital. It is barred from entering most of the industries on which there are no price controls (non-essential consumer goods mainly) and finds price controls much more difficult to evade because of the sheer size of its operations, and the divorce of ownership from management.

A small entrepreneur, by contrast faces fewer formalities, is immunized against competition from larger enterprises in no less than 128 industries, gets loans on a priority basis at low rates of interest, is often given priority in the supply of imported raw materials and components, and faces very few price controls. Even where price controls or high excise duties are imposed after he has gone into production, he finds it far easier to evade them by virtue of his smallness.

Finally, traders have the best time of all. They face almost no formalities and are virtually guaranteed large profits by the mere existence of price controls and crippling excise levies. All these policies have had a feedback effect which has further reinforced the shift of investible resources into low priority investment, into the parallel economy, and into consumption. For the dearth of investment in the core sector has created bottlenecks in the supply of crucial inputs—power, fertilizers, and essential consumer goods. These shortages have given birth to new price controls and higher excise duties on the one hand, and inflation on the other. The first has further stimulated large scale black-marketing and the second has caused a direct transfer of incomes from the unorganized working classes and the fixed income groups and in recent years from the organized working class, to the self-employed classes which are made up once again of traders, small entrepreneurs and well-to-do farmers with a marketable surplus to sell.

These trends have increased the existing inequalities of income, and the effective demand for luxury goods, while reducing the effective demand for essential consumer goods (even though the poor need these more desperately than ever before). As a result, the profitability of low priority investment has continued to grow.

NOTES

1 See Bhagwati and Desai, *Planning for Industrialization in India* Chapter I page 5 (Oxford and OECD 1970) and Chapter VI pp 115–117.
2 K.N. Raj, *Some Economic Aspects of the Bhakra Nangal Project*, Delhi 1960.
3 'Industrial Planning and Licensing Policy', Final Report Vol. I, GOI Planning Commission.
4 See for instance *Economic Growth and Social Issues: Some Indian Villages and Districts Resurveyed 1963–64 to 1975.* By Gilbert Etienne, in 'Community Development and Panchayati Raj Digest', July 1976.
5 See Report of the Central Excises (Self-Removal Procedures) Committee, Ministry of Finance, Govt. of India.

5/ The Class Origins of Economic Law

IN ADDITION TO CONFLICTING directly with the avowed aims of the government's own growth strategy, the economic policies described in the last chapter have had one other important effect: they have steadily diverted investment away from areas over which the government has more control to those over which it has less. Indeed the mechanism of controls has itself been perverted to achieve this end, by bearing down harder on large scale than on small industry, and on industry as a whole than on trade.

For instance, the government exercises complete control over the investment in the public sector, but it is precisely this sector which has been hit hardest by its pricing and tariff policies. In the same way, it exercises a very large measure of control over large scale industry: big firms find it harder to evade excise duties, corporate taxes and price controls than small ones, partly because they are being watched more closely by the government departments, and partly because their managements are salary and not profit earners, as in the case of owner-managed concerns, large or small. Yet large scale industry and the larger industrial houses have been discouraged from expanding, while medium and particularly small enterprises have been given every inducement to do so. Finally, there are very few controls on trade, and the few that exist apply mainly to the wholesale traders who are fewer in number and easier to identify.

The rapid growth of the parallel economy, and the rise in society's propensity to hoard which is partially reflected in the increased share of the tertiary sector in the GNP, can also be traced to the steady shrinkage of the areas of the economy on which the government is able to impose fiscal and other obligations proportionate to the rights enjoyed by those who work in them. The other face of this coin is the slow growth of the government's tax revenues, particularly after 1965–66, which is the direct result of a drift of investible funds out of the hands of those on whom the government can levy taxes easily into the hands of those in which it has become progressively more difficult to identify income, assess incomes and collect taxes. The decline in savings by the public and the corporate sectors and the countervailing rise in household savings and capital formation shown by the Central Statistical Office may be a reflection on this drift.[1]

Can such systematic biases be attributed to mere naivete— to an over-reliance on physical controls, a misguided faith in the honesty and integrity of government officials, and a belief in the omnipotence of the bureaucracy? Or is it the reflection of deeper social forces, and in particular of a changing balance of political power between different segments of society? The view that such a perversion of the government's avowed aims can spring from mere naivete, is hard to accept. But since it is widely held it needs to be examined in some detail.

On the face of it the government's economic policies reflect an attempt to fulfil three avowed policy aims: to secure the best possible allocation of investible resources while at the same time diffusing the ownership of productive assets; to raise the maximum of investible resources by way of taxation, and to keep the prices of essential consumer goods down for the benefit of the poor while keeping those of intermediate goods and machinery down in order to stimulate investment and keep the overall cost structure on the economy low.

It can be claimed that the government has sought to achieve the first aim by means of the licensing system, the second through heavy indirect taxation (as the direct tax base is rather narrow) and the third through price controls. If these policies miscarried it was largely because of an exaggerated belief in the capabilities of the bureaucracy and the integrity of its members.

This opinion is widely held and is voiced in a host of different ways. The often heard lament 'if only the economic ministries were staffed by economists' and the demand for the induction of more specialists in the top administrative posts of the economic and technical ministries, which was voiced more than once by the Administrative Reforms Commission, reflects the belief that economic policies have miscarried mainly from a lack of technical know-how, and therefore of foresight about their probable consequences.

In their book *Planning for Industrialization in India*, Bhagwati and Desai have noted that the Indian economy has suffered both from too many and too few controls at the same time, and that detailed physical controls in the field of industry exist side by side with a total neglect of other equally important weapons of control, such as its fiscal, tariff and monetary policies. They apparently believe that this neglect is inadvertent—the result of putting too much faith in physical controls like the licensing system for industry and trade, and on the price and distribution controls, and that this in turn is a symptom of an 'underdeveloped' administration which, lacking confidence in its ability to handle sophisticated instruments of control, prefers to pin its faith on crude, direct ones instead.

This view fails to take into account the possibility that there may be deeper political and social reasons for the over-reliance on some methods of control and neglect of others. That this is most probably the case, is revealed by the *systematic* biases which both over-reliance and neglect have introduced in the pattern of economic activity and the distribution of economic gains in society. Bhagwati's conclusion that the government's sins of omission and commission were inadvertent results from his failure to recognize that both have exerted pressures on the economy in the same direction.

The direction has already been identified: investible funds have been diverted from large into small industry, from high to low priority industries, and from industry as a whole into trade. It now remains to ask who has gained from these shifts and whether the gainers are merely scattered groups of people in society or have enough in common to qualify as a distinct socio-economic class. To take industry first: Industrial licensing has systematically favoured small over large scale industry. Together with the government's anti-monopoly legislation it has, in addition, favoured medium sized firms over the large industrial houses. Finally, while the indigenous large houses, the Birlas, Tatas, Mafatlals and others have found their way around the new laws, although with progressively greater difficulty and longer delays, these laws have borne down particularly hard on foreign companies (both the branches of the multinationals and the 400 or more other collaborations in which more than half shares have been retained by the foreign partner). The gainers have therefore been the self-employed industrialists, either owner-managers of small companies or families controlling and operating 'closely-held' public companies.

The government's import policies and its price controls have hit the core sector i.e., the highest priority industries in the country. Far from being exempted, the public sector units have been among the hardest hit. Since small producers and owner-managers are far more numerous in the non-core industries, and particularly in those producing consumer goods, these policies have also benefited the 'self-employed' among the entrepreneurs.[2] In the same way price controls and excise duties have served to enrich traders and to a lesser extent the small manufacturers. Nearly all of these people are also self-employed. Add to this the government's credit policies, particularly since the nationalization of the banks, which have systematically favoured small manufacturers, exporters (trade) and agriculture (where nearly the whole of institutional credit has been monopolized by well-to-do farmers) and it becomes abundantly clear that the government's economic policies have systematically favoured the self-employed classes in society.

Can the self-employed be considered a distinct socio-economic class? The dominant characteristic of self-employment is that there is no divorce, or at best a nascent divorce between labour and capital on the one hand, and between capital and management on the other. Correspondingly, its earnings can neither be classified as a reward for labour, nor as a payment for risk-taking (i.e., profit), but are an amalgam of the two. The self-employed thus lie midway between the large-scale professionally managed capitalist enterprises of the private sector, and the working classes. They include traders, truck and taxi operators, restauranteurs, small scale industrialists, lawyers, doctors and other professionals and the owner proprietors of closely held companies who have no shareholders to answer to.

But self-employment is not confined to the towns alone. The peasant farmer tilling his land, with or without hired labour, is also self-employed in precisely the same sense as the trader or the small-scale industrialist. Can such disparate elements be considered part of a single class? The answer will depend on whether they can be shown to share an identifiable economic *interest*—one which will make all members of the class, as a rule react to a given situation in the same way.

The answer is 'yes'. The interests and the resulting social and political attitudes of the self employed cannot be reduced, even for purely analytical purposes to those of labour and those of capital. It is not as if this class will side with labour on some issues and capital on others. If this were so, it would not have a distinct social identity. On the contrary, it has very distinct interests, which do not coincide either with those of labour or of capital. This has been brought into glaring relief by the inflation and shortages of the last ten years, which has benefited neither the worker nor the salaried professional manager who fought a losing battle to maintain their real wages. The shareholders in large enterprises have also not benefited uniformly from inflation, because of the shifts it has caused in income distribution and the accompanying changes in the pattern of consumption.

By contrast, the self-employed have as a whole benefited from inflation. The rich farmer because of higher food prices, the trader because of the opportunities it has created for blackmarketing, and the owner-entrepreneur because he has been able to slip through the government's price and tax net relatively easily.

The concept of an 'intermediate class' is not new. It was first put forward by the Polish economist Michal Kalecki[3] and its relevance to Indian conditions was highlighted by K.N. Raj in his R.R. Kale memorial lecture of 1973, entitled 'The Politics and Economics of Intermediate Regimes'.[4] Raj has summarized Kalecki's thesis with admirable succinctness as follows:

'In a paper published in 1964, Kalecki used the term 'intermediate regimes' to describe governments in which the lower middle class and the rich peasantry could be identified as performing the role of the ruling class. In the past, he observed, whenever social upheavals brought their representatives to power they had invariably served the interests of big business often allied with the remnants of the feudal system. However, certain conditions had emerged recently in many underdeveloped countries which made it possible for them to play a different role. The specific conditions he cited were the numerical dominance of the lower middle class at the time of achievement of the political independence of these countries, the extensive involvement of governments in economic activity, and the availability to them of credits from socialist countries. Given these conditions, the State could, in his view, perform the role of 'dynamic entrepreneurs', and promote 'a pattern of amalgamation of the interests of the lower middle class with state capitalism'.

'Kalecki noted also the conditions that had to be fulfilled for intermediate regimes to remain in power. They would have to gain a measure of independence from foreign private capital, carry out land reform, and assure continuous economic growth (the last of which he believed to be closely connected with the other two). The pressures exerted by imperialist countries in support of foreign private capital could be resisted with the help of credits obtainable from socialist countries. Land reform, even if open to evasion, could be used at least to deprive the feudal landlords of their strong position in political and social life. The intermediate regimes would then be able to promote economic development using the public sector as its main instrument. This, he pointed out, would be highly advantageous for the lower middle class and the rich peasant for three reasons: (a) 'State capitalism concentrates investment on the expansion of the productive potential of the country' and there is therefore 'no danger of forcing the small firms out of business, which is a characteristic feature of the early stage of industrialization under *laissez faire;*' (b) 'the rapid development of state enterprises creates executive and technical openings for ambitious young men of the numerous ruling class;' and (c) 'the land reform, which is not preceded by an agrarian revolution, in such a way that the middle class which directly exploits the poor peasant, i.e., the moneylenders and merchants, maintains its position, while the rich peasantry achieves considerable gains in the process'.

The significant points in Kalecki's thesis are his observation that in the first generation of industrialized countries, the representatives of the intermediate class had played a somewhat subservient role to big business and to feudal interests allying themselves with one or both of them. By contrast in countries attempting to industrialize today, particularly those which have only recently broken their colonial shackles, the intermediate class can under certain conditions come to dominate economic and political life in the country. It needs no profound study to see that the conditions

Kalecki has stipulated—incomplete land reforms, partial independence from foreign private capital secured with the help of assistance from socialist countries and active state participation in economic activity, are all present in India. However, both Kalecki and Raj fail to identify the one set of conditions which forge the disparate elements of self-employed and the peasantry into a single *class*. This is the existence of all pervading shortages in the economy—shortages which give rise to inflationary conditions. In such conditions, the self-employed both urban and rural, have the capacity to raise their money incomes by raising their fees or charging a constant distribution markup on the goods they sell. In this way they succeed in shifting the entire burden of the shortages onto the shoulders of other groups and classes in society. This results in a steady rise in the economic power of this class in relation to the others. The rise remains only relative so long as the real incomes of members of this class does not rise. But when they do rise, at a faster rate than the growth of national income (as for instance when shortages permit speculative hoarding and black-marketing on a wide scale) there is an absolute rise in the power of this class also. Kalecki thus notices that unrestrained competition which is characteristic of the early stages of industrialization and the philosophy of *laissez faire* weakens the intermediate class. What he fails to grasp is that the relationship is reversible and that the absence of effective competition which results from endemic shortages of capital foreign exchange and wage goods in a 'developing' country foster the growth of the intermediate class.

Again Kalecki considers aid from the socialist countries to be essential for breaking the grip of foreign private (therefore western) capital and thus freeing the intermediate class from its subserviance to the big *bourgeoisie*. But in India at any rate it is not socialist *capital* but socialist ideology which has performed this task. As has already been shown in the discussion of industrial licensing and credit policy, leftist ideology in this country has been used effectively by the intermediate class to limit the growth of the large industrial houses and what is more important to put the votaries of *laissez faire* on the defensive. The role of the left in the rise of the intermediate class is discussed more fully in a later chapter.

The perimeter of the intermediate class

So far the intermediate class has been held as virtually synonymous with the self-employed defined in the widest possible sense of the term to include the landowning peasant, at one extreme and the owner-manager of industry at the other. It is time however to define the class more precisely, using the touchstone of class interest. Immediately one does this, it becomes clear that the correlation between the intermediate class and the self-employed is not perfect.

To begin with, a line must be drawn between those land-owning peasants who stand to gain from shortages and high prices of agricultural produce and those who stand to lose. The dividing line in practice lies between those who, taking the good years with the bad, have no net marketable surplus of grain or cash crops and those who do. This dividing line is one that villagers throughout the country not only understand but use as their yardstick to distinguish the well-to-do from the poor in their own villages. Its rationale is the inelasticity of demand for nearly all agricultural produce and particularly for cereals which causes a rich farmer's money income to rise in a year of poor harvests even though his marketable surplus may be smaller, and to fall in a year of good harvests in spite, or rather, because of an increase in his marketable surplus. This is the group to which the term 'farm lobby' is correctly applied, a group that is against compulsory procurement in poor harvest years but asks for (and usually obtains) high support prices in good years. However, the strength of the class interest in profiting from shortages and obtaining government support in times of plenty, varies according to how high up the scale of affluence the farmer lies. At the bottom is the farmer who has a surplus only in very good years but has to purchase food for the family (through his saving) in bad years. At the top are the eight million families who operate 55 per cent of the total cropped area of the country, the majority of whom are able to irrigate at least a part of their land and thus be assured of a marketable surplus even when the monsoons are weak.

All of these farmers, rich or poor, have a class interest which is dramatically opposed to that of the poorer landowners in each village, who cannot grow enough to feed their families and have to buy a part of the food they eat every year. They have a strong interest in compulsory procurement to ensure a steady supply of grain from fair price shops in poor years, and in the lowest possible market prices in good years. In this their interests are at one with those of the landless and the urban working classes and fixed income groups. All in all the intermediate class can be said to include families operating around 11 million of the 70 million operational holdings in the country. This is the number of the farmers who farm more than ten acres of land. While some of them in the semi-arid regions may well be very poor, there are others with only five or six acres of rich irrigated land elsewhere who belong to the intermediate class.

The conflict between the interests of the intermediate class and the fixed income groups is self-evident, and would normally put it at loggerheads with the bureaucracy, whose members are all salary earners. But this is not entirely true. A distinction needs to be made between those who accept bribes for facilitating the work of obtaining government licences and sanctions and looking the other way when rules are broken, and those who either do not or are not in positions where they are likely to be offered such bribes. The first type of civil servant can no longer be said to have a fixed income. In a very real sense they too are self-employed because they accept money in return for services, and they are members of the intermediate class insofar as the value of the services they render condoning blackmarketing, bootlegging, smuggling, colluding in the evasion of excise levies, or speeding up the process of obtaining official sanctions, increases with the intensity of the shortages being experienced by the economy. It is not easy to put a figure on the number of government employees who have joined the intermediate classes, but if one includes the meanest of bribe takers—the *chaprasi* who takes a few rupees to put an applicant's file on top of the heap on the officer's desk—the bulk of the police force, and the majority of the staff of the economic and technical departments of the Central and state governments, who come in direct contact with the public, can be considered members of this class.

Finally, a crucial distinction needs to be drawn between those owners of capital who manage the enterprises in which their money is invested, and those who merely own shares, and leave the running of the enterprise to professional salaried managers. The former category includes not only all small trading and manufacturing enterprises but also large, family-owned, or closely held private and public limited companies. This is because if the price of their products rises, or if they conceal a part of their production to evade excise duties and siphon this part of their output directly into black market the extra income comes directly to them as 'black' money on which they pay no taxes. By contrast in professionally managed firms inflation reduces the real income of the salaried manager and even sharp increases in salaries are no help as they attract very heavy marginal rates of income taxation. By raising prices to boost profits, concealing a part of the output, or hoarding stocks of raw materials, they may hope to obtain a promotion. But this is a far weaker motive for breaking the law than that of the owner-manager. Thus, while there may be significant differences in behaviour between companies, as a rule professionally managed concerns are likely to behave with greater responsibility than owner managed concerns. In particular on the crucial question of benefiting from shortages, while the former are more likely to seek increased profits by raising production, the latter are on balance more likely to seek it through an increase in prices, or through selling their product in the black market.

By this definition, the enterprises which fall outside the perimeter of the intermediate class include the most advanced of the indigenous industrial groups, in which the professionalisation of management has made a good deal of headway, the majority of the foreign owned and controlled enterprises in India and, significantly, the whole of the public sector.

It is worth noting that the concept of an 'intermediate' class cuts across all the conventional Marxist definition of class, for it lumps together groups which the latter would regard as having sharply divergent interests. Thus the comprador capitalist, a key member of the Marxist demonology comes out as having a good deal in common with the public sector manager. The national *bourgeoisie* are shown to be far from homogeneous, and the better elements in it are not the small but the large units (at least when large size goes hand in hand with modern professional management). Again the bulk of the national *bourgeoisie* are shown to have similar interests to the *petit-bourgeoisie*, but dramatically opposed interests to the upper fixed-income groups which are normally lumped together with them. Finally, and perhaps most significant of all, the intermediate class spans town and country, abolishing the conflict between the two which is implicit in most Marxist analyses of the interplay of class interests, in developing countries.

A good example is the conflict between the farmer and the grain trader who is also very often the local moneylender. A close look at it shows that this conflict of interests is mainly between the *poor* farmers and the trader-moneylenders. The rich farmer is able to hold back his grain from the market to profit from higher prices later in the season, just as the trader does. In fact in this case he acts precisely like the trader. Again the rich farmer can take his grain directly to the urban grain markets, once again assuming the role of the trader. Finally, it is the rich farmer who has cornered the bulk of the low-interest loans given by the co-operative banks and other rural credit agencies and has, on occasion, re-loaned this money at much higher rates of interest to his poor neighbours.

Since the intermediate class cuts right across older divisions it is necessary to redefine social classes in an early capital economy. In the preceding pages the intermediate class has been defined by referring to the gainers from a regime of shortages. The other classes can be identified by seeing who loses from such a regime of shortages. The worst hit are the classes which have no defence at all against inflation—the fixed income groups, the poor farmers, the rural landless, and the unorganized workers in the towns. Less badly hit are the salary and perquisite earning professional managers in business, and the organized working class (including honest members of the lower rungs of the government services).

These last two groups are able to protect themselves or are protected at least partly against inflation, because the managers in industry are able to look after themselves, while the workers in the organized sector and government servants are protected by the dearness allowance scheme or by wage agreements.

If the intermediate class is fairly heterogeneous, its rivals are far more so. This is one reason why the former has been able to seize power with such ease. However, its rise has also been aided by a covert pact with the organized working class and the government servants, the two other cohesive and numerous groups in society. The comprehensiveness of the dearness allowance system, which covers the bulk of the workers in the private organized sector is a clear proof of the existence of this pact. Herein lies the explanation of the anomaly whereby the lower civil servants, who are the least productive members of society, are most fully protected against inflation while the agricultural worker and the tenant farmer who are arguably the most important members of the work-force enjoy absolutely no protection whatever.

The power of this intermediate class is based not only on its growing share of the national product but also on its sheer numerical dominance. Organized industry employs between eight and nine million workers. The unorganized sector in the towns employs about the same number of whom around half are either self-employed, small employers hiring three to four workers, or the relatives of such employers. Thus the total number of wage earners in industry does not exceed 13 to 14 million. Against this, the number of farmers cultivating 10 acres or more amounts to nearly 11 million. Add to this five million shopkeepers, a million or so bus, truck, taxi and scooter rickshaw operators, around four million self-employed and their relatives in the unorganized sector, a quarter of a million or more professionals, and a few million corrupt civil servants, and it becomes clear that with at least 20 million income earners and eight to ten times as many dependents and relatives in joint families who have their interests, the inter-meditate class is easily the largest single class in the country.

Once the size and power of the intermediate class are recognized, it becomes easier to understand a host of other apparent ano-malies in the government's economic legislation over the past two and a half decades. A prime example is the government's policy of giving subsidies to the well-to-do wheat farmers out of the public exchequer. Before 1974, for nearly a decade, the government had been purchasing wheat at prices which were only a couple of rupees per quintal less than those at which it sold the grain to the state governments for distribution through the ration shops. In doing so, it bore virtually the entire cost of handling transport, storage and distribution, amounting to an average of Rs 23 per quintal, from the Central exchequer. It met this cost initially by importing large quantities of very cheap wheat from the USA and using the profit it made on the sale of this wheat to make good its losses on the sale of domestically procured wheat. It only gave up this practice in 1973, when the world price of wheat shot far above local prices in this country.

It fixed such high procurement prices—higher even than the open market prices in 1968, '69, '70 and '71—ostensibly in order to assure a massive procurement of wheat, but in reality under relentless pressure from the governments of the wheat growing northern states, mainly Punjab and Haryana, which are dominated entirely by the farm lobby.

Similarly, till 1973, imported fertilizers cost far less than those produced indigenously. As a result, once again under pressure from the farm lobby, the government set very low fertilizer prices with the intention of balancing the loss incurred on domestic fertilizers against the profits made on the sale of imported fertilizers. When demand actually grew much more slowly than the government had anticipated, not only did the imports continue, but the government gave priority to the sale of the cheap imported nutrients, and left the domestic fertilizer industry to fend for itself. Foreign exchange was thus used to swell the profits not of the entire rural population, but that small segment which could afford to invest in sinking tube-wells and buying fertilizers, and thereby generate a surplus for sale in the cities.

The power of the farm lobby is also reflected in the slowly widening gap between the rate of growth of agricultural and industrial prices. Dr Ashok Mitra has computed that between 1962–63 and 1972–73, the terms of trade have swung against industry and in favour of agricultural products by around 60 per cent. 'The movement of relative prices has been such that even in the course of the past twelve months (December '71 to November '72) a standard unit—if it can be worked out—of industrial product would today fetch nearly 12 to 13 per cent less of agricultural output than a year ago'. Mitra traces the near stagnancy in private industrial employment and co-operative saving to this opening price scissors which has squeezed the profits of industry and forced it to economize wherever possible in the use of labour. It is also interesting to note the sharp contrast between the Indian and Russian experience before the introduction of the New Economic Policy. As Mitra pointed out, between 1913 and 1923, while industrial prices in the USSR went up by 276 per cent, agricultural prices rose by only 89 per cent. This reflected the Bolshevik conviction that agriculture must provide the surpluses for industrialization.[5]

In India by contrast the price scissors have opened in the opposite direction but for precisely the same kind of reasons, namely, that their movement reflects the growing power of the intermediate class. It is true that the scissors closed sharply between 1972 and 1974, when the prices of manufactured and semi-manufactured goods rose far more rapidly than those of agricultural commodities. But the stimulus for this did not come from within the Indian economy. It came from the world-wide boom in raw materials prices, notably of ores, non-ferrous metals, and crude oil.

However, the most dramatic evidence of the growth in power of the rich farmer is provided by the census of agriculture carried out in 1970–71, whose results were finally published in December 1975.

The 16th and 17th rounds of the National Sample Survey had shown that there were 49.9 million operational holdings in the country in 1961–62. The 1971 census revealed that in nine short years their number has grown to 70 million. What is worse, the fragmentation was entirely at the lower end of the scale. Whereas 39 per cent of the holdings were of less than one hectare in 1961–62, over 50 per cent fell into this category in 1970–71. By contrast, while farms of more than ten hectares accounted for 24.4 per cent of the land in 1961–62, they covered nearly 31 per cent in 1970–71. Significantly, while the land area accounted for by the large farms had grown, their number had remained almost constant at around three million. It is thus clear that in the last 9 years there has been a sharp increase in the concentration of power in the hands of a very small number of rural families.

The mushroom growth of the bureaucracy in the last twenty years is also in part a reflection of the growing power of the intermediate class. It is true, as described earlier, that the pressure for jobs has to be absorbed by the bureaucracy mainly because of the highly capital-intensive nature of public as well as a good deal of private investment, its long gestation period, and the failure of the public sector to yield profits which could be ploughed back into creating more jobs in industry. But in which segment of society did this pressure originate? The beneficiaries were certainly not the landless in the villages, or the Harijans and Scheduled Tribes. The repeated circulars to government departments to fulfil their quotas of Harijan and Scheduled Caste recruitment, and the annual reports of the Commissioner for Scheduled Castes and Tribes show that even the statutory provisions of the law have not sufficed to give them a due share of the posts in the bureaucracy.

The principal beneficiaries have been the poorer relatives of the leaders of the local power elites in the rural areas. Similarly, in the large towns, most of the recruitment to the Class III services in particular has been from among the petty *bourgeoisie*, the only group with the necessary educational qualifications (a B.A. degree or a technical diploma) but without the influence or the social status to aspire to anything higher than a clerical post. The way in which the lower rungs of the bureaucracy have armoured them-selves against increases in the cost of living furnishes an even more striking proof of the power of the intermediate class. Up to a salary level of Rs 1,000 per month at the Centre and perhaps a little less in the states, the government has provided for automatic increases in salaries designed to compensate for between 95% and 50% of the increase in cost of living.[6]

One may argue with some justice that this is only fair. But it is also highly selective. Industrial workers, who are far more valuable to society than the lower levels of the bureaucracy, do not enjoy this right except where the employers have accepted the dearness allowance scheme. Many therefore have to fight to keep their real wages from falling. By the same token, agricultural workers and tenants who perform the actual task of cultivation and are arguably the most important segment of the working class, get absolutely no protection whatever. Thus, the government has ignored the interests of the most vital sections of the labour force, while lavishing its solicitude on the least important segment.

The class bias of legislation is also revealed in the concerted attack on the fixed-income groups in the last twenty years. Over the years it is this group, consisting of academics, school teachers, senior bureaucrats, army and police officers, journalists, and salaried managers in the public and professionally managed private companies, who have borne the brunt of the government's severe direct taxation who have received virtually no compensation for the steep fall in the value of the rupee, and have been the principal victims of the government's onslaught on urban property holders. The way government has allowed the fixed income groups to be squeezed by inflation and rising tax rates, contrasts sharply with its apathy towards the problem of taxing the self-employed classes. More than three-fifths of the actual income tax payers in the country are salaried earners. Indeed the number of tax payers who fall outside this category is barely one and a half million. A more telling estimate of tax evasion among the self-employed was furnished by a background paper submitted to the Wanchoo Commission on direct taxes, which showed that there were less than 1,700 lawyers, doctors and other professional people in the entire country declaring a taxable income of more than 100,000 in 1969–70 when the number in Bombay alone must have exceeded this figure. In December 1975, the Income-tax Commissioner for Bombay disclosed that only 11 doctors in the city disclosed a taxable income of more than this amount. [7]

Income tax raids in Madras showed similarly that only a fraction of the registered chartered accountants in the city paid any taxes at all. And as for shopkeepers, taxi and truck owners and others, it is doubtful if more than a handful bother to pay any kind of tax whatever. What is even more telling is the fact that to this day, no state government, except that of Kerala has been able to levy any kind of tax on agricultural incomes, other than on plantations.

The excuse that the income tax department often puts forward, that it is overworked, that the self-employed are hard to pin down, and that far too many income, excise and sales tax inspectors are corrupt, is specious. It should be obvious that taxing the self-employed will need more rough-and-ready methods of assessment, than those applied to salary or dividend earners. But in two decades the department has made no serious attempt to formulate, let alone apply, such yardsticks of assessment. Again, for different types of income earners, there is an urgent need to work out statistical norms of earnings, and tolerance limits within which indi-

vidual deviations will be accepted *prima facie* without the need
to make a detailed examination of tax returns. The formulation
of such statistical norms requires detailed surveys of the income
earned by different types of self-employed persons. But no such
surveys have been made. The truth is that the apathy of the income
tax authorities is a reflection of the indifference of the government
towards taxing the self-employed.

The bias against the upper fixed income groups in particular
is revealed starkly in the government's sustained attack on urban
property. The attack has been launched in two ways: by imposing a
ceiling on urban property, and by passing expropriatory tenancy
and rent control laws. It is most clearly manifested in the tenancy
laws enacted in Bombay, where the lease that a tenant signs on
entering a flat, is not worth the paper on which it is printed. Under
the current laws, a tenant can move into a flat, then move the courts
for fixing a standard rent which is as little as a quarter of the sum he
has contracted to pay, and stay on indefinitely paying the same rent,
irrespective of increases in the cost of living, the market price of
real estate, and the cost to the municipal authorities of supplying
the flat owner with water, power and other amenities. As if this is
not enough, he can hand over the flat to a son or relative on his
departure from Bombay or in the event of his death.

Needless to say, over the years flat owners have found various
ways of getting around these laws, but no sooner is one found than
the government plugs it with a new amendment to the tenancy
law. And if, as a last resort, the owner refuses to rent out a flat
and prefers to keep it vacant, the government requisitions it for the
use of its officers, at a nominal rent.

It is true that all the real estate in the cities is not owned by the
members of the fixed income groups. In recent years, more and
more bungalows and apartments are being bought by the *nouveaux
riches* who usually pay a part of the purchase price in black money.
The tenancy laws hurt them also. But the social significance of the
tenancy laws lies in the fact the purchase of a house or flat is the
first and often the only avenue of investment that most salary
earners think of. This is where their life insurance and provident
fund savings go as a rule. And significantly the tenancy and rent
control laws make little or no attempt to distinguish such legitimate
investment from the speculative purchase of flats with black

money. In theory most state governments try to distinguish between the ownership of one and of several flats, on the not unreasonable grounds that most salary earners cannot afford more than one flat or house. But in practice, the slow working of the courts has robbed the flat owners of any protection that the law could have afforded them.

Several other apparent anomalies of government law and practice become comprehensible only when seen as expressions of the power of the intermediate class. Thus the often heard complaint by managers of the public sector that in spite of belonging to the state, these enterprises are subject to all the disadvantages and all the red tape that bedevils the functioning of the private sector. For instance, in the middle of the power famine of 1973 and 1974, when trying to obtain spares from abroad for their defective generators, some of the state electricity boards found that it took up to 12 months to get a clearance from the government to place orders abroad.[8]

The refusal of those who advocate the nationalization of the large private concerns to examine the pattern of shareholding in these companies is another manifestation of the power of the intermediate class. In more than half of the largest concerns in the country, the bulk of the shares is owned by government bodies like the Life Insurance Corporation, and the long-term lending institutions set up and run by the Central and state governments. Thus under the existing company law, these companies are already government companies. Yet they are subjected to bitter attack and prevented from growing while every facility is given to wholly privately-owned smaller concerns to expand further. The government's obstinate refusal to distinguish between the 'good' and the 'bad' concerns in the private sector, can also be explained only as a reflection of a bias against 'bigness' and efficiency rather than against private ownership.

The Hazari committee on Industrial Licensing found definite proof of attempts to manipulate the licensing laws to pre-empt productive capacity in various industries in the case of only one of the 28 larger industrial houses in the country. The Dutt committee on Industrial Licensing, which followed up the work done by Hazari could find even a presumption of guilt only in the case of four large industrial houses. Yet, the government fastened on these few instances to tar all the large companies in the private sector with the same brush and made them the pretext for introducing a spate of new restrictions under the Industrial Licensing Policy Amendments of 1970, and the Monopolies and Restrictive Trade Practices Act.

Finally, coming back to the realm of agriculture once again, the power of the intermediate class explains why a government ostensibly wedded to socialism did not set up state farms in the vast tracts of 'new' land brought under cultivation in the U.P. Terai, and in the command area of the Rajasthan Canal in the 'fifties and 'sixties, even though this would have solved the problem of ensuring a minimum marketable surplus for financing its development projects and feeding the urban working classes. In every case, it preferred instead to distribute this land to private owners, thereby swelling the number of owner cultivators in the country. (A large part of of this land was originally given to displaced people from East and West Pakistan in small plots but soon found its way into the hands of the so-called progressive farmers.)

NOTES

1 See Chapter 1.
2 An interesting study of the unorganized sector in Bombay by Joshi & Joshi shows firstly that out of 27,500 employers in 1961 in the manufacturing 26,100 operated establishments employing less than 25 people. Self employment was highest in food and beverages, tobacco, textiles and metals, engineering(mainly repair work and the manufacture of small components for various appliances). See *Surplus Labour in the City*, Oxford University Press 1976, pp 51–7.
3 This paper, first published in Polish was translated into English and published in 1967 in *Co-existence* (Pergamon Press), Vol. IV. It has been recently reprinted in a posthumous publication of Michal Kalecki entitled *Selected Essays on the Economic Growth of the Socialist and the Mixed Economies*, Cambridge University Press, 1972.
4 Published as a pamphlet by Orient Longmans 1973 and printed in the *Economic and Political Weekly* 7th July 1973.
5 Dr Ashok Mitra, 'A Growing Scissors Crisis: Two Separate Inflationary Trends', *Times of India*, 26 December 1972.
6 Recommendations of the 3rd Pay Commission Report, Vol. IV, p. 5, Government of India Publications.
7 See *The Times of India*, December 3, 1975. In May '79 Prime Minister Morarji Desai deplored the fact that only 1400 people declared a taxable income of over Rs| 2,00,000.
8 See article in *The Times of India* by the author 'The High Cost of Neglect'. February 21, 1974.

6 / The Rise of the Intermediate Class

THE ECONOMIC LAWS described in the last two chapters do not merely reflect the growing power of the intermediate class, but are also its vehicle for the acquisition of more power. This becomes clear when one traces the rise of this class in a more systematic manner.

In the rural areas it can be traced to the first round of land reforms enacted in nearly all states in the 'fifties and early 'sixties. These reforms failed to give the land to the tiller, but created instead a class of peasant proprietors. Since this has been described in detail many times already, only its brief outlines need be given here.

The first round of reforms had three features in common: It placed a ceiling on individual instead of family holdings, allowed the resumption of land for personal cultivation up to this ceiling, and gave the tenant the right to buy land in excess of the ceiling, but as a rule, fixed rates of compensation which were well beyond the reach of the actual tillers of the soil.

The first two clauses enabled the *zamindars* to resume land up to the ceiling permitted to each member of the family from the tenants who had previously cultivated it, and to sell a good part of the surplus to smaller farmers who after counting heads in their families found they could still buy a good deal of land under the terms of the law. Finally, what little land was left after these adjustments was taken over by the erstwhile middlemen who had previously collected land rents from the peasants on behalf of the *zamindars* and were almost the only other people who could afford to pay the high rates of compensation fixed by the state governments. Needless to say all three groups took good care to see that no tenant could lay claim to hereditary tenurial right in the future, by simply throwing out all non-statutory tenants, (the vast majority) and reemploying them as agricultural labourers.

Thus a class of well-to-do owner-cultivators came into being literally overnight. As Ladejinsky wrote after a field trip to the Kosi area in north Bihar, there were operational holdings of several hundreds of acres, but registered in the names of 16 or more members of a family.[1]

It is worth noting that these peasant proprietors exactly correspond to the original concept of the *kulaks* in Russia—the richer, more aggressive peasants in the Mirs who bought out the landed gentry after the 1861 emancipation of the serfs, and took over the lands of the poorer peasantry who had the misfortune of falling into their debt. Their attitudes and their self-righteous defence of their property rights are also very similar to that of their now vanished Russian counterparts. A description of the *kulak* class given by Eric R. Wolf, could as easily apply to the new class of peasant proprietors in India.

'. . . twenty years after the Emancipation the equalising operations of the village had not succeeded in stemming the process of differentiation. The well-off, composing 20 per cent of all households, had clearly achieved a dominant position in concentrating land allotments, and in purchasing or renting additional land. . . Moreover, they had bought land of their own, often from the nobility which between 1877 and 1905 lost through sales nearly one-third of their land. . . .'
'Among these well-off peasants there were also many who became moneylenders to the poor.' "There are in these Russian villages," says Leroy-Beaulieu, "men who would be called in the West *exploiteurs*, vampires: enterprising, clever men, who fatten themselves at the cost of the community. The *mujik* has for them the frightfully expressive name of *mir-eaters* (miro-yedy). In many governments—those of Kaluga, Saratof, and others—most villages are pictured as being under the control of two or three wealthy peasants, who beguile the commune out of its best lands 'for a song'—or for no compensation at all. . ."
'The frequent failures of crops in the southeast are a standing danger to the needy, a standing opportunity for the unscrupulous rich. The insolvent debtor is compelled to give up to his creditor, often for a nominal price, a lot which he has no longer the means of tilling.'[2]

With a few changes of names and dates, the above description could be that of India today.

The new peasant proprietors who usually came also from the dominant caste groups in the village, were able to convert their economic strength into political power not only because of their pre-eminence within their castes, but also through their control of nine-tenths of the job opportunities in the village and through the operation of the *panchayati raj* system, which gave the *zilla parishads* (district councils) control over sizable amounts of development funds as well as the right to decide who got these and other inputs first. The hold of the new class on the *zilla parishads* was further strengthened by the fact that in all states where the *panchayati* system was introduced, with the exception of Maharashtra, elections to the *zilla parishads* were indirect, with the *gram panchayats* electing representatives to the *mandal* or *anchal parishads*, and these in turn electing the members of the *zilla parishads*. Even in Maharashtra, although elections to the *zilla parishads* were direct, the local peasant proprietors were able to consolidate their hold on power through control of the co-operative movement, notably the sugar co-operatives in the state.[3]

The growing power of the peasant proprietors has been reflected in their success in getting the Central government to fix high procurement and low fertilizer prices, as described earlier. But the money which has flowed into their hands has helped them to further consolidate their power. One visible effect is the growing ability of the district party bosses in the Congress to insist on choosing the party's candidates for the state legislature.[4] Another is the steady increase in the percentage of agriculturalists in the Lok Sabha, from 14.7 per cent in the first to 33.8 per cent in the fifth Lok Sabha.[5] As Kochanek pointed out for the Congress members of the second Lok Sabha, most of the agriculturalists owned sizable holdings of land. (Half of the seventy-one per cent who had some connection with the land, owned more than twenty acres of land, while 9 per cent owned more than 100 acres.)[6]

If the rise of the intermediate class in the rural areas can be traced to half-baked land reforms, its upsurge in the towns can be traced to equally half-baked attacks on big business. Indeed. as K.N. Raj has pointed out, a common strand linking the intermediate class in both the rural and the urban areas is the fear of bigness *per se*. The systematic bias in economic legislation against bigness and, as a corollary against complex technology has already been described in detail. Here it only needs to be restated that this paralysed the large modern companies in the private sector, discouraged them from entering or expanding production in the core sector and thus created all-pervasive shortages of key raw materials and intermediate goods. These shortages have given birth to large-scale blackmarketing on the one hand and inflation on the other. The two have conspired to lower the real income of the working classes, the fixed income groups and the salaried professional managers of big business and the public sector, while enriching the self-employed who form the backbone of this class in the cities. The intermediate classes have thus grown stronger both absolutely and in relation to other classes and over time they have used their growing economic power to capture political power by means of wholesale bribery and through political donations in black money to the ruling parties at the Centre and in the states.

The infiltration of the political machinery has been rendered very much easier by the government's decision in 1968 to ban business concerns from giving donations to political parties. Once again the immediate motive was to deny funds to the opposition notably the Swatantra Party, which commanded a good deal of support among the large industrialists in Bombay and Ahmedabad.

But the more significant feature of the move was that it was not accompanied by any attempt to set up an alternative method of financing political activities and meeting election expenses. As a result since the parties' need for funds kept growing, all of them were forced to go back to the very same business concerns and trade and industrial associations to ask for funds, but this time in black money. The move undoubtedly helped the Congress party by effectively destroying the financial base of the non-communist opposition. For as the ruling party, the Congress was in a position to virtually blackmail business concerns into meeting its demands on the one hand, and to set the law enforcement agencies on any concern which it suspected of giving funds generously to an opposition party, on the other. But in the search for influence, this move gave a decided edge to those whose control of their company's finances was so complete that they could raise black money easily. The favours that the government has showered on certain closely held Indian concerns, and in particular the tirade by many ministers against firms with foreign equity participation, springs as much from this as from any avowed leftist ideology or fear of 'foreign domination.'

Nor had the ruling Congress party hesitated to tap small enterprises and wholesale and retail traders through manufacturers' and trade associations. The student revolt in Gujarat in February 1974, was sparked by alleged deals struck by the Congress chief minister, Chimanbhai Patel with the wholesale traders in edible oils, which would allow them to rig up the price of groundnut oil in exchange for contributions to the state Congress party. The government's apathy toward taxing the trading community springs at least in part from its knowledge that even when a manufacturer gives a donation to the party 'in black' it usually does so by collecting black money from its selling agents—wholesale and retail.

The growing political power of the intermediate class can also be seen in the emergence of a whole range of key political positions, and powerful lobbies in the legislatures, other than that of the farmers. The political power of the 'sugar barons' in UP, and of the chairmen and functionaries of the sugar co-operatives in Maharashtra has been commented on frequently in the press and in academic works. What is less well-known is the way in which the operators of the power-loom sector of the textiles industry have infiltrated into the Congress party with many MPs and MLAs drawn from their ranks, and now forms a powerful lobby within the Central and many of the state parties. The pressure it has been able to exert on the government, by harping constantly on the dangers of the concentration of economic power in the hands of the owners of the large mills, and their alleged misdeeds in transferring depreciation funds to other industries, is one of the main causes for the continuing bias in the government's laws against the large-scale sector. In fact, nearly every small industries association has a powerful and effective lobby in New Delhi. Significantly, when the government proposed to lift price controls on soap and vanaspati in 1974, the move was *opposed* by the representatives of the small-scale producers while it was supported by the big producers.

It is a commonplace of Indian politics that newly mobilized

caste groups have usually shown their power first by giving their votes to the opposition parties. Thus for instance, the rise of the SSP and the Jana Sangh in U.P. can be traced to such a mobilization of caste groups.[7] In the same way the success of the SSP in Bihar in the 1967 elections resulted to a considerable extent from its mobilization of the powerful Yadava community in south Bihar. But the preoccupation of political sociologists with caste has obscured the fact that a similar mobilization pattern can be distinguished among class groups also. With next to no field work having been done on the basis of class as opposed to caste classifications, it is difficult to furnish concrete data to support this conclusion. But some qualitative observations do point to such a phenomenon. The success of the Jana Sangh in the parliamentary elections in Delhi in 1967, when they captured five out of the seven seats from the Union territory, and the oft-voiced opinion that the Jana Sangh in Delhi at least is a party of 'shopkeepers' gives some ground for the thinking that the intermediate class in many areas, first flexed its political muscles by voting for the opposition.

A better documented instance is given by Angela Burger, who examined elections to the state legislature in six U.P. constituencies in 1962. In the case of Rudauli she ascribed the success of the Jana Sangh to the existence of 'a network of shopkeepers.' The case is interesting because although the Jana Sangh won because of its superiority in the rural areas of the constituency, it did so almost entirely on the basis of wholehearted support from an urban-cum-rural network of wholesale and retail traders. Eight of the ten activists who worked most diligently for the candidate were shopkeepers. However, the fact that he was a *bania* by caste also undoubtedly played a part in mobilizing the trader network.[8]

The rise to power of the rich peasant proprietor is better documented. A striking example is furnished by the opposition aroused by the land-tax bill which the U.P. government introduced in 1962 in the state legislature. The storm of controversy which this raised for over six months until the Chinese invasion cut it short in October, and which was resumed in 1963, is described by Paul Brass.[9] The bill, brought forward by Mr C.B. Gupta's ministry to increase land revenue by 50 per cent for holdings of more than one acre, divided the state Congress and created a rare unity among the opposition parties. It is significant that the state government's decision, under the dual threat of factionalism within the Congress and the combined onslaught by the opposition, to raise the exemption limit to eight acres and thus exempt 90 per cent of all land holdings in the state, did not assuage the opponents of the move. This shows clearly that the concern of the opponents was not for the small but for the medium and large farmers! This is further underlined by the fact that opposition did relent when the government reduced the land revenue surcharge to 25 per cent even though it simultaneously lowered the exemption limit back to one acre.

Table 6.1
Occupations of the Members of the Lok Sabha

Occupation	1st LS No.	%	2nd LS No.	%	3rd LS No.	%	4th LS No.	%	5th LS No.	%
Full-time Social & Political workers	121	24.7	109	22.0	106	21.2	112	21.6	92	17.6
Lawyers	107	21.9	112	22.6	109	21.8	86	16.6	93	17.9
Scientists, Engineers, Doctors	21	4.3	15	3.0	20	4.0	23	4.4	16	3.1
Teachers	37	7.6	30	6.1	36	7.2	38	7.3	36	6.9
Business	53	10.8	47	9.5	55	11.0	58	11.2	39	7.5
Journalists	38	7.8	33	6.7	19	3.8	27	5.2	30	5.7
Agriculture	72	14.7	93	18.8	114	22.8	135	26.0	176	33.8
Services	24	4.7	22	4.4	24	4.8	25	4.8	12	2.3
Information not available	16	3.2	34	6.9	17	3.4	15	2.5	27	5.2
Total	489	99.8	495	100.8	500	100.0	519	100.0	521	100.0

Sources: S.L. Chopra and O.N.S. Chauhan, 'Emerging Pattern of Political Leadership in India, *Journal of Constitutional and Parliamentary Studies* IV: 1 (1970), p. 126. *Journal of Parliamentary Information* XVIII: 2(1972), p. 372.

However, even this proved unacceptable to the farm lobby in the long run. In 1963, after the Chinese threat had passed, the

agitation was resumed, and led eventually to the removal of the
chief minister, Mr C.B. Gupta, from office under the 'Kamaraj'
plan. One of the first acts of the new chief minister, Sucheta
Kripalani was to remove the surcharge altogether.

The nature of the principal dissidents is as interesting as the
course of the agitation. In the state Congress, the principal op-
ponent was Mr Charan Singh, the minister for Agriculture. Four
years later, Mr Charan Singh, seceded from the Congress, and
became the leader of a new party, the Bharatiya Kranti Dal, which
gained major successes in successive elections on the basis of very
strong support from the rich and middle-farmers of western U.P.
who are predominantly *jats*. His hold on them remains strong
even today. Opposition also came, interestingly enough, from
Mr K.D. Malaviya, member of parliament from U.P., who was
then a minister in the Central government. Mr Malaviya was then
regarded as a radical in the Congress party, and was an ardent
advocate of state enterprise and was known for his pro-Soviet
leanings. Yet he too recognized the growing power of the inter-
meditate class and fulfilled Kalecki's dictum of promoting 'a pattern
of amalgamation of the interests of the lower middle class with
state capitalism.'

The alignment of the opposition parties also furnished further
proof of the role they played in initially mobilizing this intermediate
class. Brass records that the leading role in the opposition to the
bill was taken by the Jana Sangh and the Samyukta Socialist
Party. In other words, the same party that mobilized the intermediate class in Delhi in 1967 and the shopkeepers of Rudauli in
1962, was also most ardently wooing the rural *kulak* in U.P. in
1962 and 1963.

Nor does the story end here. In 1966 and 1967, both before and
after the general elections, state governments vied with each other
in totally abolishing the land revenue. (Ironically, Mr Charan
Singh, who headed a motley coalition of parties and became chief
minister of U.P. in 1967, also met with disaster while trying to reim-
pose the land revenue on agricultural holdings).

The swift rise of the SSP and the Jana Sangh in the 1967 elections,
may be ascribed at least in part to the support it was able to mobilize

from this class. By the same token factionalism may have developed within the Congress, culminating in the breaking away of dissident groups in as many as four states at the same time (U.P., Bihar Bengal and Orissa), because the party was unable at first to recognize the growing power of the intermediate class. It should be remembered that even in the mid 'sixties, the Congress was still considered a champion of big business. The newspapers of 1966 and 1967 and the parliamentary debates of the time were full of references to the disproportionate influence of the House of Birlas in party circles. As Kochanek has pointed out, the big business link was forged as far back as in the 'thirties and the pre-independence years saw a large influx of businessmen into the Congress party. Indeed Mahatma Gandhi habitually stayed at Birla House in New Delhi.

But after its election reverses in 1967, the Congress was quick to come to terms with the intermediate class. It did so by breaking its links with big business and eventually turning openly hostile to it. The steps by which it did so are well known: in 1967 it dissolved the managing agency system, forcing the larger industrial houses to break up the management of their industry groups and thus weakening their influence over the constituent enterprises. It banned donations by companies to political parties—a step that incidentally affected the larger, professionally owned concerns far more than the family owned enterprises. In 1969, it used the Dutt Committee's report on industrial licensing to raise the bogey of a 'concentration of economic power' (a phrase that it has never satisfactorily defined) and amended the industrial licensing policy and passed the Monopolies and Restrictive Trade Practices Act to put curbs on the further expansion of the largest concerns in the private sector. It is interesting that the dividing line between the large industrial concerns and the others was drawn solely on the basis of the value of their fixed assets and not on capital employed. Since trading concerns have few fixed assets but employ vast amounts of working capital, the bias that this has created against bigness is a selective one that operates more against industry than against trade.

The rapid adjustment that the Congress made after 1967, is one probable reason for the failure of parties like the Jana Sangh and the SSP to pick up further strength. The performance of both parties in the successive midterm polls in U.P., Bihar and Punjab, and at the Centre has declined steadily, both in terms of seats and also, for the most part, in terms of their percentage of the total votes.

The preceding analysis is by no means free from shortcomings. For one thing, it is based on woefully little empirical evidence. As a result the conclusions that I have drawn are highly tentative, being more in the nature of promising hypotheses than firm conclusions. Yet they fit so neatly with the class bias of legislation described earlier, that it would be impossible to ignore them altogether. Regardless of whether they are fully borne out by future research or not, the preceding analysis does highlight the urgent need for a far deeper study of political and economic development in this country using the toolbox of class conflict rather than caste antipathies. Caste may have been an adequate frame of reference for the earlier phase of the socio-political development in India till 1962, when the rate of economic growth and of the expansion of productive employment was by and large satisfactory. In this phase, class antipathies were muted or as yet unborn. However, caste alone is not an adequate tool for analysing developments during the second phase, which started with the Sino-Indian conflict of 1962 or a little later. Since the mid 'sixties in particular, economic stagnation, inflation and the emergence of all manner of shortages, have pulled the various classes rapidly apart, exposing the underlying conflict in their interests. It would have been surprising if this was not reflected in a growth of class tensions in the political arena. Indeed the growing strain on the democratic system since 1973, the birth of the movement of dissent led by Jayaprakash Narayan and the demise of parliamentary democracy cannot be understood except in terms of the rise of an intermeditate class in India.

By its very nature, this class is parasitic. This is not to say that its members do not perform a necessary function in society. The well-to-do farmer and the small scale industrialist produce goods for sale (except when the farmer is a non-cultivating landowner). The trader distributes the goods that the others produce. In the same way the professional classes perform a variety of essential functions in society. But the class as a whole is parasitic in the sense that most of its members actually gain from the shortages that are caused by economic stagnation, or a poor monsoon, and all of them have the capacity to shift the burden of these shortages onto other segments of society.

Thus the intermediate class fattens on the debilitation of the economy. What is more, a large part of this class produces not goods but services, and, therefore, contributes very little to the net *material* product of the economy. But, as the figures cited earlier show, it has been able to raise its share of the national cake, very rapidly from 28.7 to 35.4 per cent in as little as ten years. In a poor country the increased value of services cannot by any stretch of imagination be deemed a rise in welfare. On the contrary, the rise in transport and distribution margins in an economy where nearly everything is in short supply is the surest indication of the parasitic nature as well as the growing economic power of the major part of the intermediate class.

Here then lies the root cause of the economic stagnation of the last 10 years. It is that in the short run at any rate, this stagnation has increased the power of the dominant class in society, and that the class has sought to consolidate its hold on power by perpetuating this stagnation. But the prolonged stagnation is at last beginning to cause political repercussions in other segments of society.

It is not entirely a coincidence that political unrest in the country touched a new peak in 1974, the same year that saw its economic fortunes reach their nadir. The truth is that as its economic problems have grown more intractable, they have cast a lengthening shadow on the political scene. The challenge to authority which began to manifest itself in student-led riots in Gujarat and Bihar and threatened to spread elsewhere in north India in 1974 is a direct outcome of a growing feeling of hopelessness and a mounting fear, particularly among the young, that the future holds out no promise to them but only a threat.

In the last twelve years, the number of people employed by the organized private sector has increased by about four to five hundred thousand. By contrast, the number of job seekers on the live register of the employment exchanges has increased from under five million to over ten million in just the last eight years What is more, inflation has halved the real incomes of the wage-earning and salaried groups and the unorganized sections of the working class, and robbed them of half their life's savings in the short span of two years, between 1972 and 1974.

As a result, while millions of jobless young men face the bleak prospect of remaining dependent on their families for years to come, many parents are losing hope of getting their children married and of being looked after by them in their old age. Even those who are prepared to support their grown-up children find their capacity to do so greatly reduced by the fall in the value of their savings.

Inflation and the mounting unemployment therefore threaten the very foundations of society. But even this would not have caused so many young people to question the very legitimacy of the present system of government, had they not become aware of the fact that some people at least have done very well out of the prolonged economic stagnation, mounting shortages, inflation and growing unemployment.

However dimly they may perceive it, more and more of the young people in the cities have come to realize that it is the government's own policies that are responsible for widening the gap between the economic power enjoyed by a small segment of society and the burdens borne by the mass of the people and that while most people have suffered cruelly, some clearly identifiable groups have been able to turn the decline in the fortunes of the country to their own advantage and have become extremely rich.

It is this which makes it possible for a blackmarketeer to buy an imported car from the State Trading Corporation for a lakh of rupees while a secondary school teacher cannot afford to buy the cheapest seasonal fruit for his family. Yet the school teacher often pays a larger share of his income by way of direct and indirect taxes than the blackmarketeer. It is the manifest injustice of this situation which has undermined the legitimacy of the present economic system.

The growing illegitimacy of the economic system has caused a progressive loss of faith in the political system. This would not have happened if the government had made a visible effort to prevent the divorce of economic power from responsibility. But far from doing so, politicians and bureaucrats alike have sought to profit from the situation. Instead of preventing the transfer of income from the poor to the rich they have sought to divert a part of this flow into their own pockets and instead of punishing the law breakers they have protected them, for a price.

Thus every control has created a new avenue for corruption. Smugglers, blackmarketeers and bootleggers have bought immunity from the law by bribing politicians and policemen, tax evaders have bribed income tax and excise inspectors, and businessmen have obtained investment and import licences by bribing members of the ruling party and paying black money to political parties to finance their election campaigns.

To those who are not among the direct beneficiaries of this corrupt system, society presents an ugly picture indeed. It is one of rule by a rapacious elite whose prime interest is the perpetuation of its hold on political power and its monopoly of the fruits of economic development; and which has now so completely infiltrated the government as to be indistinguishable from it. Its self-interest is manifested in hundreds of ways, large and small. Government servants have first claim on ration cards, milk cards, housing, the allocation of cars and scooters, and accommodation on trains and aeroplanes. Job security in the bureaucracy is absolute, and no group of wage earners is so well insulated by law against rises in the cost of living.

Thus here also one finds the same perversion of national priorities which has so severely hampered the growth of industry. Government servants, who as a group add the least to the country's material product, enjoy more rights than any other section of society. Workers in organized industry have to fight for every increase in wages, even those designed merely to offset the rise in cost of living. The country's intelligentsia, which means its schools, colleges and science laboratories, has fared a good deal worse. As for the tenant-farmers and agricultural labourers who actually till the bulk of the country's arable land, and are therefore the most important segment of its working population, they have neither security of job nor security of tenure.

The government fixes absurdly low prices for crucial materials like steel and cement not so much to protect the consumer who, it knows, will have to meet a good part of his needs in the black market, but to ensure that its own departments are able to get all they need at the low price that it has fixed. And public enterprises get loans at half to two-thirds of the interest rates that the private sector pays.

The government has turned visibly into a predator, feeding more and more voraciously on the economy but giving less and less to it in return. In recent years it has even appropriated the whole of the tax and non-tax revenues raised from the public for its own consumption, for since 1970–71, the non-developmental and non-Plan expenses of the Central and state governments have almost exactly equalled the sum of its tax and non-tax revenues.

Over everything there hangs the stench of corruption. The smuggler kings and the dacoits in Madhya Pradesh both had their political patrons. More and more of the cinema houses, restaurants, hotels and luxury apartment buildings in Bombay are now owned by smugglers, bootleggers and hoarders. Worst of all, there is no social stigma in ruling circles against these people. They are to be seen in the best clubs and at the most prestigious social functions, and their houses are frequented by ministers, secretaries to government and senior police officers.

Is it surprising that the vast majority of the urban population, which has not been coopted into this corrupt elite, and particularly the young people who face an uncertain future, have come to believe that the present system has nothing to offer them, and that the only way that they will get something is to fight for it in the streets? For it hardly needs to be stressed that a system of government can be considered, good, or morally legitimate, only to the extent that it tries to secure a balance between the rights that it confers on individuals and groups, and the obligations that it imposes upon them—between the contribution that they make to society and the demands they make upon its pool of resources. By the same token, no system of government which condones or connives at creating a wide disparity between the two is likely to retain its legitimacy in the eyes of the people for long. Such a political system can only survive through the ever increasing use of force and repression.

The catalytic roles of the left in the
rise of the intermediate class

No description of the rise to power of the intermediate class will be complete without a reference to the way in which the left has unwittingly played the role of a stalking horse in the achievement of its designs. It has done this by invoking the sanction of Marxism-Leninism and thereby cloaking the policy aims of this class in a mantle of intellectual respectability and humanitarian concern.

The pro-Moscow Communist Party's interpretation of the class character of the ruling class in India is that:

'The state in India is the organ of the class rule of the national bourgeoisie as a whole, in which the big bourgeoisie holds powerful influence. This class rule has strong links with the landlords. These factors give rise to the reactionary pools in the state power.'

The pro-Peking Communist Party's interpretation is somewhat broader:

'The present Indian state is the organ of the class rule of the bourgeoisie and the landlord, led by big bourgeoisie, who are increasingly collaborating with foreign finance capital in the pursuit of the capitalist path of development. This class character essentially determines role and function of the state in the life of the country.'[10]

The extremist CPI(ML) (Naxalites) cannot see anything Indian at all in the Indian ruling class and accuse it of having 'mortgaged the country to the imperialist powers, mainly U.S. imperialists and Soviet social-imperialists.' The two domestic elements responsible are 'feudalists and comprador-bureaucratic capitalists.' ('Programme of the Communist Party of India' (Marxist-Leninist), *Liberation* May-July 1970).

Leaving aside the CPI (ML) formulation, the differences between CPI and CPM are really a matter of emphasis. The national *bourgeoisie* include big and small business with and without foreign links. The landlords are not considered a dominant ruling class by the CPI.

The CPM reduces the importance of the small *bourgeoisie*, but includes the landlord. From these basic formulations have emerged a set of attitudes on major issues of economic policy that are tailor-made down to the last detail to suit the needs of the intermediate class. Thus, the left has consistently championed the wholesale nationalization of big business, and the expulsion of foreign monopoly capital from the country. Again, it has championed price controls, investment controls, anti-monopoly legislation, the setting up of prohibitive tariff walls, the banning of a wide range of imports, punitive direct taxation and heavy indirect taxes, all in the name of the small man. But it has done so without once following the logic of its own reasoning to its conclusion and finding out just who is the 'small man' whom these laws are supposed to benefit.

In the same way, it has supported each and every wage demand (including even the demand for more pay raised by the pilots of Indian Airlines in January-February 1974 who were even then earning more than Rs 4,000 a month exclusive of allowances) and wilfully blinded itself to the glaring fact that the organized working class is the elite of the country's labour force and accounts for at most half of the urban labour force, and that in a situation of all pervasive shortages and endemic inflation, higher wages for those who already have jobs may mean fewer jobs for new entrants into the labour market.

Most important of all, it has consistently championed the cause of small scale industry against big business, without once considering that the small industrialist today is precisely the property-conscious, self-righteous capitalist entrepreneur of the 19th century who aroused Marx's wrath.

Leftist intellectuals in this country are not entirely unaware of the trap into which the 'progressives,' both communist and social democrat, have fallen. The following excerpts from a perceptive essay by Ashok Rudra and Pranab Bardhan reveal this very clearly.[11]

'One may, of course, say that a party should not be judged by what it writes in its manifesto or what rhetoric it uses in public speeches or even by its electoral support base, but by what it actually does. If that is the criterion used in making the left-right distinction, it is to be noted that most of them (the political parties) communist or non-communist, act as pressure groups for the interests of largely the top two deciles of the population. These include those of the better-off farmers and traders, white-

collar workers and such sections of industrial labourers who
have come to form a kind of "labour aristocracy".'

'Most of the vociferous demands of these parties, whether for
more "remunerative" prices for farmers, or for higher wages
and salaries in the organised sector, for tax exemptions on the
lower middle class or against betterment levies on farmers, for
various subsidies and underpriced inputs, for expansion of
higher education or of jobs in the bureaucracy, all cater to the
interests of the richest quintile of the population. Many of these
demands are no doubt made in the name of the small man and
there are substantial regional variations in the pattern of such
demands or in the style of their articulation, but there cannot
be much doubt about who the ultimate beneficiaries are.'

On the specific role of the left parties, Rudra and Bardhan have
the following observations to make:

'It is of course true that there are many instances of the left
parties trying to lead struggles for the poor and exploited workers,
particularly around the industrial belts. But the fact remains
that the overwhelming majority of the poorest people in India
are unorganized. Except in a few localized pockets in the country
the vast masses of poor peasants and landless labourers have
been outside the pale of leftist movements. The leftist agrarian
organizations have, if anything, effectively served only the
interests of the rich and middle peasants, their declared inten-
tions not withstanding. The fake character of the left-right
distinction is particularly glaring when it comes to economic
matters. Thus, if an economist stands more for controls, licensing, takeovers and nationalization, he is a "progressive," in
case he is against these, he is obviously a "reactionary".'

The authors have no illusions about who benefits from the policy
measures which the left have supported.

'Price controls in steel, cement, automobiles and the like directly
benefit the consumption of the rich, yet by supporting them one
is supposed to uphold a "progressive" cause...'

'Quantitative trade restrictions provide an automatically protected market for inefficient domestic producers of luxury goods
like air conditioners, refrigerators and automboiles, and yet
anybody criticizing them must be having a "free-trade", laissez
faire bias...'

And on the class nature of the members of the bureaucracy
and the public sector they come very close to the concept of the
intermediate class elaborated in this book:

'Leftists often refuse to extend their class analysis of the state to the expanding public sector and the sprawling bureaucracy. Administered allocations of premia-carrying licences and permits strengthen the economic and political power not only of those who use those licences and permits but also of the relatively better-off white-collar workers who dispense those licences and permits; in fact this serves as a leverage they use in sharing the spoils with the industrialists.

'Nationalization (even when it is not used simply to bale out owners of "sick" mills) is used largely to expand the job prospects and security of white-collar workers, to improve wages, housing and other amenities of the unionised working class and to provide underpriced intermediate and capital goods for the private sector.

'Yet any expansion of the public sector is to be called a victory of the proletariat and any criticism of the way the public sector is run or the way the potential surplus is frittered away is to be construed as support for the cause of monopoly capitalists.

'To support controls, without asking who controls and to support take-overs without asking who takes over and for whose benefit, appear to us to be basically un-Marxian in approach...'

The origins of this *ersatz* socialism are rooted firstly in its essentially foreign inspiration, and secondly in an attempt to apply a particular definition of social classes to an environment for which it was never intended. The character of the Indian left has been moulded to a large extent by its ideological origins. These have been described succinctly by Nigel Harris[12].

Briefly speaking, the left has subscribed to the fundamental Marxist beliefs that the working class is the prime instrument of social change in any society, that this class is exploited by the capitalist who pays him a fixed wage based on demand and supply conditions in the labour market, and appropriates the surplus value he generates; that this process leads to a concentration of capital in the hands of a few and the alienation of the working class. It is on this ideological basis that they support workers demands for more wages on the one hand, and legislation restricting the growth of the larger industrial enterprises in the private sector on the other.

Yet, even assuming this analysis is correct, to what proportion of society does it apply? The private organized sector employs less than five million workers. No one has any clear idea of the number of workers in the unorganized sector. If we employ the ratio between the two sections worked out by Joshi and Joshi in their study of the unorganized sector in Bombay, it probably employs between four and four-and-a-half million persons.

On the other hand, the big capitalists are only a handful, and they control at best a quarter of industry in a country where industry contributes barely 18 per cent of the national product. How does one classify the vast numbers who do not fall into either category— the nine million civil servants and the up to twenty million self employed?

The mistake of the 'left' was its failure to realize that the self-employed constituted a separate class with distinct and identifiable interests. Leftists of all persuasions either ignored it altogether or assumed in some unspecified way that its interests could be 'reduced' to those of capital or labour, the two basic categories in their intellectual toolbox.

This is what led to their failure to distinguish between the big *bourgeoisie*, including professionally managed Indian and foreign companies, and the national *bourgeoisie* which included the bulk of the manufacturing enterprises in the organized sector. Most of the conditions of exploitation—lack of job security, violation of factory safety rules, evasion of pension, provident fund, housing and other provisions of the law—are far more common among the national *bourgeoisie*, but the CPI, and to some extent the CPM also joined hands with this class to attack the big and comprador *bourgeoisie*, in whom the divorce of ownership from capital had already tempered some of the worst excesses of early capitalism.

'The Indian Left was also linked to its ideological parents abroad, to Stalinism (the Communist Parties) and Social Democracy (The Labour and Socialist Parties). In both cases, what was meant by socialism had been steered very far from its historic moorings.

'In the original version (of Socialism) the freedom of the majority could be secured only by abolishing the private ownership of the means of production, by the working class, taking—by whatever means—control of economic power. In the later version, the extension of State power, of the public bureaucracy, was the essence of "socialization." The State was substituted for the majority: its power stood proxy for that of the working people. The two versions were linked by a whole series of phrases designed to muddle rather than clarify. For in speaking of the State as "the nation", its policies as "the national will", what social class controlled the State was concealed. Nationalization without workers' power merely assists the preservation of the power of the existing ruling class by sacrificing one small section of private capitalism. This ideological "sand in the eyes" was designed to conceal the real change between the original and the later versions of "socialism"—namely, the reconciliation of Stalinism and Social Democracy to the existing distribution of power.'

'For the Communists, the extension of nationalisation, state planning and loyalty to Moscow effectively encompassed the most important tasks for socialists. For the Social Democrats, extension of nationalisation, State planning, and defense of "democracy" (for which read, association with the United States) was the essence of the struggle for socialism. In India, the pursuit of these aims plus economic development, provided there was no foreign intervention, would gradually bring the promised land. For most people, the foreign association—the Soviet Union or the United States—was all that remained of the great historic debate between Revolution and Reform.'

Thus the Indian Left's commitment to nationalization and to state entrepreneurship in general, was rooted in Stalinism, while its support for the demand of the organized working class for land reform, centralized planning, small scale industry and a regime of controls, was rooted in social democracy. Ironically, as Harris points out, few if any in the Left movement realized that the identification of workers' power with state capitalism which had become an ideology to them was originally a matter of expediency to Stalin himself. Recalling the birth of the Soviet Union, Harris points out that:

'Despite a victorious working class revolution, Russia remained economically backward... The New Soviet republic survived under the constant threat of imperialist attack. The future of the Russian bureaucracy depended upon the future power of the Soviet Union, upon its military capability to repulse invasion. Military capacity is a function of industrial capacity. Industry can be built only by massive sustained investment which, in conditions of economic backwardness, means forced savings, freezing—or even lowering—the level of consumption of the mass of the population. In Marxist terms, it means extracting as much surplus value from the workers as is possible in order to accumulate capital. To undertake such a process, the bureaucracy had to be entirely beyond the control of the masses who were squeezed, otherwise they would never agree to such a process. The bureaucracy had to assume a privileged position in relationship to the means of production. Industry might formally be "owned" by everyone, but it was controlled by the functionaries of the State with absolute strictness, not to say ruthlessness...'

The tragedy of Indian socialism is thus a part of the larger tragedy of world socialism described by Harris. It has been put even more succinctly in an essay by the Polish philosopher Zygmunt Baumann.[13]

'It hardly occurred to Marx that socialism would arrive before capitalism had "exhausted" its creative potential, and he believed that this potential was sufficient to raise the productive forces of the society to the level of abundance. In this perspective, socialism could be located squarely in the political and cultural sphere of the social organization; it would be possible, indeed, only in so far as the capitalist venture, in its own crude and ruthless manner, liberated society from economic scarcity, and, therefore, from slavery to Nature and necessity.

'The Marxist idiom, however, was taken over and used as a revolutionary call to arms in countries which hardly fit the Marxist description of a society "ripe" for socialism. The peasantry has been invited to carry out the Marxist revolution; the same peasantry whose disappearance Marx counted among the main conditions for anybody to enter the kingdom of socialist reason. In consequence, the Marxist leaders of the peasant revolution (in Russia) were confronted, the day after they had captured state power, with a number of vital questions which had never been considered by Marx in the context of the socialist system and were obviously incompatible with the Marxian notion of socialism as the final act of human liberation.'

Thus the Indian socialists failed to realize that the big *bourgeoisie* and the comprador capitalists whom they condemned so heatedly were a product of mature capitalism and far closer to the point of socialist transformation than the national *bourgeoisie* with whom they were prepared to join hands. The fact that their very bigness made them more amenable to state control and supervision brought them a stage closer to the socialist goal, for it was at least possible for the state to make them shoulder a large measure of their social obligations in a way that became progressively more difficult as we progressed down the rungs of the national *bourgeoisie*.

Finally, in reconciling themselves to an alliance between the organized working class and the national *bourgeoisie* the CPI in particular failed to realize that it was not the workers who were taking over the reins of power but the exact reverse and that just as the intermediate class had hidden behind communist rhetoric to destroy its big enemies—those that originally came higher up the income and status scales—it had bribed the organized working class with protective legislation and dearness allowances to safeguard its flank during the early years of its rise to power.

The crushing of the railway strike in May 1974, which many observers have correctly interpreted as the beginning of the chain of events which led to the proclamation of the 'emergency' in June 1975, heralded the end of this opportunistic alliance. Significantly, it was not the representatives of the workers but those of the intermediate class in the ruling Congress party who triumphed in the end.

The failure to take cognisance of the intermediate class and to recognize its size and power, has reduced Marxists to talking about what is at most a peripheral struggle in the country today. But in focussing attention on the periphery they have drawn attention away from the central phenomenon of our times—the rise of the self-employed to dominant status in society.

The orthodox Marxist delineations of class and its later elaborations are irrelevant in Indian conditions because they were mainly intended to apply to mature capitalist economies and not to those in the very early stages of capitalist development. Labour can yield a surplus value for appropriation by the capitalist only when it is paid a fixed wage independent of its productivity. Exploitation of this kind therefore becomes a *central* feature of the economy only when the majority of the people in the country become wage earners. In the same way, the concentration of economic power becomes a central feature only when monopoly capitalists account for the major part of the national product. In such an economy, peasant proprietors will have long given place to capitalist farmers, owning and operating vast holdings of land. The wholesale traders will be organized in nationwide combines capable of pushing up or lowering prices throughout the urban markets of the country almost at will, and the corner grocery store will long since have given place to the supermarket chain. The majority of the population will be living in the cities, and the bulk of this majority will be wage-earners. But even the bare description of such an economy is sufficient to show how very far removed it is from the Indian reality.

NOTES

1 *Economic and Political Weekly*, September 1969, Review of Agriculture, p. A-147.

2 Eric R. Wolfe, *Peasant Wars of the Twentieth Century*, Faber and Faber 1972, p. 64.

3 Stanley Kochanek, *The Congress Party in India*, Princeton, 1968, Ch. 15, pp 370–1. Kochanek quotes a study by Mr Sirsikar showing that 83 per cent of the members of the zilla parishads in Maharashtra were agriculturists. Another study by D.C. Potter of Panchayati Raj in Rajasthan shows the strength of agriculturists declining from 83 per cent to a substantial 29 per cent as one moves from the villages to the district councils.

4 Stanley Kochanek, op. cit. pp 438-9. Kochanek quotes R. Roy, 'Selection of Congress candidates', *Economic and Political Weekly*, Feb. 18. 1967, p. 409.

5 The following table shows this clearly for the Lok Sabha. Kochanek op. cit. p. 3 cites a table prepared for the U.P. Legislature which shows a similar but less marked trend.

6 Kochanek, op. cit. p. 383.

7 Angela Burger, *Opposition in A Dominant Party System*, Oxford University Press 1969. See pp 54–6 for the caste compositions of various parties in 1962.

8 Angela Burger, op. cit. p. 56.

9 In Myron Weiner (ed) *State Politics in India*, Princeton 1968, pp 100–09, chapter on Uttar Pradesh.

10 B. Dasgupta, 'The Class Character of the Ruling Class in India', in *India: State and Society* (ed.) Mathew Kurien, Orient Longman.

11 'Totems and Taboos of Left Mythology' By P. Bardhan and A. Rudra, *Economic and Political Weekly*, 26 April 1975.

12 Nigel Harris, *India and China: Studies in Communism and Underdevelopment*, Vikas Publications, 1974 Ch. I.

13 *Controversies in Sociology: 3*, (ed) Prof. T.B. Bottomore and Dr M.J. Mulkay 'Socialism: The Active Utopia'. Zygmunt Baumann's essay '*A Socialist Experiment*', p. 77.

7/ The Emergency and After

THE PRECEDING CHAPTERS were written between July 1975 and October 1976, when the repressive measures of the 'emergency' were being most severely enforced in India. Since I was keen to see this book published in India, I deliberately refrained from making any mention of events after June 1975, and for the most part was content to cite statistics, and describe economic developments only till the end of fiscal year 1974–75. I did not feel that this detracted in any way from the relevance of my analysis, and was confident that readers who took the trouble to follow my arguments closely would have little difficulty in applying my politico-economic model to the emergency, and in discerning the forces which brought democracy to an end. To recapitulate briefly, I had attempted to show that stagnation after 1965–66, was not the product of an interplay of purely economic forces, but of the rise of an 'intermediate' class composed of the traditional petty bourgeoisie (including the owner-managers of manufacturing enterprises whether large in physical terms, or small) and the well-to-do farmers, which had a short term vested interest in stagnation. In its rise to power, this class first gave its support to the non-ideological opposition parties, notably the Jana Sangh, the Samyukta Socialist Party (SSP) and breakaway Congress factions like the Samyukta Vidhayak Dal (SVD) which later became the Bharatiya Lok Dal, but was successfully wooed by the Congress after it suffered its first major setback, in the 1967 elections. It was further shown that to safeguard its flanks during its rise to power this class infiltrated the bureaucracy by means of bribery, and made an ally of the organized working class by means of the dearness allowance scheme which gave it automatic protection against increases in the cost of living. This alliance was strengthened by the adoption of a socialist rhetoric which duped the bulk of the left in the country into becoming, in ideological terms, the Trojan Horse for its attack on the professional, upper-middle classes consisting of professional managers of 'late-capitalist' concerns, the senior members of the civil services and the armed forces, and the academics, journalists and lawyers and other members of the intelligentsia. It was further shown that this 'intermediate' class was parasitic, in so far as it thrived while the economy sickened. The corollary to this proposition—that the rise of the intermediate class, unless accompanied by a qualitative change in its vision of society, and of its role within it, contains the seeds of its own destruction, provides the starting point of any application of the above model to an understanding of the emergency.

Very briefly the events that led to authoritarian rule may be summarized as follows: Economic stagnation after 1966 particularly in the non-agricultural sector had led to a slow down in the growth of government revenues in real terms. The shortage of food and other wage goods, which was partly a result of this stagnation, made inflation chronic. Thus each year the government, now firmly in the hands of the intermediate class, found it more and more difficult to maintain its compact with organized labour and the lower civil servants to pay them their dearness allowances. They did so first during the plan holiday (1966–69) by cutting back planned investment. Then during the fourth plan (1969–74) by means of reckless deficit financing. For two years, exceptional harvests moderated the inflationary impact of this deficit financing.

But in 1972–1973, another large budgetary deficit conspired with a poor *kharif* crop and world-wide inflation to give a violent new lease of life to the inflationary spiral. The rise in oil prices gave another savage upward thrust to it, with the result that between January 1972 and January 1974, the price level rose by no less than 40 per cent. This spell of inflation finally wrecked the alliance between organized labour and the intermediate class. Around November 1973, the word went out from Delhi that further demands for wage hikes should not be entertained.[1] The government itself crushed a series of strikes by the pilots of Air India and the employees of Indian Airlines and the Life Insurance Corporation. The repression of organized labour culminated in the ruthless breaking of the railway strike in May 1974.

Once the government had dissolved its links with the working class, it felt itself free to make a number of structural changes in economic and political laws with the aim of curbing consumption and increasing saving and investment. The freezing of additional emoluments other than regular wage increments, the compulsory deposit scheme which affected mainly the upper salaried groups, the sharp increase in the bank rate to 9 per cent, and the minimum lending rate to 11.5 per cent followed. These measures impounded around Rs 450 crores of income and reduced the flow of credit in the economy. They therefore helped in (but were by no means wholly responsible for) the containment of inflation in October 1974. The period which followed saw two opposed trends: on the one hand the decline in prices which resulted from these measures brought universal relief. The use of MISA against smugglers and hoarders also proved popular, although the law itself was morally repugnant and was correctly foreseen by many even then as a precursor of worse things to follow. But at the same time they aroused the hostility of the organized working class and greatly reinforced the feeling of insecurity instilled in the members of the intermediate class by the mounting agitation of the students, the unemployed and the unemployables, in Gujarat and Bihar in the first months of 1974.

Mrs Gandhi's decision to declare the emergency must be viewed against these contradictory trends. The undoubted popularity of many of the strong measures she took in this period had enabled her to regain much of the political ground she had lost during the inflation of 1972 to 1974. In early 1975 the general consensus in the country was that an election would see her returned to power with only a slightly diminished majority. On the other hand the intermediate classes, whom she now represented, had lost their most powerful ally, the organized labour movement, alienated the left intellectuals in the country, and could no longer hide their bid for political dominance behind a veil of socialist rhetoric.

As will be shown later, most of the leftist writing on the emergency has assumed implicitly that the above trends complemented and reinforced each other. Their argument is that strong economic measures cannot be initiated by a democratic government. Thus the declaration of the emergency was the necessary condition for launching the economic programme of the government. This view is wrong. One has only to read the editorials in the major newspapers of the country, and numerous subsequent references to the Maintenance of Internal Security Act (MISA) in the weeks after they were promulgated, to realise the extreme ambivalence that even the most perceptive commentators felt towards them. Among the people not only was there heartfelt relief at the decline in prices, but a great deal of satisfaction that the smugglers and hoarders were getting their just deserts.

If the above analysis is correct it leads to two important conclusions. The Allahabad Court's verdict convicting Mrs Gandhi of electoral malpractices and debarring her from membership of the Lok Sabha for six years definitely acted as the trigger for the declaration of the emergency, and that without it, the emergency would never have occurred. However, behind it lay a steady shift in the balance of political power towards a vast class which had a vested interest in stagnation, and whose self-preservation demanded the suppression of all manifestations of the political and social unrest which was born of this stagnation. The emergency was thus the culmination of an interplay of class forces triggered by the process of economic development itself. From this there follows the disturbing possibility that if the end of the emergency has not ended the dominance of the intermediate class, then the return of democracy may also turn out to be temporary—an Indian summer before the permanent onset of winter. The analysis which follows is deliberately carried on beyond the emergency upto the end of March 1978 in order to examine whether this danger does exist. Subject to the difficulties inherent in interpreting current events as they unfold around us, the conclusion arrived at is that it does, and that consequently the threat to democracy, to human freedom and to the hope for gradual, if unspectacular social change is by no means over.

The Causes of The Emergency—Some Interpretations

Before going into the causes of the emergency in greater detail, it is worth examining some of the explanations for the events of those 19 months which are now current in both popular and academic literature.

The official explanation of the Congress party, that the emergency was the only way of protecting democracy and the rule of law against a concerted attack by the opposition parties, abetted by mysterious foreign governments or agencies, need not be taken seriously. But two others, which can be taken to represent the 'liberal' and the 'socialist' interpretations need to be examined more closely since both contain important insights.

The 'liberal' interpretation tends to put a large part of the blame squarely on Mrs Gandhi's personality. In its less sophisticated form it is indistinguishable from the charge made by the members of the ruling Janata party, that Mrs Gandhi declared the emergency solely to stay in power in the face of the Allahabad Court judgement. It claims that the so-called threat to law and order in June 1975 was vastly exaggerated. Similarly J.P.'s call to the police and army on June 20th 1975 not to obey illegal orders to commit violence on the people which Mrs Gandhi used as a pretext for clamping down her authoritarian rule, could scarcely have been considered a call to revolt. Such calls had been issued by the Congress itself on many occasions during the struggle for independence. Mrs Gandhi's actions only underlined that the Congress of 1975 was not the Congress of 1942. It is true that Justice Krishna Iyer the 'vacation' judge of the Supreme Court had granted a conditional stay of execution of the judgement, which permitted her to remain Prime Minister (although without the right to vote in the Lok Sabha) till her appeal against the Allahabad judgement could be heard by the full bench of the Supreme Court. But, the argument runs, a seriously weakened Mrs Gandhi might not have been able to get her own party to pass the retroactive legislation that she needed to make absolutely sure that the Supreme Court would give a judgement in her favour. Not only was such retroactive legislation likely to be repugnant, but the first days after the Allahabad judgement had shown that the parliamentary Congress party was not unanimously of the opinion that Mrs Gandhi was indispensable. In fact a sizable rump favoured a rapprochement with J.P., and both Mr Chavan and Mr Jagjivan Ram had earlier turned down Mrs Gandhi's suggestion that there should be a 'caretaker' prime minister nominated by her until her appeal was heard. Mrs Gandhi, the argument therefore runs, declared the emergency not so much to counter a threat to law and order from the opposition but to cow her own party into passing the spate of retroactive legislation which was actually enacted in July and August 1975.

The above interpretation is by no means comprehensive. It

ignores the role played by mounting social unrest and economic
stagnation in bringing about a situation in which the entire cabinet, Congress parliamentary party and rank and file in the States
welcomed the emergency, and industrialists, traders, trade union-
ists and many members of the intelligentsia vied with each other
in showering compliments on Mrs Gandhi for her 'bold and
courageous action'. It also underplays the highly provocative role
played by the opposition in the period after the Bangladesh war
when it was willing to support almost any kind of demand, and
lead any protest or *morcha*, in order to stay in the public eye.
In fact the opposition rediscovered a purpose and regained some
internal discipline only after JP launched his movement for reform
in Bihar and Gujarat. Nor does the above interpretation account
for the growing personal rancour that marked all references by
the opposition leaders to Mrs Gandhi, and by her to them. Mrs
Gandhi's increasingly frequent references after 1972 to mysterious
foreign powers and reactionary vested interests who were ganging
up against her, undoubtedly contained an element of paranoia.
But the opposition also did everything it could to provoke this
paranoia. In the 14 days that elapsed between the Allahabad Court
judgement and the declaration of the emergency, she was the sole
target of their attacks. The argument, conceded by Justice Krishna
Iyer while granting Mrs Gandhi an interim stay of judgement,
that the office of the prime minister is the focus of power in a government and that power, unlike legal rights cannot be given back by a
decision of court, cut no ice with the opposition leaders.

The Janata party's interpretation does however have the merit
of highlighting the personal element in her decision to overturn
democracy, which has been touched on above.

A far more sophisticated 'liberal' analysis of the events which
led upto the emergency, given by Prof. Rajni Kothari, needs to
be seen against the background of his analysis of Indian politics.[2]
At the risk of some oversimplification it may be said that he ascribes the emergency to the breakdown of the politics of consensus
in India. In his view the process of politicization in India has consisted of two separate movements. Those in power have drawn
into their fold the elites of more and more ethnic, religious, caste,
linguistic and interest groups. These have then performed the

function of mobilizing the remaining members of their groups to vote for particular persons or parties. Such a process requires that there should be at the very least a broad consensus among the elites coopted into the political leadership. The consensus must of course be greater within each party, but some element of it must exist even between members of rival parties, so long as they subscribe to democratic methods of government. It is this consensus which Mrs Gandhi destroyed by her mode of governance. Kothari described the breakdown of this consensus in a highly prescient article published in the *Times of India* at the end of December 1974. He predicted that the only possible outcome, if the current trends continued, was a sharp increase in the level of violence in the country. Less than a week after it was published, L. N. Mishra, then the Union Minister for Railways and chief fund raiser of the ruling Congress party, fell victim to an extraordinarily clumsy, but nonetheless successful assassination attempt at Samastipur in Bihar.

One result of the rising level of violence, Kothari believed, would be an increasing pressure on the still young political institutions of the country. Kothari traces, in the chain of events leading up to the declaration of the emergency, Mrs Gandhi's step by step destruction of every political institution in the country, ending with parliament itself. Thus she split the Congress in 1969 and in the ensuing years systematically undermined the position of every Congress chief minister in the country, most of whom she replaced with her own nominees. In this process she destroyed first the Central and then the state party machines, and reduced the Congress to a caucus party.

In the years after 1971, she severely curtailed the independence of the judiciary, first by putting more and more statutes beyond the purview of the courts and then in 1975 by flouting the convention of choosing the senior-most judge of the Supreme Court to be next chief justice of India and appointing another judge of her choice. Again, having gained the largest majority ever received by a Congress government Mrs Gandhi chose in 1971 to enact important laws mostly by presidential ordinances which were later presented to parliament for ratification. In this way she reduced parliament as a whole to a rubber stamp. The jailing of sitting members of parliament, the imposition of censorship on the press, and the massive attack on the judiciary during the emergency were thus only the last act of a long drama.

In his article in *Seminar*, a monthly magazine published in Delhi, in January 1976, Kothari concentrated only on the destruction of the Congress and the democratic institutions of the country from 1969. But his analysis can profitably be extended back to 1967, to show how, even before the Congress split, the ruling party had accomplished the destruction of the non-communist opposition. The two most important moves it made during that period were to ban donations by companies to political parties, and to deprive the princes of their privy purses. Since these were overwhelmingly the most important sources of finance for the Swatantra and the Jana Sangh, the enactments deprived both of them of their financial base. The public controversy aroused by both these moves, which centred around textbook political and legal issues like the nexus between business and politics, and the breaking of solemn covenants made by the Indian union with the princely states, missed the main point altogether. What had actually happened was that in the 1962 elections, many of the princes of central and western India had revolted against the Congress (whose proteges they had been till then). A large number had stood as Swatantra or Jana Sangh candidates and even more had stood as independents, and won thumping victories. In 1967 the princely revolt went a stage further, and they came to play an important part in the Jana Sangh and Swatantra parties in Rajasthan, Madhya Pradesh and Gujarat. In Madhya Pradesh, the Congress suffered a severe erosion of strength, and in Gujarat and Rajasthan it lost its majority.

The Congress leaders could hardly have failed to perceive the threat. In the Swatantra party, in particular, it perceived a rival which, although small, could attract away a disproportionately large share of the donations which businessmen were earmarking for political parties. In the same way, the rulers had begun to use their privy purses to finance political activities inimical to the ruling party.

The unwillingness of the undivided Congress to tolerate this shift in loyalties and live with the attendant threat to its hegemony marked the beginning of the breakdown of the political consensus.

However, the breakdown first became visible in the wholly un-principled manner in which the Congress launched an all-out attack to unseat oppositon SVD (Samyukta Vidhayak Dal i.e. Coalition) governments in the states. No threat and no inducement was considered too low to use, including outright bribery of MLAs to change sides. This attack was launched within days of the 1967 elections, on a relatively minor note when Mohan Lal Sukhadia, the leader of the Congress party in Rajasthan was given time, before he faced the new house, to buy over a number of MLAs from the opposition parties with promises of ministerial posts, to convert a minority into a tenuous majority. In the next nine months, it engineered the fall of SVD governments in Haryana and Bihar, and the first CPI-CPI(M) led United Front government in West Bengal. In this way the opposition coalitions were denied the time they needed to learn to live together. It is true that the opposition also engineered defections in Congress governments such as that of Madhya Pradesh. What is more, several SVD governments were no more than rag-bag coalitions including parties from the CPI(M) to the Swatantra, which could not possibly have survived very long. But this does not change the fact that the Congress initiated the process of engineering defections and was as a rule too impatient to wait till the coalitions fell of their own weight.

The fortunes of the opposition parties touched their nadir between 1971 and 1974. They were virtually penniless, and thanks to Mrs Gandhi's success in dealing with the Bangladesh crisis and persuad-ing most people that she was a champion of the poor, they were without a programme and without support. In desperation they were reduced to joining almost any agitation in support of no matter what cause, to garner a little transient support, to shore up the morale of their cadres, and quite literally to remind the people through the press that they still existed. When they found in the JP movement of 1974 a bandwagon they could at last hitch themselves to, their pent-up bitterness burst forth. The highly personal nature of their attacks on Mrs Gandhi in the ensuing 15 months was a direct reflection of this bitterness.

The process of 'de-institutionalizing' democracy thus began not with the Congress split in 1969 but more than two years earlier after the electoral reverse suffered by the Congress in 1967. What is more, the blame for it cannot be placed on Mrs Gandhi alone, but on the entire leadership of the undivided Congress. It is important to bear this fact in mind because the purely political moves described above paralleled the determined and successful bid initiated by the undivided Congress to woo the intermediate class, which has been described in Chapter VI. Extending the analysis back to 1967 also helps to highlight the question which Kothari does not ask, and which his brief analysis in *Seminar* does not answer: If Mrs Gandhi's personal style of government cannot be held responsible for the breakdown of political consensus, why did it happen? While Kothari has undoubtedly a fairly shrewd idea of the causes, it is important to note that they cannot be deduced from the analysis given above, which is rooted in structural functionalism. The chief weakness of all such analyses lies in their basic premise, that societies tend to perpetuate themselves—that the processes of political acculturation, mobilization, interest aggregation, and political differentiation through the growth of institutions serving explicit political goals, which mark the transition from traditional to modern societies all serve to perpetuate the status quo. Such analyses fail, almost by definition, to offer a worthwhile explanation for the breakdown of a social or political system.

'Leftist' Interpretations Of The Emergency

The above critique shows that while explanations of the emergency that focus on the personality or motives of Mrs Gandhi, or on specifically political processes, give us valuable insights into its causes, they do not explain why the political consensus broke down, why this process began in the days of the old undivided Congress whose leaders were past masters of the art of compromise, and most important of all, why virtually the whole of Mrs Gandhi's Congress welcomed the emergency. They do not also explain the rapid growth of paramilitary police forces, particularly after 1966 and the fact that this occurred with the almost complete approval of the ruling classes and the intelligentsia; why these same groups again supported the use of Draconian laws like MISA against smugglers, grain traders, and currency black marketeers in 1974 despite the grave risk that they would be used against political opponents, and why even the intelligentsia was initially sharply divided on the merits of declaring the emergency.

For an answer to these questions it becomes necessary to bring economic and social trends explicitly into the picture. The chief merit of the current 'leftist' explanations of the emergency lies in the central role they ascribe to these trends.

The less serious of these explanations lays the blame for the emergency on the pressures exerted on India by the international community, notably through the International Monetary Fund and the World Bank. This thesis has been spelt out by Jeremiah Noviak, in an article for the July 1977 issue of *The Asia Mail* (USA) which was also published in the *Times of India* on 1st, 4th and 5th July 1977. Noviak's thesis is that when India applied for a loan from the IMF to tide over the impact of the rise in oil prices, the IMF, the World Bank and the Aid-India Consortium insisted 'in part because of prodding by Mr Daniel Patrick Moynihan, '...that Mrs Gandhi give up her quasi-socialistic policies (even the communists called her pre-1974 policies 'quasi-socialist') and turn to more 'western' policies—policies (which) were more in keeping with the make-up of the members of the Consortium, all of whom are western countries.'

This 'western' policy consisted, according to Noviak, of a freeze on wages, cuts in public consumption expenditure, a high interest rate and increases in exports, designed to stabilize prices, curb imports and bring the balance of payments back into equilibrium. In political terms, the crunch came with the first part of this deflationary programme. For it required the government to take stern measures to discourage demands for increases in money wages and thus to impose cuts in real wages and salaries on its own employees and those of the private sector. Since these were bound to be unpopular, and since the general elections were around the corner, Noviak argues that Mrs Gandhi felt she could implement them only by suppressing democracy altogether.

There is a superficial plausibility to what has been said so far. The IMF package for international stabilization does centre around deflation, and deflation is bound to be unpopular. But Noviak goes one step further and tries to paint a picture of the Indian government dancing like a puppet on strings pulled from Washington. 'But before either the IMF funding or the (World Bank aid consortium) loan was approved, Mrs Gandhi had to act decisively. She did this by crushing the railway workers' strike in May 1974.' In the same vein Noviak says "The IMF noted these deflationary-cum-liberalizing policies with satisfaction in the IMF survey, September 2nd 1974, and word went out in business circles that India had 'turned around.'"

Noviak also ascribes the mass sterilization programme to the World Bank with not a shred of evidence except remarks made to him by a few Indian officials. To explore the connection, if any, between these agencies and the family planning programme falls well outside the purview of this chapter. Noviak's willingness to trust hearsay in this matter shows how far he is prepared to suppress academic scepticism in order to find evidence for his theory of an international conspiracy against Indian 'socialism.' In fact, he seeks to strengthen his case by comparing Mrs Gandhi to Salvador Allende of Chile.

'Consider her position. In 1974 she found herself in an economic position not unlike that faced by Mr Allende in Chile. Either she came up with a suitable programme or she would not get IMF-Consortium support. Mr Allende did not conform to the IMF-World Bank and his credit was cut off. Forces in Chile then took power, implemented the 'proper programmes' and were reinstated. But first Mr Allende was murdered.

'Confirmation of this sequence was also found in Bangladesh in 1974–75. In June 1974 almost the same day as India received its consortium loan Bangladesh received a standby credit from the IMF. A 'standby credit' is issued with even harsher conditions by the IMF than the credit to India.

'As the result of the terms of this credit Sheikh Mujib found that in January 1975 he had to declare himself president and take dictatorial powers. Even then he could not gain control over the bureaucracy and his own economy. On July 28th 1975, two weeks before he died, the IMF issued this press release "The Fund approves a standby arrangement for the People's Republic of Bangladesh...in support of a financial programme to *stabilize* the country's economy...this is the second standby arrangement since Bangladesh became a member of the fund".

'Two weeks later Mr Khondakar Mustaq Ahmed, a pro-western Bengali led the revolt. In October 1975 he issued a "white paper" which spelt out an economic programme not unlike the PN Dhar-V.K.R.V. programme.

'And for another case, in May 1972, the Philippine government obtained a standby arrangement even harsher than usual. At that time a group of economists, led by Gerardo Sicat, proposed a programme similar to that of P.N. Dhar and V.K.R.V. Rao (see Sicat's *New Economic Directions*, 1975). In September 1972, Mr Marcos declared an emergency.

In all, 14 standby arrangements were implemented in 1974, 15 in 1973, 13 in 1972 reaching as high as 25 in 1976. These IMF arrangements require changes in policy that are almost impossible to implement without authoritarian rule. And Mrs Gandhi was not the first, nor the last, to implement an IMF stabilisation programme under dictatorship.

And by the way, Bangladesh, Chile, the Philippines and other countries began well financed population programmes after the dictatorships. No doubt somebody will study why population and economic stabilization programmes go together.'

Noviak's attack on the international agencies is along the lines of a great deal of recent leftist writing on the Machiavellian nature of foreign aid.[3] It is not my purpose to discuss the broader attack on the motives of aid-giving countries and agencies, some of which seems to me to be well founded. All I wish to point out here is that it completely fails to explain the causes of dictatorship in India and that its failure stems from the fact that the model of political-economic development from which it is derived, which lays great stress on the role of foreign capital and the export sector is not appropriate to India.

Noviak goes wrong on three counts. The first is his interpretation of the nature of Mrs Gandhi's government and policies. The second is his chronology and interpretation of developments in India. The third is the importance of the IMF's promptings in the framing of Indian policy.

To take Mrs Gandhi's regime first, enough has been said in the earlier chapters of this book to show that it would be the height of naiveté to call it socialist in any meaningful sense of the term, much less compare it to the Allende regime in Chile. The detailed analysis of economic policy in the foregoing chapters shows clearly that Mrs Gandhi's was an *intermediate* regime, devoted to protecting the interests of the self-employed. The urban component of this

class includes a nascent indigenous capitalist class of owner proprietors whom Marxists would call the national bourgeoisie, who
are thrown up by the process of economic growth itself. The idea
that this type of government is socialist is hardly worth entertaining.
In fact 'national capitalist' would be a far more accurate definition.
With regard to Mrs Gandhi's allegedly socialist measures between 1969 and 1973 a close look at the most socialistic of them—
bank nationalization—shows that the new recipients of bank
loans were almost entirely from the self-employed classes such as
truck and taxi operators and small scale industrialists and that the
structure of rural credit remained biased in favour of the middle to
large farmer.

Many other measures in the field of industrial policy, such as
the monopolies act, succeeded in discouraging new investment and
thereby reinforcing the *de-facto* monopoly enjoyed by the existing
producers.

Noviak's thesis that Mrs Gandhi 'switched to the western model
of development' is naive in another way. It takes it for granted
that such 'switches' are possible, which in turn means that governments operate in some rarified atmosphere, above the hurly-burly
of class struggle. It fails to ask what classes or interests were behind
the earlier policies, how strong was their hold on the government,
and how great was their capacity to react to drastic changes of
policy. In fact, for an analysis rooted in an off-shoot of Marxist
thinking, it is completely un-Marxian in approach. As I hope to
show later the 'emergency' is better understood not as the spring-
board for a change in economic policy, but a pre-requisite for the
continuation and intensification of the existing policies, designed
to perpetuate the dominance of the intermediate class.

Having started from defective premises, it is hardly surprising
that Noviak has had to distort the chronology of events to fit his
hypothesis. The most important distortion relates to the supposed
connection between the breaking of the railway strike and the
approval of the first IMF SDRs. The negotiations for the loan were
concluded in April as Noviak himself admits at a later point in his
article. The IMF announced the release of SDRs on May 1, 1974.
The railway strike however did not take place till May 8th. It is
true that the government had made it clear that it would not con-

cede the strikers main demands for the payment of a compulsory minimum bonus under any circumstances. But on April 25th it had conceded a number of other demands which would cost the exchequer Rs 80 crores. What is more, talks were going on until almost the last day in the hope of arriving at a compromise and it was generally believed that the railway men would settle for around half of their maximum demand of around Rs 470 crores. There was thus no way in which the IMF could have been sure on May 1st that the Indian government would not make further concessions to avoid a strike. The question of making the release of SDRs conditional on crushing the strike, therefore did not arise.

Even had it wanted to, the IMF could not have imposed any stringent conditions on its loan. This was because the April agreement was for the release of only the first tranche of SDRs. Noviak does not seem to be familiar with the operation of the IMF's system for granting loans to cover balance of payments deficits. The conditions which the borrowing country must fulfil become progressively more stringent with each successive tranche. The release of the first tranche is little more than a formality. His ignorance of IMF procedures is also revealed by the fact that all the examples he cites of countries on which the IMF imposed severe conditions—Bangladesh, Philippines, Britain and Italy—involve standby agreements, an entirely different sort of loan arrangement begins which only after a country has exhausted all the three tranches of its SDRs. At this stage the IMF does impose stringent conditions including an obligation to deflate the economy, but by the time a country reaches this stage its balance of payments deficit begins to look highly intractable, and the IMF's concern becomes more understandable. India never got to the point when it had to ask the IMF for a standby loan.

In his attempt to make facts fit his hypothesis, Noviak goes on to pile error upon error. He claims that the Aid-India Consortium's loan on June 14th was also conditional on the adoption of deflationary policies. Nothing could be further from the truth. The consortium had been granting long term loans for two decades. In the years before the fuel crisis this came to around $1.2 billion. In 1974–75, the amount actually rose to around 1.4 billion dollars. The question of not granting a loan never even arose as it would have had the most disastrous international consequences, by no means confined to relations between the rich nations and India. On the contrary it was a foregone conclusion in Delhi at least four to five months before the consortium met that it would give more and not less aid. In fact Mr Macnamara, the IBRD's president had written to the donor countries recommending higher commitments, long before the railway strike. As it turned out, the small increase sanctioned by the aid-giving countries, was rather disappointing, and could in no circumstances be considered a reward for breaking the railway workers' strike.

Noviak's interpretations of key events and the governments reaction to them are, at times rather fanciful. According to him, Mrs Gandhi called out the troops at the time of the railway strike because she did not rule out the possibility of an insurrection in support of the railway workers. This is wishful thinking. To put it bluntly, the railway strike was unpopular. It coincided with the closure of schools and colleges all over the country, the beginning of the Summer holidays for the affluent, and most important of all with the annual leave of millions of industrial workers who go home in May to supervise the sale of their *rabi* or spring harvest, the picking and sale of mangoes, and so on. It also disrupted the flow of foodgrains immediately after the *rabi* harvest. There was thus hardly a single influential segment of the population—the farmers, the mill workers, the capitalists and upper salaried managers and the intelligentsia, which was not severely inconvenienced. In fact, the resulting climate of universal condemnation was one reason why as large numbers of railwaymen disobeyed the strike call right from the start, forcing the strikers from the second or third day to concentrate on paralysing only the major switchyards like Mughalsarai in Uttar Pradesh and Tughlaqabad (near Delhi).

Noviak is also completely off the mark in thinking that 'the Bangalore policies and the crushing of the railway strike were among the major causes of the increased political agitation of 1974–75...' It is true that the number of man-days lost because of industrial disputes rose to an all-time high of 40 million in 1974 but a very large part of this—perhaps a third to one half—was accounted for by the railway strike, which went on for over three weeks. The

view that 1974 was no worse than the preceding years is also sub-
stantiated by the fact that the number of industrial disputes went
down to 2938 in 1974 against 3243 in 1972 and 3370 in 1973.[4]

Noviak's notion that the economic programme begun at
Bangalore 'needed the emergency to be fully implemented' also
does not make sense. The Bangalore programme included some of
the most severe economic measures implemented by any democratically elected government anywhere in the world. These included
the impounding of dearness allowances, the introduction of a
compulsory deposit scheme, and a sharp increase in the minimum
lending rate of 11.5 per cent, which meant that marginal borrowers
were having to pay 16 to 18 per cent for short term loans from the
banks. It also included, although Noviak does not mention it, the
passing of laws like the Maintenance of Internal Security Act which
were morally repugnant, but were initially welcomed because they
were used against known smugglers and hoarders who had for
long been the targets of public ire.

By contrast the measures taken after the declaration of the
emergency, were according to Noviak 'more irrigation projects,
more relaxation of controls on business, lower taxes, higher price
supports for farmers, an export surplus.' Apart from the fact that
an export surplus is not a policy but a consequence of policy, the
above list does not contain a single politically controversial measure.
It is hard to perceive what *interest* the working class had, for instance, in thwarting a *further* relaxation of controls or lowering
of taxes, particularly when it had already accepted the first moves
in this direction in the budgets of 1973 and 1974. Compared to the
strong wine of the "Bangalore" policies, this was plain drinking
water. It is strange at first sight that Noviak does not mention the
only truly important change with serious policial implications
which the government made during the emergency. This was the
repeal of the compulsory bonus. It is possible that Noviak did not
see the significance of this measure, which greatly widened the rift
between the intermediate and the working classes that had opened
with the crushing of the railway strike.

Noviak's estimate of the importance of the IMF in firstly framing
a deflationary policy and secondly 'foisting' it on the Indian govern-

ment is grossly exaggerated. He admits that there existed in India itself a sizable body of economic opinion in favour of a deflationary policy package, which he has dubbed the V.K.R.V. Rao-P.N. Dhar policies. He fails to point out that with minor variations of emphasis the sentiment was almost universal, and that the demand for a curb on dearness allowance payments as the first step in a programme to curb the growth of government consumption expenditures was being made continuously since the early 'seventies in virtually every important national daily. As has been explained in Chapters 3 and 4, the reasons for this lie in the perception that the growing structural imbalance in the organised sector between what might be termed revenue-producing employment (i.e. employment in mining, industry, and power generation and revenue-consuming employment (which includes the whole of the government sector outside the public enterprises, the railways and the posts and telecommunications) was primarily responsible for the stagnation of output and employment after 1966. By 1974, the government knew it had reached the end of its tether. The state governments were virtually bankrupt and were paying their employees by taking huge unauthorised overdrafts from the Reserve Bank of India. The level of public investment in real terms had declined in 1973–74 and was set for another drop in 1974–75, and there were no less than five instalments of the dearness allowance outstanding, totalling around Rs 750 crores! The IMF's prompting may have reinforced these compulsions, but it is doubtful whether the government even noticed their added weight.

Nor was there anything particularly Machiavellian about the 'deflationary' package. To begin with, when a government is running a chronic balance of payments deficit, there is no way of curing it except through deflation. Under the gold standard this was supposed to happen, and in the nineteenth century did happen, automatically. Since the collapse of the gold standard, a balance of payments deficit has to be cured either by deflation or devaluation. The choice rests with the national government, and deflation enters the picture only when it rules out devaluation, whether for good reasons or bad. The advanced countries, whose economies are flexible and whose export industries can increase output at short notice, have usually chosen devaluation. Indeed even in the case of the British standby agreement of 1976, which Noviak cites as an example of 'open covenants openly arrived at', the government, by making its discussions with the IMF public, actually *caused* a steep fall in the value of the pound. This decision, unlike the covenant Noviak refers to, was one in which the British public was not consulted.

However for the less developed countries, whose imports and exports are usually inelastic, and in whose case devaluation can actually worsen a balance of payments deficit, deflation may be the only alternative. Such deflation can be brought about gradually in response to obligations accepted by the government while obtaining successive tranches of SDRs or standby credits, or suddenly and traumatically when foreign suppliers one day abruptly cut off all credit to the debtor nation and force its industries to grind to a halt. As a spur to dictatorship the second is likely to be far more powerful than the first. To accuse the IMF and World Bank of having brought about dictatorship in any country, is thus completely absurd.

Had Noviak studied the Indian economy closely he would not have attached such importance to the IMFs promptings, or read such devious motives into them. But then he would also not have given the credit for the stabilization of the Indian economy so wholeheartedly to the harsh measures taken by Mrs Gandhi. The main cause of this decline in prices which began in the beginning of October 1974 was not the deflationary policy announced by Mrs Gandhi just three months earlier. Although it must have warned wage and salary earners not to expect the decline in their real incomes to be made up in the near future, and thus caused some reduction in their expenditure on goods other than foodstuffs, it had not really had time to bite. The real reason was the huge import surplus which began in December 1973 following the second hike in oil prices. All through 1974 and 1975 the country was running a monthly trade deficit of around Rs 100 crores. Since the marginal rate of saving in India is 28 per cent it means that one rupee worth of import surplus reduces domestic purchasing power by three and a half rupees. By October 1974 the effect of this continuous and 'multiplied' contraction of domestic purchasing power was beginning to be felt. In 1974 and 1975 the country recorded a trade deficit of around Rs 1,200 crores a year. Against this, the income impounded by means of its deflationary package was no more than Rs 300 crores in 1974–75, and Rs 450 crores in 1975–76!

The Orthodox Marxist Explanation

What may be termed an orthodox Marxist analysis of the emergency is best presented by David Selbourne.[5] This has two merits: it sees the emergency not as an aberration but as a logical culmination of certain tendencies in the Indian polity and, as a corollary, largely if not altogether discounts the influence of international agencies or governments (as distinct from international capitalism). Shorn of its purple prose, Selbourne's analysis sees the emergency as the culmination of a conflict between two classes in Indian Society—the rulers and the ruled, or if one prefers, the exploiters and the exploited.

The vast mass of people fall into the latter category, and despite a little improvement in odd corners of the economy, their condition, Selbourne points out, is no better now than it was at the time of independence. The reason is the 'cruel and violent' exploitation of the mass of the people by the exploiting classes. Yet as resignation and acceptance, preached assiduously by Hinduism wears thin,[6] dissent and revolt have begun to surface, and a progressively more embattled elite has responded by unleashing violence on an ascending scale on the hapless masses. The emergency is thus seen as the latest station on a long railway line.

On the identity of the exploiters, Selbourne is explicit. 'The poor' he says, 'are held in a vise-like grip, held not only by the exigencies of poverty and structural destitution, but by functional political necessity. That is, one section of the ruling classes must resist the agrarian revolution which is needed by another for the development of capitalism; has no choice but to hold down the rural poor in preservation of their own political and economic interests. The other seeks to build and partially succeeds in building an indigenous capitalism, while itself held in thraldom (circumscribed by shortages of resources, insufficient investment and its inherited position within the international division of labour) to the world economy, with its disorderly succession of slumps and recoveries, inflation and recession, and its control of both capital and market. These are also the first intersecting and colliding circles of dependency, instability and potential violence played out upon the body politic of India (p. 11).

The rural exploiters, according to Selbourne are a 'minority of peasants who can be termed Kulaks' (p. 3). Their urban counterparts are 'the private sector . . . itself dominated by a handful of indigenous and growingly prosperous (as well as corrupt) monopolists who are in turn supported by a state patronage which they have the political and economic power to manipulate' (p. 5). Selbourne sees 'the whole of the edifice of exploitation resting as it must on the backs of Indian industrial labour, itself surrounded by a growing reserve army of the unemployed. . . .' He therefore sees the vast mass of the people as 'citizens of a client state of the ruling bourgeoisie and landlords which is itself in turn deeply mortgaged . . . encumbered by international indebtedness while struggling to assert its independence, as might a fly in a web. . . India is thus a barely moving pyramidal structure of inequality, uncorrected by economic distribution.' (p. 6)

The above thesis suffers from three defects, two of them in the realm of sociological theory and its application and the third in the realm of facts. The first is the problem common to all attempts to apply Marxist's abstract dichotomous theory of classes to concrete historical situations, that in reality apart from the main classes formed around the central line of conflict, which itself is defined by the dominant mode of production, there are (a) transitional classes which are either left over from a passing mode of production and set of property relationships, or herald a future set of property relationships (b) quasi class groups and (c) differentiated sub-groups within each class.[7] All of these together make it possible for a variety of middle or intermediate classes to exist. The central chapters of this book have been devoted to defining such classes in the current Indian context and examining the effect of economic growth on them. No one, least of all Selbourne, would deny that India is a society in a state of transition. Yet nowhere in his analysis is there a serious attempt to define such transitional classes, the central set of property relationships, and hence the central line of conflict. Implicitly Selbourne hews to the orthodox concept that central class conflict is around the ownership of property—land in the case of the farmers and capital in the case of industry. But for the reasons which have been given in Chapter V this is unsatisfactory for India and perhaps for a number of other nascent capitalist economies. In rural areas, defining class relationships around the ownership of land leaves the position of 50 million or more marginal and submarginal landowners ambiguous. In the towns the same ambiguity applies to the position of the bulk of the self-employed such as small shopkeepers who are capitalists but are not paid a fixed wage determined by the market demand and supply for labour.

The second problem, which is integrally linked to the first is that once the existence of a variety of middle or intermediate classes is recognized, it becomes difficult to define which are the 'permanent' or central classes and which are the transitional ones. To put it in another way, once we recognize the existence of several lines of conflict how do we decide which is the central line and which are the subsidiary ones?

The above shortcomings in Selbourne's analysis could have been ascribed to a somewhat uncritical application of Marx's theory of social classes to the complex Indian reality, had he not chosen his facts and adopted a method of presentation which were designed systematically to overstate the misery of the population, to understate the extent of progress made in the last three decades and to exaggerate the degree of repression unleashed by the 'ruling elite' on the masses, and on organized movements of dissent. The examples of such bias are almost too numerous to quote. Selbourne makes much of the fact that food items make up one quarter of India's total exports, grown and harvested by the 'hungry and the chronically undernourished'. But he fails to point out that most of the food does not fall into the category of essential mass consumption items. In 1973–74 (one of the two years whose figures he has cited), two thirds of the food exports consisted of tea (5.8% of total exports), coffee (1.8%), oil seed cakes (6.8%), and pepper (1%). All of these are technically food items, but their export can hardly be deemed to make a significant contribution to undernourishment.

In fact oil cakes, the largest single export item, are not fit for human consupmption.

The exports which do have an impact on domestic consumption are fruits and vegetables, vegetable oils, sugar, and fish products. Together these made up almost exactly 10% of the total exports in 1973–1974, by value. Against this Selbourne should have pointed out that cereals and cereal preparations made up 16 per cent of the imports of the country and since imports greatly exceeded exports in that year, the absolute value of cereal imports was ninety per cent more than the value of the above mentioned exports. What is more, after food, the most important item on the import list in 1973–74 (apart from crude oil) was fertilizers!

It may be argued that since imported cereals are consumed mainly by city-dwellers, and the fertilizers are bought mainly by well-to-do farmers, neither import benefits the really poor. But this proposition is hard to sustain. Even when destined for the cities food imports reduce the effect of the pull of urban demand on prices in the villages. Again, the use of fertilizers increases the supply of both food and work in the villages.

There are other factual errors, unimportant in themselves, but which help collectively to overstate the misery of Indian masses and the oppression unleashed on them. For instance, he points out that the output of cloth in India was the same in 1975 as in 1944 (p. 4) but forgets that in 1944 British India had not been partitioned, and the available figures therefore are for the entire subcontinent, including Pakistan. Since there are precise and easily available statistics for the period from 1951 to 1975–76 which indicate that while the output of mill-made cotton cloth has stagnated, that of the powerlooms and handlooms has increased dramatically, Selbourne's failure to cite them is somewhat surprising.

Selbourne's attempt to prove that the private sector dominates the industrial economy and is itself dominated by a handful of indigenous, growingly prosperous (and corrupt) monopolists is also weak. His evidence is that 'the public sector, while providing the costly infrastructure for the activities of private capital takes only a 16 per cent share of the domestic product' (p. 5). The table in *India 1976* from which he culls this figure speaks of the *contri-*

bution of the public sector to the gross domestic product, i.e., what the public sector provides to the total pool of consumable goods and services in the country.

But this figure, far from highlighting any underpricing of public sector products is intended to show what an *important* role it is playing in the national economy. For, of the GNP, agriculture accounts for no less than 45 per cent and is entirely outside the hands of private monopoly capital. The secondary and tertiary sectors, consisting of industry, trade and services, account for 55 per cent of GNP and the public sector accounts for almost one third of this. What is more, around a third of the industrial production in the private sector, nearly all of trade, and most of road transport is in the hands of the self-employed—people who are neither workers nor capitalists; and most certainly not monopoly capitalists. After deducting the contribution of the self-employed, it is doubtful whether the entire contribution of private 'monopoly' capital, however, loosely defined, to output in the secondary and tertiary sectors of the economy, is equal to that of the public sector. The picture of dominant private monopoly capital exploiting the public sector is therefore somewhat fanciful.

There are other such errors: A united left-front government was not elected in West Bengal 'three times, in the space of four years'. But twice in 1967 and 1969. In 1971, the second UF government was dismissed and a government was formed by one of its constituents in alliance with the Congress party. In 1972, after the liberation of Bangladesh; the Congress won a massive victory and although Mr Jyoti Basu complained bitterly of rigging and intimidation, the CPM did not try to substantiate these charges in the courts.

Again, Selbourne says that there were 60,000 casual 'daily rated' workers in the railways, earning £5.00 a month at the time of the railway strike. But the railwaymen's own figures were 30,000.[8] What is more these were employed in civil construction projects. Since the construction industry falls very largely in the unorganized sector and is the largest employer outside agriculture, any move to 'departmentalize' construction workers in the railways would lead to rising wage rates (in relation to productivity) and lower employment generation in this sector.

Selbourne quotes a newspaper report citing a West Bengal state labour department survey for the year 1975, to show that real wages in agriculture had declined. Such data pertaining to a single state and more often than not to comparisons between single years, has been challenged more than once and is highly debatable. A much better documented study, quoted by Keith Griffin shows that even in Punjab the proportion of the population below the poverty line rose between 1960–61 and 1970–71 from 18 to 27 per cent. But Griffin himself is no longer convinced of the reliability of such an index.[9] In any case wage-rate data cannot be cited as evidence of growing exploitation by the land-owner. For this it is necessary to show that the share of wages in the total produce has gone down. But figures compiled by Professor P.R. Brahmananda[10] for the economy as a whole show a rise in the share of wages in national product and a falling share of profit in the 'sixties and 'seventies, even though the real wage rate had declined. This indicates that employment has grown more rapidly than the rate of growth of GNP. In the specific case of the Punjab, wage rates have been kept down to some extent by the rising influx of migrant workers from other states. Since 1971, over 100,000 agricultural workers have been coming from adjoining western Uttar Pradesh alone.

Selbourne wants his descriptions of poverty to shock the reader, and he succeeds admirably. But what precise analytical purpose do they serve? It is no secret that the country is poor, that a large part of the population is underfed and underclothed and that there has been a shift in relative income distribution from the poor to the rich. But a mere impressionistic and highly selective description of poverty serves little purpose. Meaningful socio-political analysis requires a comparison of the conditions of the people at two points in time to see if things are getting worse or better. As shown earlier, Selbourne's few attempts at citing comparative statistics are often inaccurate and always selective.

Against the statistics he has cited, it is possible to present a battery of others which show that the state of the people has improved considerably in the last thirty years. The most significant of these, which finds no mention in his book, is the rise in average life expectancy from 27 in the 'forties to 52 or thereabouts in the 'seventies.

It is true that this has led to an explosive growth of population, which has prevented any substantial improvement in standards of consumption. But the decline in infant mortality, in the incidence of epidemics, and of preventible diseases in general, cannot be dismissed as being of no consequence. One may say that India took its improved welfare in the form of more babies, and longer lives, and not in terms of higher standards of living, but there is no denying the initial increase in material welfare which made this 'choice' possible.

The truth is that per capita availability of just about every wage good in India increased rapidly after the war till about 1965–66. After that it has either stagnated or declined. A meaningful analysis of the Indian polity needs to explain why this turnabout took place in 1966–67, not earlier or later. To postulate that India's economic history is just one long saga of stagnation or decline is patently misleading. And any theory built on such a hypothesis will be equally untenable.

However Selbourne did not start with hypotheses based on empirical evidence. His aim throughout has been to make facts fit a preconceived theory. His impressionistic descriptions of poverty, his repeated use of words such as 'cruel' and 'violent' to describe India's history (p. 14) is not the product of naivete or raw shock. The latter may have rung true two decades ago, but today the use of such purple prose is patently designed to serve an end. The author does not hesitate to spell this out: 'Indeed the setting of this book and its continuous theme is the condition of the people; a condition with other factors, *propelling India towards revolution*, surviving the succession of one faction by another and one illusion by another—*the last and perhaps greatest that of the transformation of India by election (p. xii)*. (Italics added).

For Selbourne India is slated for revolution. Change cannot come in any other way. Above all, it cannot come via the ballot box. This is a thesis he set out to prove before he came to India. It came before the empirical evidence. It had little to do with the emergency, just as his year's stay in India only happened to coincide with the emergency. It explains his selectivity in presenting statistics and the bias in his inadvertent errors.

What is more important, it is the key to his use of the word 'violence' in a context where the obviously more correct term is oppression'. Violence in normal parlance means causing bodily harm to another person. A man is considered violent when he is using or likely to use physical force on another person. Oppression has a much wider meaning and does not necessarily involve physical violence. That Indian society is oppressive cannot be denied. But to say that in India the rich are constantly committing violence on the poor, or waging war against them, makes no sense unless one radically redefines the words 'violence' and 'war'. Such a play on words is not innocent. There is more than one way to fight oppression, such as *morchas*, *gheraos*, voting behaviour and passive resistance. But there is only one way of defending oneself against *violence* and that is by taking up arms in self-defence. The use of words like 'cruel' and 'violent' is thus designed deliberately to create a climate of opinion in which the poor are freed from the normal human inhibition against taking human life.

For the votaries of violence, it is necessary above all to prove that elections cannot bring about a shift in political power. This is perhaps the main reason why Selbourne does not analyse the role of caste in the electoral process, the mobilization first of the backward classes and later, however imperfectly, of the harijans and scheduled castes (witness the rise of the Soshit Dal in Bihar in 1967 and the Jharkhand party, also in Bihar, in 1962). Readers of M.N. Srinivas and other sociologists know the extent to which low caste status overlaps with low economic status. To completely discount the mobilization of the lower castes is to take a singularly jaundiced view of the mobilization process.

Selbourne has claimed that elections are a fraud because the voters are manipulated. When they rebel (and he cites Bengal as an example) they are ruthlessly suppressed. He has not examined the voting pattern in the two elections which a united left front won in that state, or indeed the composition of this united front. If he had he would have found them a strange medley of parties with strongly parochial as well as clearly class-oriented ideologies. He would also have found that the two communist parties together polled no more than 25.13 per cent of the vote in 1967, far less than the 40.97 per cent of the Congress. Both in 1967 and 1969, the left front won because of the operation of the simple majority voting system, which rewarded its electoral unity and penalized the Congress for its internal dissensions. This has not only happened in Bengal but in many other states. In Tamil Nadu for instance where it was faced by an all-party alliance led by the DMK in 1967, the Congress won 21 per cent of the seats with 41·49 per cent of the popular vote. And in March 1977 elections with 18 to 34.6 per cent of votes in the northern states (excluding Kashmir and Assam) the Congress won only five seats out of the 261 that it contested!

There is a strong left movement in Bengal, but it did not, till June 1977 command a majority of the popular vote. In the Lok Sabha elections in March 1977 the CP(M), by now the only left party with any degree of credibility in the eyes of the people, polled 27.12% of the vote. It was only in June 1977 that the CP(M) obtained a majority of the vote in Bengal, and no attempt is being made to oust them, as no attempt has been made to oust the 7-year-old CPI-led government in Kerala. Selbourne's thesis that when *the people* use the ballot box to rebel, they are ruthlessly suppressed, cannot be sustained.

He also often seems to forget that Bengal is not the whole of India. The two communist parties enjoy far less support in other states. Is the whole population then voting for the status quo? Or are they in some way beguiled into forgetting their class interest by the vested interests? Selbourne would obviously claim the latter, but can he, or for that matter, anyone claim to know what they want better than they do?

In fairness to him, it must be stated that this proposition is not as absurd as it sounds. People often do not recognize their own best interests. This is particularly true when they are comparing clearly visible short term gains with only dimly perceived long term losses. But to adopt this position with respect to the better part of 650 million people one needs to be imbued with a special kind of confidence. Selbourne clearly derives this from his allegiance to Marx's concept of historical materialism. Since class conflict is the prime mover of social change, those who do not recognize the dictates of their class interest are either blind or bemused. They are not free.

The weakness of this position stems from the weaknesses inherent in a purely dichotomous vision of society. As Giddens has pointed out, for Marx the dichotomy between the haves and the have nots was an analytical tool. For Selbourne it is a historical reality. In practice Marx admitted the possibility of several dichotomies existing at the same time in any given society and giving rise to a number of transitional classes. Selbourne, at least in his book on India, does not take this possibility into account.

Not only does he never talk about such classes, but if he had, it would have admitted the possibility of transitional and shifting loyalties and alliances, even between sections of the 'haves' and the 'have-nots'. These would have blurred the lines of conflict in Indian society and increased the possibility of social amelioration through co-operation as against stark conflict, in other words by means of the ballot box rather than the gun.

The Emergency—The Intermediate Class On The Defensive

The exact process of thought by which, Mrs Gandhi arrived at her decision to impose the internal 'emergency' on the country need not detain us very long. There can be little doubt that the Allahabad Court judgement convicting her of minor infringements of the electoral laws in 1971 gave her the push which sent her over the brink unto dictatorship. But the imposition of authoritarian rule itself was not sudden. On the contrary, authoritarian trends had begun to manifest themselves from the very beginning of Mrs Gandhi's rule, if not earlier. These trends exactly paralleled the onset of economic stagnation, the virtual end of job creation in the organised sector of industry, the rise of labour unrest, and the sharp increase in student violence that took place after 1966. The onset of stagnation in that year has already been described at length in chapter I. It is worth noting that the number of man-days lost in industrial disputes rose dramatically from five to seven millions in the years 1961–1964, to between eighteen and twenty millions in the middle and late 'sixties.[11] Student unrest too did not rise gradually but erupted suddenly in a spate of strikes that paralysed more than a dozen major universities throughout the country in the summer and autumn of 1966. This outbreak took the entire establishment by surprise, provoking a spate of articles and editorials in the press. Most of these did little more than admonish the students to finish their studies first—a telling indication of how little the articulate sections of the population were prepared for or understood these events.[12]

The decade after the end of the third Plan also saw a sharp increase in the size of the police forces. The central and state Reserve Police, whose sole purpose was the maintenance of order, as distinct from law, were rapidly expanded during this period. In addition two specifically paramilitary police forces, were created, the Border Security Force and the East Frontier Rifles, which were intended mainly to patrol the extensive borders with west and east Pakistan, but which were more and more often used for the maintenance of order. The net result of these new additions was that the police eventually came to number around 200 battallions. The late 'sixties also saw a number of changes in the law which were not without significance. The external emergency declared first during the Sino-Indian border conflict in 1962 was reinforced during the Indo-Pak war of 1965 and then continued for five years after that. It was lifted only briefly before being clamped down again during the second Indo-Pak war in 1971, and was in force even in 1975 when Mrs Gandhi declared the 'internal' emergency (hence the term 'double emergency' often used at the beginning of the period). Under this and the accompanying Defence of India Rules, the government enjoyed wide powers of arrest and detention without trial. In all this time Preventive Detention, first brought in by the British, continued to be used. Under it the government could keep a person in jail for up to six months *at a time* without trial. Not content with all these powers, the government also passed an Unlawful Activities Act, at the beginning of 1968, which allowed it to ban particular organisations, and to keep its members in prison without a proper trial for up to two years at a time. In the period up to 1974 these laws were used almost exclusively against the Naxalites in Bengal and Andhra Pradesh, and against the members of the Plebiscite Front (Sheikh Abdulla's party in Kashmir).

Another far from insignificant change occurred in 1968 when Mr Chavan, who was then the home minister, insisted on and succeeded in establishing the Central government's right to send in the Central Reserve Police or call out the army to protect its property in states where it felt that the state government was not in a position to ensure its safety.[13] This reserve power, which has on balance, been sparingly used, was aimed at preventing opposition governments, notably the Marxist dominated regimes of Bengal and Kerala, from turning a blind eye on demonstrators who wished to damage Central government property, such as the railways and stations. In the same vein, to guard the railways, the central government set up a special railway protection force, and followed this up with an industrial security force to protect the public enterprises, and other centrally-owned industrial undertakings. Although law and order was a state subject, these forces remained exclusively under the command of the Home Ministry in New Delhi.

The above description is by no means exhaustive, but it shows clearly that the central government was arming itself with more and more coercive powers as far back as the middle and late "sixties". Those, like Selbourne who insist in seeing Indian society purely in terms of a simple dichotomy between the 'haves' and the 'have-nots' have proceeded from the observation of these trends to the conclusion that this was a direct product of the growing feeling of insecurity among the former, and reflected their determination to continue their exploitation of the 'have-nots' by resorting to a steadily rising level of coercion.

But this interpretation leaves out of account the fact that the government built up its paramilitary police forces not to reinforce the army but to minimise its use against the civilian population, for the maintenance of order. Its ostensible reason for doing so was to prevent the politicization of the army, and to avert the ensuing threat to democracy. It is an undeniable fact that as unrest grew, and the number of police firings rose, the army was called out less and less often. This paradox hardly fits the model given above, and can only be explained if one accepts that there were deep divisions between those whom the orthodox left clubs together as the 'haves'. The most likely explanation, as I have pointed out elsewhere is that the army was not a part of the intermediate classes, and its senior officers in particular belonged to the old upper-middle class elite which had inherited power from the departing British.

Army officers, with their fixed salaries, and with virtually no opportunities for graft, were among those who had been worst hit by the inflation and stagnation of the 'sixties and 'seventies. As a result, their loyalty to any intermediate regime was naturally suspect. Such a regime required a coercive instrument cast in its own mould and the police, heavily riddled with corruption, fitted it far better than the armed forces. This distrust continued and indeed became heightened during the emergency, when Mrs Gandhi was careful not to involve the army in her repressive acts.

Those who postulate a linear development of repression culminating in the emergency also tend to ignore the vast increase in popular participation in the political process, which occurred in the period between 1947 and 1967, and which continued until the declaration of the emergency.

There was a steady rise in the proportion of electorate that voted from 45.67 per cent in the first to 61.33 per cent the fourth general elections (after this, the separation of the parliamentary from the assembly elections makes comparison difficult). The phenomenon of the 'protest' vote against Congress first manifested itself clearly in 1967, when the huge turnout at the polling booths coincided with a severe reverse for the Congress. This pattern was repeated with a few exceptions in each state, where the highest percentage of votes polled for the state assembly and Lok Sabha were associated with the sharpest declines in the Congress' share of the vote.

The introduction of Panchayati Raj in 1961, was another move towards decentralizing the exercise of power and increasing popular participation in decision-making. It is true that for most of this period—perhaps the whole of it—the political mobilization was carried out by land-owners, moneylenders, and other job-givers in the rural areas, and that precisely these classes came to dominate the Panchayati Raj system, but if the 'haves' were united in their desire to oppress the 'have-nots' what was the need for all this fuss in the first place? Why open a Pandora's box, if you know you will have to shut it again one day?

The democratization of India, and later the reversal of this trend can only be understood once again in terms of the conflict between elites, one on its way in, and the other on the way out. At the risk of some oversimplification, one can say that in the first two decades of independence, increasing democratization was a weapon used by the rising intermediate classes against the old upper middle-class elite of the country. This latter elite, which was highly mobile, drawn from all over the country and spoke English, was thickly represented in the armed forces, the upper echelons of the police, bureaucracy, the professions, foreign-owned business concerns, and in the universities, inherited power from the British. By contrast, the commitment to adult franchise and later the linguistic reorganisation of the states originated entirely within the Congress party. Both these measures, which immensely increased popular participation in government, resulted from pledges given by Mahatma Gandhi in the 'twenties and 'thirties to a host of local movements for self-determination, such as the Akalis, the Vishal Haryana and Andhra movements, and the nascent political parties in the princely states in exchange for joining the national freedom movement. Kochanek has outlined how these tactics paid off in the 'twenties and 'thirties, and resulted in a wholesale invasion of the party by what he terms the 'Old Guard'. An ironic side effect of this expansion was the reduction of the Gandhians in the Congress to a permanent minority.

The middle-class elite's perception of the threat to their dominance posed by democratization, is catalogued by Myron Wiener in an early essay on South Asia.[14] It leaves one in no doubt about the suspicion with which the technocratic-bureaucratic elite viewed the process of democratization, and the attraction felt by some of its members for authoritarian methods to sort out the prevailing anarchy. Indeed one needs only to have lived through the late 'fifties in India, to remember the horror inspired by the linguistic reorganization of the states in the members of this elite, the armed forces and the professionals, all of whom viewed it as a prelude to the break-up of India.

In the first phase therefore, democratization was designed to take power out of the hands of a microscopic urban, but essentially nationalistic elite, to a much larger parochial intermediate class of well-to-do farmers and urban self-employed. It is only when the same mechanism threatened to disperse power still further to the legions of the poor that the government, by now firmly a tool of the intermediate class, began to forge the instruments of repression which it eventually unleashed on the populace during the emergency.

The manner in which, from the late 'sixties onwards, Mrs Gandhi's government systematically dismantled the edifice of democratic institutions has already been described earlier in this chapter. Suffice it to say that by 1974, when the students went on the rampage once again in Gujarat and Bihar, parliament had been reduced to a rubber stamp for retrospective endorsement of the actions of the government, the autonomy of all but a few state units of the Congress party had been shattered, the financial base of the opposition had been destroyed, and the Supreme Court had been partly tamed by the nomination of Mr A.N. Ray as Chief Justice superseding three more senior judges, in contravention of the existing convention of choosing the senior-most judge of the Supreme Court as the next chief justice.[15]

Even the actual declaration of the emergency could not have come as a total surprise to Mrs Gandhi's colleagues in the cabinet. In October 1974, when JP had declared a three-day *bandh* in Patna, the entire cabinet had seriously debated the advisability of arresting him.[16] It is idle to suppose that had it done so, it would have been able to stop there. And in November 1974, the government began placing very large orders in the US for crowd control equipment such as tear gas and, significantly, rubber bullets. These orders were placed not through the State Trading Corporation, but through at least one (and possibly several) small international trading concerns which had handled very little government business in the preceding years.[17]

This lack of surprise may be one reason why no one in the Congress and for that matter almost no one in the opposition parties, the judiciary and the bureaucracy, opposed the imposition of the emergency. But a far more important reason is that all of these groups had, in their own ways, felt seriously threatened by the situation as it had been developing since 1973, and particularly in 1974 and 1975. Each had their own expectations of the emergency and sought to use it to reestablish its position in society. Among the bureaucrats, and not a few army officers, there was a widespread belief that the emergency would restore discipline to the nation. Many officials in the districts sincerely believed that it would free them from the annoying interference of local politicians, and let them get on with their work. In the same way, most professional managers in industry, although initially wary of the emergency came eventually to accept it because it gave them relief from persistent labour trouble, and a chance to produce more and increase their profits. To both these groups, which formed the majority of the upper salaried and professional classes in the country, the emergency seemed at first glance like a chance to reestablish the social values they stood for, and an opportunity to arrest the erosion of their political and economic position in the country.

Among the opposition parties, the attitude of the CPI was particularly interesting. Since 1964, this party had been consciously following a policy of forging an alliance between the working class and the 'national bourgeoisie' in order to attack the comprador bourgeoisie and the rich kulaks (see Ch. 6). This policy seemed to be paying dividends in the period after the Congress split when a strong 'socialist' wing emerged within Mrs Gandhi's Congress, which was indistinguishable in its attitudes from the CPI. Mrs Gandhi herself seemed to be lending a more ready ear to their proposals, and was passing laws to curb the growth of the large industrial houses, to control the growth of monopoly power in the private sector and to nationalize the wholesale trade in wheat. However, the oil crisis, Mrs Gandhi's sharp move to the 'right,' severe action taken by the government in the ensuing months to suppress labour unrest in the public sector, culminating in the breaking of the railway strike in May 1974, made them realize how transient their gains had been.

In these circumstances the assassination of Mr L.N. Mishra, the Union Minister for Railways on January 5th 1975, came as a heaven sent opportunity for it to raise the alarum of a 'rightist' plot against Mrs Gandhi, the government, the poor of the country and against 'progress', itself. Since this allegation became a constant refrain in Mrs Gandhi's speeches in the months which followed, particularly between June 12 and June 25th, the CPI first believed that its ruse had worked, and that it would now be able to direct national policy through Mrs Gandhi. They were soon to be undeceived.

The other opposition parties were not free from ambivalence in their view of the emergency either. Among the non-communist parties there was always an element that believed that Mrs Gandhi was misguided rather than evil, and that it was possible to hold a dialogue with her in order to show her the error of her ways. Towards the end of 1975, a number of lesser leaders of the rightist parties, including Mr Minoo Masani of the Swatantra party, drew up a declaration which they presented to Mrs Gandhi, and in which they admitted that the opposition had gone 'too far' in the days preceding the emergency. They expressed the hope that such a public recantation would pave the way for lifting the emergency and building a new national consensus. Masani, who had always been close to big business interests in Bombay was no doubt impressed by the reduction of industrial unrest, and the inflated production figures that the government kept trotting out. His ambivalence therefore reflected the ambivalence of big business in Bombay.

The true nature of the emergency did not take long to emerge. Among those arrested during the first weeks, were not only political workers, suspected smugglers, hoarders and other criminals, but also large numbers of university teachers, and trade union activists. In the first phase, the state governments in particular also picked up a large number of journalists, but within a few months all but a handful of them were released following a review of the list of detenus by the Central government. By then the ruling caucus had begun to understand that in order to muzzle the press it was necessary only to silence the journals, and not the journalists. The attack on political cadres, particularly the RSS, was only to be expected, but the onslaught on journalists and trade union leaders showed that the government was singling out all those who could be expected to articulate radical dissent in the country. Nor did Mrs Gandhi lose much time in disillusioning the bureaucracy and the senior army officers. Both were shown in the most distinct way possible that they would not be allowed to question any decisions of the Government. Senior Government officials like Nirmal Mukherjee secretary to the Ministry of Home Affairs were transferred summarily to relatively unimportant departments for daring to remonstrate against the wholesale abuse of government powers. Air Marshal P.C. Lal, former chief of the Air Force and chairman of Indian Airlines, who resigned because a junior director was being promoted over the heads of two extremely able senior colleagues because he was in the good books of the prime minister's son Mr Sanjay Gandhi, was harassed, and his house was raided by the income-tax authorities in an attempt to find something that the government could pin on him. In the same way, judges who gave decisions against the government were demoted and sent away on 'penal postings' to far off places. Naval and Army officers were repeatedly insulted and humiliated by Bansi Lal, whom Mrs Gandhi brought as Defence Minister in place of the highly respected Swaran Singh, in October 1975. The message was clear: it was not theirs to reason why. Few failed to understand it.

The disillusionment of the CPI did not take long to come. The first action of the government after it declared the emergency was to impose a ban on the unions' right to strike. This was followed in the next five months by the revocation of the compulsory bonus, and a revision of the formula for calculating profit for the purposes of bonus, which was intended to safeguard the company's capital stock, by allowing the deduction of a number of prior commitments under this head, before it became liable to paying the bonus.

To present all the events which disclosed the class bias of the legislation during the emergency and led to the disenchantment of all but a few of the leaders of the CPI, would take too long. Since they followed on each other's heels the effect on the CPI was of a sustained barrage. But perhaps the most significant statement of the entire period was the interview given by Sanjay Gandhi to 'Surge', a small periodical published from Delhi. This interview was picked up by the Press Information Bureau of the government and circulated to all the papers in the country *with instructions to print it in full.* In this interview Sanjay Gandhi launched a vicious attack on both the communist movement in the country and, significantly, on the public sector. Mr Gandhi called the communists perhaps the most corrupt people in India.

He also said that the public sector was inefficient and should be allowed to die a natural death. The first of these remarks sent a shock wave through the CPI, and brought its leaders face to face with the truths they had been trying their best to ignore ever since the beginning of the emergency. On the day when the interview appeared, Mrs Gandhi was out of Delhi inspecting extensive floods which had occurred in Orissa. On her return that evening she was met by a delegation of CPI leaders. By 8.00 p.m. that night, instructions had been sent out to the newspapers to 'kill' the interview, but by this time the damage had been done. Most Delhi papers had already carried the interview in the morning edition and news-papers in other cities had published excerpts in the morning followed by fuller texts in the afternoon papers. There was a great deal of speculation at the time about the extent to which Mrs Gandhi was aware of the contents of the interview, and some observers concluded that she was actually using Sanjay as a stalking horse to open a broadside on the communists. Whether this 'maximal' interpretation is true or not, there can be no doubt that Sanjay Gandhi who looked over the typescript of his interview carefully and even incorporated changes, could not have felt that he was stepping far out of line with his mother's thinking. Nor is it neces-sary to ask who influenced whom in this respect. In view of the close relations between mother and son, the question is immaterial.

In any case the interview was no isolated episode. It was part of a process of disenchantment, which can be traced back to the oil crisis, and the suspicion that grew in Mrs Gandhi that she had been made use of by the communists and their fellow-travellers in the Congress to pass legislation whose effect was to disrupt production, without making society significantly more egalitarian. It would have been surprising indeed if her return to growth-oriented economic policies in 1974 had not been accompanied by a growing distrust of the CPI. This process of disenchantment found expression in the early months of 1974, when she sponsored the creation of a Nehru study forum within the Congress, to act as a counterpoise to the Congress Socialist forum.

The change in her advisers and confidants which occurred during the emergency is another indication of this disillusionment. The very first days saw an attempt to discredit P.N. Haksar, who was then the deputy chairman of the Planning Commission, and I.K. Gujral, minister for information. It is true that both fell foul, in the first instance, of Sanjay Gandhi. But Mrs Gandhi's in-difference to their fate can be traced back to the fact that both were radicals, who had played a prominent role in shaping policy after the Congress split in 1969. At the time of declaration of the emer-gency, Mrs Gandhi's closest advisers included Siddharta Shanker Ray, Chief Minister of West Bengal, D.K. Borooah, Congress President, and at a somewhat lower level Rajni Patel, President of the Bombay Pradesh Congress Committee, who was emerging as the chief fund raiser of the party after the death of L.N. Mishra. As the months passed, all three fell out of favour. Patel's home in Bombay, and his wife's business establishments were raided by the police in an attempt to find evidence of concealed income. Ray fell out of favour with Sanjay Gandhi after he resisted the latter's attempt to build a base in the powerful Youth Congress in West Bengal. Matters came to a head at the Gauhati session of the Congress held in November 1976, when persons known to be close to Ray criticized the rise of a personality cult in the Congress, a not very veiled reference to Sanjay. Within a month of the attack, Ray was humbled, agreed to relinquish the key portfolio of home minister in the West Bengal Government, and was believed, according to one popular magazine (Blitz) to have agreed to resign as Chief Minister by March.

Mrs Nandini Sathpathy, another 'radical' and erstwhile confidante whom Mrs Gandhi had foisted on the Orissa Congress as chief minister of the state, also fell out with her and was forced to resign in December 1976. Finally, although nothing actually happened to Borooah, by early 1976 his exclusion from all decisions taken at the Prime Minister's house was virtually complete.

The decline of all these advisers was closely correlated with the rise of Sanjay Gandhi as a decisive power in the Prime Minister's house. In June 1975, Sanjay was still a shadowy figure in the PM's establishment, important mainly because, as Mrs Gandhi put it, he 'saved' her from resigning after the Allahabad Court verdict, and made her decide to 'fight'. Sanjay showed his power on the very first day after the declaration of the emergency, when after an altercation with him I.K. Gujral found himself transferred within twelve hours from the ministry of information to the ministry of planning (leaving the way open for the emergence of V.C. Shukla). Even so, till late in 1975, Sanjay was seen mainly as an *eminence grise* behind the throne. His interview with 'Surge' magazine marked his debut on the political scene as a quasi-independent focus of power. Hindsight permits us to see that as a debut it was stamped with the same bungling ineptitude which marked Sanjay's brief and disastrous political career, and led to his mother's and the Congress' downfall. However, the views Sanjay expressed in the interview gain importance precisely because of the purpose which it was meant to serve. There is thus no reason to doubt the accepted view that the eclipse of the Congress radicals was the direct consequence of Sanjay Gandhi's antipathy to 'fellow travellers' within the Congress party.

The fall of the radicals was accompanied by the rise of a new breed of henchmen at No. 1 Safdarjung Road. These included Bansi Lal, chief minister of Haryana, Mohammed Yunus, an erstwhile civil servant with close ties to the prime minister's family, and Yashpal Kapoor and R.K. Dhawan, past and present personal assistants to the prime minister. Kapoor and Dhawan may be dismissed as bagmen of the new mafia in Safdarjung Road, but both Bansi Lal and Yunus enjoyed the trust of Mrs Gandhi. The significant difference was that they did not enjoy *only* her trust. They also had close links with Sanjay. In the case of Yunus, it was through his son Adil, a boyhood friend of Sanjay. Both had been involved in an endless series of juvenile 'pranks', including the repeated theft of cars in 1964. This came out in January 1965 when Sanjay and Adil stole a car and got into an accident. Both were hurt, and Adil Yunus was taken to hospital with a fractured skull. Sanjay made a confession, but the matter was hushed up. Bansi Lal, on the other hand, had enjoyed a special place in Sanjay's heart ever since he summarily evicted dozens of farmers from around 450 acres of prime agricultural land near Gurgaon in Haryana to enable Sanjay to build his Maruti car factory.[18]

Sanjay's rise to power was given a firmer base when he enrolled in the Youth Congress and became a member of its national committee on 9th December 1975. This was only a cover for a take-over and revitalization of this body, with the objective of creating a parallel power base for the son within the Congress. The Chandigarh meeting of the Congress three weeks later set the seal on his rise to power. Sanjay was the unquestioned star of this meet, and put even his mother in the shade. The welcome given to him by the delegates, and the abject servility with which even chief ministers like Zail Singh of Punjab and Bansi Lal of Haryana treated him, showed that a new *Duche* was emerging in the Congress party, and perhaps the nation. This impression was further reinforced by the welcome Sanjay got in Calcutta in February 1976.[19]

With Sanjay, there came into prominence a new breed of businessmen, all of whom enjoyed close personal ties with him. These included self-made industrialists like Raunaq Singh, a manufacturer of metal products, tyres, and the like whose boast was that he had begun life on a salary of Rs 8 per month, and younger 'business-men' like Prem Sagar and Kamal Nath who had been Sanjay's cronies at school or elsewhere. All of them were the very epitome of the self-employed owner-proprietors in industry and construction. Sanjay's exhortations during the five months between December and April, and again during the high summer of '76, made his politics amply clear. He continued his attack on the left parties and deplored 'rightism' and 'leftism' equally, called for discipline and hard work, pronounced himself against nationalization and often made derogatory references to the public sector.

It was in the area of economic policy, however, that the class bias of the emergency became most evident. The ban on strikes and the revocation of the compulsory bonus could have been interpreted as moves designed to raise production and stimulate investment by increasing corporate retained profits, had these measures not also been accompanied by the voluntary disclosure scheme, which allowed holders of black money to 'launder' it after paying the requisite tax on it. Significantly this tax rate of 30 to 60 per cent was far lower than the rates paid by honest taxpayers. The ostensible purpose of the scheme was to reduce the amount of black money in circulation. But the very notion of voluntary disclosures is repug-nant as it amounts to condoning a crime and putting a premium on dishonesty. The real purpose was therefore to aid the self-employed who hold most of the unaccounted income in the country. The lower tax rate on black money made this preferential treatment blatantly obvious.

Had the government really wished to destroy the parallel economy it would have resorted not to the voluntary disclosure scheme, but to demonetization. To be effective this would have had to be extend-ed to hundred rupee notes and not just to notes of Rs 1000 and above as was done in 1949, and again by the Janata government in 1978. It is true that since hundred-rupee notes made up well over half the currency in circulation, this would have been administra-tively very difficult to handle, and would have caused a severe disruption of the flow of transactions in the economy. But this very disruption would have dealt a mortal blow to the parallel economy.

What is more, since transactions by cheque would have remained unaffected, it would not have hurt the legitimate economy very much. The severity of the blow that it would have dealt to the parallel economy was revealed by the demonetization of notes of Rs 1000 and higher denominations, which was carried out in January 1978 by the Janata government. Of an estimated Rs 145 crores of such currency notes which were in circulation, the Reserve Bank exchanged only Rs 78 crores worth. Allowing for the fact that some more would be tendered later under various special exemptions, more than a third of the cash was destroyed. But demonetization, which had been repeatedly advocated, was not even contemplated by the government. Its policy thus turned out to be a stick for labour and a carrot for the black-money owning self-employed.

The true nature of the regime also revealed itself in what the government did not do, or even promise to do. This is made clear by the twenty-point programme itself. Announced by Mrs Gandhi on July 1, 1975, it seemed on the surface to offer something to everyone in the country. To the rural poor it offered a moratorium on debt, housing sites for the landless, and upward revision of minimum wages; the abolition of bonded labour; the implementation of the ceiling on land holdings, a rapid distribution of surplus lands, and special help for the handloom industry. To the farmers it offered irrigation for five million hectares of land, and 2600 megawatts of additional power. To the urban poor it promised to bring down the prices of foodstuffs and consumer goods by compelling traders and manufacturers to post their prices and by increasing production (mainly through the ban on strikes and lockouts). It also offered to improve the quality of controlled cloth, impose a ceiling on ownership of urban land and on the plinth area of new dwelling units, and new schemes for workers' participation. To the entrepreneurs it promised to increase the maximum size of investment that was exempt from industrial licensing, and the institution of an all-India truck licence to permit road hauliers to ply all over the country. For the middle classes the income tax exemption limit was raised from Rs 6000 to Rs 8000, and strong measures were promised against smugglers and hoarders. Finally the students were promised a supply of essential commodities in their hostels at controlled prices, i.e. cheaper meals, cheaper books and book banks, and enlarged apprenticeship schemes to absorb them in industry.

But a closer look shows that most of these programmes either could not be implemented, or would make no more than cosmetic changes in the economy. For instance, the abolition of the existing debt of the marginal farmers and landless in the rural areas meant nothing, and indeed could not even be enforced, so long as the poor had no alternative source of credit. This they did not have because, while the cooperative and commercial banks had expanded credit to farmers in the previous decade to the point where by 1975 they were meeting fully half the total credit needs of the rural sector, the number of borrowers had remained stagnant at around 11 millions, or about the same as the number of families farming more than four hectares of land. It is no surprise that after two decades of co-operative banking, the poor remained as deeply in debt to the moneylenders as they were before (Times of India editorial, 26-8-75). Similarly, while some instances of the abolition of bonded labour did receive a good deal of publicity, it soon became apparent that a practice rooted in grinding poverty, a rising population, increasing pressure on the land, and the near-total destruction of secondary industry in the villages, could not be eradicated until the tide of impoverishment itself had been stemmed. The futility of trying to implement land reforms in a polity dominated by the big farmers hardly needs to be underlined. Finally, although Mrs Gandhi's government announced the allocation of Rs 308 crores for the development of the handloom industry, and set up some intensive development and export-oriented centres, it completely failed to increase the output of cheap handloom cloth for the home market. While pricing and capacity constraints were partly responsible for this, several state governments did not help matters by diverting central grants intended for promoting the handloom sector towards the setting up of textile development corporations intended to finance the further growth of the powerloom sector.[20]

In the same way, the relief to urban consumers was notional rather than real. The fears aroused by the emergency did lead to a dishoarding of stocks and a sharp fall in prices in the first weeks, but these soon began to climb again. They were stabilized only in November 1975, when the biggest harvest the country has ever reaped began to arrive in the market. The subsequent fall in prices between November 1975 and March 1976, was entirely due to the arrival of the new crop in the market. From the end of March, prices began to rise once again and had risen a full 12 per cent by March 1977 when Mrs Gandhi's government was finally hustled out of office by the electorate. The raising of the income tax exemption limit was only a belated and grudging recognition of the fall in the value of money in the previous three and a half years. What is more, whatever little effect this exemption had on incomes of those in the lowest tax brackets was nullified by increases in the excise duty on sugar, and a phenomenal rise in the price of onions, potatoes, vegetables and meat, following a concerted bid to export these to the middle-east. In fact in October 1975, despite a poor early crop, state trading bodies vied with private traders to capture a large part of the available onions, in order to fulfil their export contracts, and succeeded in driving up their price by around 100 per cent, in three weeks. Since the price of potatoes also went up by around 60 per cent, the effect on the urban poor, for whom these are a staple part of their diet, can easily be imagined.

The offer of cheaper books and food to the students was a miserable substitute for the offer of jobs. The apprenticeship scheme too was already fairly fully stretched, since it had been in operation since 1961. It is not known how many more young people were taken on by the large industrial establishments during the emergency. But since the scheme offered training for just one year, for the vast majority of the new apprentices it only meant a short postponement of unemployment.

Significantly, the only promises of any substance were those made to the farmers (more irrigation and power) and to the truck operators and small entrepreneurs. However, irrigation and power were already in the fifth plan, and the promises involved at most marginal increases in allocations. As for the all-India trucking licence, and the higher exemption from industrial licensing for small units, both measures were clearly designed to benefit the urban intermediate class. In fact, the greater freedom granted to the road haulier to take on long distance haulage could only hurt the railways, which were state-owned. There can be few more telling instances of the class bias in economic legislation.

In looking at the 20-points, one is struck by the way in which Mrs Gandhi's advisers went out of their way to *avoid* proposing economic changes that would affect the basic power structure in society. This comes out clearly, when we compare the 20-point programme with the thirty-point- programme proposed to the government by the central executive of the CPI at a meeting in which it welcomed Mrs Gandhi's 'swift stern measures against right reactionary and counter revolutionary forces'. The CPI asked for speedy land reforms, including the restoration of tribal lands taken over by the moneylenders, stern measures to unearth black money, a strengthening of the public distribution system, and most important of all, the nationalization of the drug, oil, sugar, textiles, and jute industries, with a further expansion of the public sector.

The various nationalization measures and the restoration of tribal lands would, unlike the 20-points of Mrs Gandhi's programme, have caused structural changes in the economy, namely a pronounced shift towards state capitalism and a reduction in the power of the moneylender-turned-farmer. All of these recommendations were given short shrift by the government, and although two subsidiaries of multinational oil companies were nationalized during this period (Esso and Burmah Shell), this was in pursuance of decisions taken a long while before the emergency was declared.

In contrast to the CPI, leftists of various persuasions abroad, and leaders of the CPM in India interpreted the emergency as a lurch to the right. This was certainly true if one looked only at the political actions of Mrs Gandhi's government. As pointed out by A.K. Gopalan, who was jailed for a week at the start of the emergency, the government jailed thousands of CPI-M workers, notably in Kerala.[21] But this is not true of the government's economic measures, or at any rate, not unless one redefines the term 'right' to exclude large-scale industry. To benefit this sector, the government would have had to do one or more of the following things: Reduce corporate tax rates; lower excise duties; abolish some, if not all, price controls; lower interest rates, or repeal the conversion clause. But there were no such concessions.[22] The corporate sector benefited only by the banning of strikes, and the abolition of the compulsory bonus. But as pointed out earlier, these measures were designed as much to put organized labour in its place, as to aid the capitalist. If the latter benefited, it was at least partly as a byproduct of the government's hostile stance to labour. The emergency was thus neither a move to the left as the CPI had originally hoped, nor a shift to the right, as the CPM had alleged. It was designed to consolidate the power of the 'centre', a centre composed of the entire intermediate class of the country.

The need for such a consolidation, and for casting off the trappings of democracy arose because economic stagnation, which was indispensable for the rise of this class, had finally alienated the students, the intelligentsia and the organized working class, and ruptured the political alliance between the workers and the intermediate class. The resulting increase in insecurity fed the desire for increased control. In this condition the Allahabad Court judgement only served to trigger the latent paranoia not only of Mrs Gandhi's, but also of this 'elite'.

NOTES

1 This was told to the author repeatedly by private sector entrepreneurs in Bombay during 1974.
2 *Politics in India*, Little Brown & Co. Ltd. 1970. Published in India 1972 by Orient Longman & Co.
3 See Paul Baran; *The Political Economy of Growth*, Monthly Review Press, N.Y., 1973, Chapters six and seven. Theresa Hayter: *Aid as Imperialism*, Penguin 1970, and Michael Kidron *Foreign Investments in India*, Oxford University Press 1965.
4 See Footnote 10.
5 *An Eye to India*, Penguin, 1977.
6 Selbourne, op. cit. Chapter II in which purple passages describing the misery of the people are juxtaposed with selected texts from the Hindu scriptures.
7 See Anthony Giddens: *Class Structure in Advanced Societies*, Hutchinson University Library Paperback 1977, pp 30–1.
8 Reported extensively in the newspapers of the period.
9 These figures were quoted by Griffin in a Seminar at Queen Elizabeth House, Oxford, in May 1977. His qualifications were also made during questioning at the same seminar. In any case the estimates and the controversy surrounding them is well known.

10 P.R. Brahmananda: Inaugural address at the Annual meeting of the Indian Economic Association Madras, 1977, entitled '*The Falling Economy (sic) How to Revive it*', Indian Economic Assn. 1978, p. 104. Share of wages declined from 71.99% in 1950–51 to 66.28% in 1963–64, but rose to 72.32% in 1968–69 and stayed around 71–72% thereafter.

11. The exact figures are to be found in the *Indian Labour Statistics* Ministry of Labour and Rehabilitation Government of India in 1966 and subsequent years. The rise in labour unrest coincides dramatically with the break in economic growth in 1966, at the end of the third Plan. The following are the detailed figures:-

Year	No. of Disputes	Man-days Lost (in Millions)
1957	1630	6.429
1958	1524	7.797
1959	1531	5.633
1960	1583	6.536
1961	1357	4.918
1962	1491	6.120
1963	1471	3.268
1964	2151	7.724
1965	1689	6.173
1966	2556	13.846
1967	2815	17.148
1968	2776	17.244
1969	2270	16.678
1970	2889	20.563
1971	2752	16.545
1972	3243	20.544
1973	3370	20.626
1974	2938	40.262*
1975	1843	21.563

12 There were 744 outbreaks of student disturbances between 1968 and 1971, (*Youth Times*, Bombay, Dec. 29, 1972) there was also an increase in the number of police firings, an average of 103 per year between 1947–1967 to 140 per year between 1964 and 1969.

13 This was later enshrined in the 42nd Amendment to the constitution during the emergency, and has been repealed by the Janata government.

14 Almond and Coleman, *Politics of the Developing Areas*, Princeton, 1960.

15 Reestablished by the Janata government in February 1978.

*(railway workers' strike)

16 Conversations with Mr K.C. Pant at the time when this was being debated, Pant was then the Minister for Irrigation and Power in the central government.

17 One such was Muller & Philipps (India)—conversation with the Managing Director, February 1975.

18 The details appeared in the newspapers reporting the Janata government's probe into the affairs of the Maruti car factory headed by Justice A.C. Gupta.

19 On Sanjay's meteoric rise, see David Selbourne, op. cit. pp 300–9.

20 Editorial in *Times of India*, 'Not Enough', 21.6.1976.

21 A.K. Gopalan's speech in Lok Sabha: 21 July 1975 Selbourne op. cit. p. 382.

22 There was a reduction of 5 per cent in Corporate taxes in the 1976–77 budget for all except a few types of manufacturing companies, but this was on condition that this money was set aside in a special fund for investment.

8 / The Return of Democracy—1977

THE ELECTIONS which swept Mrs Gandhi's government out of power were hailed variously as a second revolution, a new dawn of freedom, a decisive break with the past and a new beginning in tackling the problems of the country. These claims were grossly exaggerated.

The fact that the Congress' share of the vote fell to 37.4 per cent from 43.1 per cent obtained in no more than 420 constituencies out of 518 in 1971, and that Mrs Gandhi herself lost her seat, indicates that the election did mark an important break with the past.

But in a number of important ways it also reflected the strengthening of trends that first became visible as far back as the 1967 elections. The most notable feature of the first three general elections in 1952, 1957 and 1962, was the remarkable constancy of the Congress' share of the total vote, which had varied from 44.7 to 47.8 per cent of the vote. In 1967 it fell to 40.7 per cent, a drop of around five per cent below the mean of the previous elections. From then onwards the swing in the ruling party's share of the vote has widened rapidly.

In 1971, the swing in favour of Mrs Gandhi was anything from eight to twelve per cent, (depending on what assumption one makes about the Congress' share of the vote in the 100 constituencies where it did not put up a candidate). This was followed by a drop of between eleven and fourteen per cent in 1977. Taken in conjunction with the other trend clearly visible until 1967, and still in evidence in recent years, of a steady rise in the percentage of votes polled, the widening swings indicate a rising level of political awareness, and the weakening of traditional loyalties, such as to caste, ethnic and religious groups, which had accounted to a great extent for the stability of the vote in earlier years.

The elections held in March 1978 in Assam, Meghalaya Maharashtra, Andhra and Karnataka, have further confirmed these trends. Mrs Gandhi swept the polls in Andhra and Karnataka capturing 43.4 per cent and 39.3 per cent of the vote, as against

9 and 17.2 per cent obtained by the official Congress. It also crippled the ruling Congress party in Maharashtra where it obtained 24.5 per cent of the vote against 17.8 per cent for the official Congress. Since the Janata party's share of the vote in these four states did not show any significant change (it went down by 5 and 4 per cent in Maharashtra and Andhra but rose by 10 per cent in Karnataka), it is clear that there has been a polarization of the vote between the ruling party at the centre i.e. the Janata, and the one *national* opposition party which could create a clearly different image from it.

It is difficult to overestimate the significance of this election. By spurning the official Congress in all three states, although it was the ruling party in two of them (Andhra and Maharashtra), the electorate showed that it was casting its vote *even for the state assemblies* on the basis of national and not provincial considerations. Again it ignored or bypassed the entire machinery of political mobilization that was studied at such length by liberal political sociologists in the 'fifties and 'sixties. Above all, in preferring Mrs Gandhi's Congress to the official Congress, it opted consciously for a heightening of political conflict in the country.

The polarization of the vote, the bypassing of the traditional machinery of mobilization, and the growing importance attached to a choice at the national as opposed to the local level, are also not new developments. In 1971, Mrs Gandhi was able to smash the Congress(O) in much the same way, by going over the heads of the organization, and virtually destroying it in the process. However, she at least was the prime minister, and commanded the loyalty of the bulk of the undivided Congress. What is more, in most states the entire Congress party machine aligned itself with her. Its internal cohesion was not therefore damaged. By contrast. in 1977, the Janata routed Mrs Gandhi's Congress even though it had no money, no organization, and most of its candidates were unknown to the voters who put them into the Lok Sabha. In 1978, Mrs Gandhi turned the tables on the official Congress in the same way: except in Karnataka her party had only a skeleton organization, and not very much money.

All this points to one inescapable conclusion. Since 1967, the electorate, which had previously been placid and stable, has become

steadily more volatile. Since that year, every verdict has resulted
from what is, in some measure, a protest vote. In 1967 a five per
cent increase in the total number of votes polled coincided with a
five per cent drop in the Congress's share of the vote. In 1971, the
huge vote for Mrs Gandhi was an endorsement of her revolt against
the organization men of the undivided Congress. In 1977 the
vote for the Janata was a protest against the excesses of the emergency, and the prolonged stagnation of the economy. The 1978
elections and particularly the fall in the share of the Janata's vote
in Maharashtra by five per cent in spite of the party having contested
twenty five per cent more seats, can be interpreted as the beginning
of popular disenchantment with its performance in the previous
year.

It is thus clear that one by one all the stabilizers built up over
the previous two decades have broken down. The development of
a party organization at the grass roots, co-optation by the political
parties of the traditional caste-cum-class elite, the use of state
funds for political patronage via the Panchayati Raj system, none
of these is of much use any longer for capturing the vote. Instead,
an even more impoverished and desperate electorate is swinging
more and more violently, with every puff of the political wind. In
desperation people are now clutching at straws, and are willing
to give their trust to anyone who is willing to offer them even a
faint hope of a better future. The Janata party came to power on
one such swing of the vote. There are signs that the pendulum
has already begun to swing the other way.

It does not need much insight to trace this growing instability
to the stagnation which set in after 1966. It is no accident that the
incidence of labour trouble, student unrest and police firings all
went up sharply after 1965–66. In particular the sudden increase
in industrial unrest coincided exactly with the reversal of economic
trends in 1966. There is thus good reason to attribute the growing
restiveness of vast segments of the electorate to the dominance of
the intermediate classes. The growing unrest in the late 'sixties
was therefore a forerunner of the revolt of the Provincial Armed
Constabulary in Uttar Pradesh in June 1973 and the student revolt
in Gujarat and Bihar in 1974. What is more important, the sharp
resurgence of labour trouble in 1977 was not the result of the end

of the emergency and the return of 'soft' government, but a part of the decade old pattern. The growing instability of the vote is thus a manifestation, at a deep, almost subconscious, level, of the embryonic revolt that is taking place in the country. This is a revolt of the classes which fall outside the intermediate strata — and have become perennial losers on account of inflation and chronic shortages.

The Janata government thus came to power on the crest of an upsurge against the intermediate regime of Mrs Gandhi. Its tragedy, and the reason for its relative inaction in its first year of power, is that most of its cadres, and a majority of its leaders, were recruited at a time when the intermediate class was giving its support to the non-communist 'oppositon', and are therefore drawn very largely from this very class. Proof of this is furnished indirectly by Angela Burger in her micro-studies of UP which showed that the older of the opposition parties, such as the Praja Socialist party, had stopped attracting new recruits even by the mid-sixties and that only the Samyukta Socialists, and the Jana Sangh were still gaining new adherents. There is good reason to suspect that the decline of the Jana Sangh and the SSP in the years between 1969 and 1977, also led to a fall in fresh recruitment even by these parties. In fact by 1975, it is extremely doubtful whether any of the future constituents of the Janata party, other than the Jana Sangh was attracting new recruits in significant numbers (the Jana Sangh could, and no doubt did, draw on the RSS).

The Janata party is thus a prey to conflicting pulls—the demands of the electorate which voted it into power, and the class interests and perceptions of its own cadres, including most of its leaders. The record of its first year in office shows that on balance the pull of the intermediate class is beginning to prevail over the pressures from an increasingly restive electorate. The growing disillusionment of the intelligentsia is a direct outcome of this trend.

On the political front the pull of the intermediate class was most clearly visible in the alacrity with which the party welcomed defectors from the Congress, both before the June 1977 elections for nine northern state assemblies, and again before the elections of March 1978. This opened the way to its entry, and just as after 1967 this class had given its support wholeheartedly to the Congress, it has now to a large extent transferred its allegiance to the Janata. The party's readiness to accept the defectors, and to make them its candidates in these elections, often in preference to old-time party members who had spent all or a large part of the emergency in jail, played a very large part in alienating the intelligentsia and the students who had flocked to its support. The fact that ten per cent of the electorate deserted the Janata in the northern states within three months, and that it did not succeed in improving its position in the south and in Maharashtra, shows that it did not go down too well with a large part of the electorate either.

The above judgements may appear to be too sweeping and there is no denying that the evidence for them is slender. To some extent, this is unavoidable when the events being discussed are only months or even days old. But there is supporting evidence for the hypothesis that the intermediate class has captured the Janata in Mrs Gandhi's behaviour after the elections and her subsequent victories in the south.

Unlike the Janata leaders, Mrs Gandhi grasped the implications of her defeat instantly. The coalition of forces which defeated her was composed of the intelligentsia, the students, the urban working class, and the rural poor. Each of these groups had its own special grievances—unemployment, falling real wages, and the excesses of the family planning drive during the emergency. But basically, this coalition consisted of all those who had suffered under the intermediate regime of the previous two decades. Mrs Gandhi lost no time in changing her political stance. By visiting Belchi, the Bihar village which saw the worst atrocity against Harijans of the Janata period, and other places where such crimes had occurred, she sought to give the impression that she cared for the poor and to indict the Janata government as a coalition of the higher landowning castes which was bent on oppressing the poor. She has sought to instil a similar fear in the Muslims, and was the first national leader to visit the coastal districts of Andhra after the cyclone in November which killed 35,000 people. It is true that her appeal to the minorities is couched in the traditional language of caste and religion. But the Harijans and the Muslims in the rural areas are also among the poorest of the poor—victims of institutionalized oppression by the landed castes. What is more important, by these tactics she has succeeded in putting the Janata on the defensive. This would not have been possible if the Janata had not allowed itself to become identified with the intermediate class. Nor would the panic of the leaders have been so great, if they had not been aware, however indistinctly, that Mrs Gandhi was threatening to capture the allegiance of precisely the people who had put it in power. Mrs Gandhi has thus located the Achilles' heel of the Janata party—the conflict between its class origins, and the expectations of those who put it into power.

Even the importance that the party has attached to setting right the wrongs of the emergency reflects, albeit indirectly, the influence of the intermediate class, for it is partly motivated by a reluctance to alter the economic structure inherited from the Congress. Its first act on coming to power was to lift censorship on the press. It followed this with the appointment of a committee to enquire into the reorganization of the news agency, *Samachar*, which Mrs Gandhi's regime had created through a marriage at gunpoint of the Press Trust of India and the United News of India. It also set up a committee to reorganize All India Radio and Television with the aim of making it truly autonomous, and seven commissions of enquiry to go into the abuses of the emergency. It promised to do away with the infamous 42nd amendment to the Constitution, enacted by the previous regime, which exempted the government from judicial review over a very wide area of legislation, and to repeal the Maintenance of Internal Security Act under which the previous government had imprisoned tens of thousands of people without even producing them before a magistrate and without telling them why they were being 'detained'.

The Janata expected its political liberation programme to win it a large measure of support. Till well into October, it felt certain that steps in this direction would be welcomed by the average people. Its first shock came when the sudden arrest of Mrs Gandhi in October touched off a wave of sympathy for her and hostility towards the government. This fiasco became the launching pad for Mrs Gandhi's political rehabilitation and her bid to recapture the Congress party. The Janata's second shock came in the elections of March 1978, which showed that all the revelations about the high-handed abuse of power by Mrs Gandhi and her caucus had made no impression at all on the 40 million people who voted in Andhra, Karnataka and Maharashtra. Clearly the electorate wanted something more than a mere return to the way things were before the emergency.

What the people wanted was radical economic change, but this is just what the Janata fought shy of giving them. *One year after coming to power, the Janata government had not made a single change of any consequence to the framework of economic laws inherited from its predecessor.* In fiscal policy, it had only increased both direct and indirect taxation without making any significant changes in the structure of these levies. In monetary policy it had preserved the entire structure of high and differentiated interest rates which came into being in 1974.

There had been little relaxation in price controls, although at the time of writing, the government was considering the replacement of administered prices with a more flexible system which would relate these to the earning of optimum rates of return on investment at specified levels of capacity utilisation.

On the other hand the government had made a number of fresh concessions to the intermediate class. In September 1977 it reduced the price of fertilizers by a further Rs 100 per tonne of nutrient. The main beneficiaries were the richer farmers in the rural areas. In the same month, it lifted the ban on the inter-state movement of rice ostensibly to spare the government from having to add to its unsold stocks of food by reviving the private stockholding of grain. But the government's granaries were bulging with wheat and not rice. What is more, the move led to a drastic decline in the procurement of paddy, which stood at only 3.5 million tonnes at the end of January 1978 and was not expected to exceed five million tonnes for the entire season. Finally, the move virtually sabotaged an attempt by the West Bengal government to start a statutory rationing system to cover the entire state, and not just the cities. This would have required a much larger quota of rice, and the state government objected strenuously to the removal of the ban, but to no avail. The prime beneficiaries of this move were the rich farmers and the grain traders.

One of the first endeavours of the new government was to propitiate organized labour and its own white collar employees.

It did this by releasing the additional dearness allowances and other emoluments which had been frozen by Mrs Gandhi's government since 1974, and paying them in cash. It followed this with the restoration of the compulsory bonus of 8.33 per cent of the wage, which employers had to pay irrespective of whether they made a profit or not. Since it was over the railwaymen's demand for a compulsory bonus that Mrs Gandhi had broken the alliance between her intermediate regime and the working class, in reintroducing the compulsory bonus the Janata left no doubt that its aim was to reforge this alliance.

There was considerable opposition to both these measures within the party. The government's original intention had been to add the dearness allowances held back by the previous regime to the employees' provident funds. It only gave in when this move was stiffly resisted by the trade unions. Similarly, the government initially reintroduced the compulsory bonus for a single year only. Although this decision remains unchanged it is a foregone conclusion that the bonus has come to stay. However, some recent developments indicate that the truce between the government and organized labour may be short-lived. Mr Morarji Desai contemptuously dismissed a petition presented to him by the representatives of the Maharashtra government employees during a two-month strike by them from December 1977 to February 1978 and a few weeks earlier S.M. Joshi (leader of the Maharashtra Janata party) was provoked by mounting labour unrest in the state to declare that strikes ought to be banned. But for the moment, the Janata has succeeded in establishing a tenuous peace with labour movement.

The government's 'softness' towards the organized working class contrasts sharply with its harsh treatment of the upper fixed-income groups. In 1974, Mrs Gandhi's government had introduced a compulsory deposit scheme to mop up a part of the purchasing power in the hands of this group. Theoretically the scheme applies to all those who earn more than Rs 12,000 a year. But, since the government has no accurate way of assessing the income of the self-employed, the main burden has fallen on the upper salary-earning groups. Under the original scheme, the CDS was to have remained in operation for two years, after which each annual instalment was to have been returned in five equal instalments over a further period of five years, with an interest of 11 per cent a year. In 1978, since the CDS had been in force for four years the annual repayments, which began in the third year, had started to mount and threatened to exceed the annual deposit. To prevent this from happening the Janata government had sharply increased the compulsory deposit rates from 1978–79. Since there was no time limit to the new scheme, the measure had caused an across the board cut in real income for the affected salary earners. Had the economy been in the grip of acute inflation, an increase in CDS rates would have been justified, but the government took this step when there was a recession and prices were falling, i.e. just when it could have both got rid of a growing burden of debt and interest payments and stimulated demand in the economy without any fear of a rise in prices. It is therefore difficult not to conclude that the move is inspired by class antipathies rather than a tender concern for the economy.

The interests of the intermediate class are also clearly discernible in the Janata's policy towards industry and the public sector. For six to eight months after the March elections, senior party leaders made frequent derogatory references to the public sector. These were often accompanied by specific allegations: for instance they accused Bharat Heavy Electricals of making substandard turbo-generator sets for the power stations, and the coal washeries of supplying very poor coal to the power stations in Bihar and ruining the boilers. In June 1977, a ten per cent price preference given by the Congress government to state-owned enterprises in 1971 was withdrawn. Thereafter the government began to look with a benign eye on a variety of requests for importing equipment which the public enterprises were capable of making within the country, on the grounds that it was cheaper, available under foreign credits, or could be obtained more quickly. One such instance was the government's decision to import Rs 12 crores worth of coal-mining machinery under Polish credits. For this purpose the state-owned Coal-India Limited cancelled contracts for the purchase of equipment worth no less than Rs 12 crores from a state unit.

The government also toyed for some time with the idea of importing power generating equipment, even though Bharat Heavy Electricals was short of orders for turbo-generators. It finally sanctioned the import of one 500 MW turbo generator set for the Tata power plant serving Bombay. At the time of writing, the government seems to have decided to set up fertilizer plants with production streams of 1300 tonnes a day for which most of the equipment will have to be imported when the know-how for building 900 tonne units already exists in the public and private sectors.

The Janata government has also repeatedly warned the public enterprises that they will not get as ready an access to public funds for financing their future expansion, as in the past. What is more, the government proposes to restrict not only its own purchase of equity shares but also the supply of credit from the long term lending institutions.

The government has served a similar notice to large concerns in the private sector, and issued guidelines for restricting the debt to equity ratio on new investment. But what is significant is that the public sector is now being treated with some of the same hostility which was previously reserved for the large private sector alone. In this the Janata's attitude, whatever its ostensible causes, is not very different from that of Sanjay Gandhi. In fairness to the government, it must be admitted that its members have greatly modified their earlier attitudes and that consequently the 'rehabilitation' of the public sector is far advanced. But their initial distrust is significant for it tends to confirm the hypothesis, put forward in Chapter V, that with the deepening of economic stagnation, the intermediate class has begun to withdraw the support it had given to the public sector.

The way in which the Janata government has come to champion the interests of the intermediate classes is also reflected in subtle changes of emphasis between the economic policy resolution announced in November 1977 and the industrial policy resolution announced about a month later.

The core of the economic policy paper is a simple statement that 'what can be produced by cottage industry shall not be produced by the small-scale and large-scale sectors and what can be produced by the small-scale sector shall not be open for large-scale industry.' Although dubbed 'Gandhian', 'reactionary', and 'Utopian', this proposal can, for a large range of basic consumer goods industry, stand the most rigorous tests of modern cost-benefit analysis.

Apart from the fact that goods like soap, shoes, textiles, bricks, bread and earthenware pottery can be produced more cheaply in the house or backyard than in a factory, the purpose of the original policy was to give productive work to millions of future village artisans whose fathers and grandfathers were thrown out of work and forced to become agricultural labourers by the relentless encroachment of modern, power-driven industry.

In this way it hoped to increase the income of the poorest segments of the rural population, and greatly increase their capacity to buy consumer goods. The resulting increase in demand would, after a time lag, have strengthened the demand for capital and intermediate goods. The end result would have been a balanced and healthy industrial growth, in which investment occurred in response to demand generated by the whole of the country's population, and not just of the fraction that lived in the towns. Still less would it have been a byproduct of the fickle and ultimately enfeebling demand of buyers in other countries.

Given this objective, the original policy paper had correctly appreciated the need for drawing a firm line between industries which did and did not use power. In the Indian context this meant discouraging not only the large but also the small-scale sector in industries which cater to the basic needs of the masses. But this is precisely the move that has been aborted in successive stages by pressure from the 'non-Gandhian' elements of the Janata party.

In October, the Planning Commission had identified no less than eight industries where production could be reserved for the cottage sector. The economic policy paper retained only two of these—textiles and footwear—but added soap. In all these industries the commission promised not only to freeze but to phase out large-scale production (siginficantly, even then it was silent on the question of phasing out the small-scale, power driven sector).

By contrast, the industrial policy promised only to freeze the output of power-driven units, and that too, only in the textile industry. In soap and footwear, the government only promised to take steps to increase the share of the cottage sector in total production. The idea of phasing out even factory production in any industry has been quietly dropped.

This steady lowering of sights may be the product of a growing realization in the Janata party that the task of handing back a large number of consumer goods industries to the cottage sector is much more difficult than it looked at first sight. But had this been the case, the government could have got around the problem by setting more modest targets over a wider range of consumer goods industries. It does not justify the progressive reduction of the number of industries in which a start is to be made.

The small-scale sector is the only real beneficiary of the new industrial policy. While the increase in the number of items reserved for this sector from 180 to 504 seems to reflect a more detailed definition and classification of industries, rather than any major widening of the area reserved for the sector, it will be the *direct beneficiary* of the sharp restrictions placed on the expansion of the large scale sector on the one hand, and the failure to get the cottage industries off the ground on the other. A striking precedent for this type of expansion already exists in the growth of the power loom sector. The ceiling placed on the production of textiles in the large mills in 1951 was designed to foster the growth of the handloom sector. But by 1961, while the output of the handlooms had risen only marginally, the powerloom sector had grown from 23,800 looms to over 140,000 looms.

Although the government has promised to foster cottage-scale technology in shoes, soap and other consumer goods, the hard fact remains that the first consequence of the new policy will be the refusal of a large number of pending applications from the bid companies for the expansion of their capacity or for setting up new units in these industries. Since there is no simultaneous ban on the growth of output in small units, the gap will immediately be filled by the small-scale and the newly created 'tiny' sector. The story of the textile industry is therefore likely to be repeated in a score of others in the next few years.

The Janata government's obsession with price stability is a clear indication of the low priority it attaches to economic growth. In this it is in no way different from the previous Congress regime, whose proudest boast during the first year of the emergency was that it had brought prices down. The relative priorities attached by Mrs Gandhi's regime to 'growth' and 'stability' are revealed by its reactions to the economic trends during the two years of the emergency. In 1975–76, prices came down by around seven per cent and industry recorded a poor growth rate of 4.7 per cent. While the government made much of the fall in prices it was not in the least put out by the slow rate of industrial growth. But in 1976–77, prices rose by no less than 12 per cent. This touched off something close to a panic in the government, which was not in the least allayed by the fact that there was a spurt in industrial growth by 10.6 per cent, the highest rate achieved since the end of the second plan.

The Janata party has shown that it has the same priorities. Almost the only 'achievement' to which leaders repeatedly drew attention during their first year in office, was the decline in prices that had taken place since June 1977. That this began during the 'lean' season from June to October, when the stocks of food and agricultural raw materials begin to run out and prices normally rise, did not arouse any concern. Nor were they unduly worried by the steep decline in the rate of industrial growth from 8.9 per cent per annum in the first three months of 1977 to 5.2 per cent in the next seven months. In language that was reminiscent of the previous ten years' reports, the pre-budget Economic Survey of the year 1977–78 ascribed the fall to strikes, lock-outs, and shortages of critical inputs like power, rather than to structural defects in the economy which are leading for a growing dearth of demand. The conclusion is inescapable: growth is acceptable only if it occurs without a rise in prices.

At first sight this may seem fanciful. But the indecision of the government over how to make use of the mounting food and foreign exchange reserves in order to accelerate growth bears this out. Any step-up in investment will, in the short run, lead to a rise in prices unless the consumption of wage goods by those who are already employed is somehow reduced simultaneously, or additional wage goods are imported. But what if food, the most important of these wage goods is actually rotting in the government's godowns; if the textile industries are short of orders; if the country has over six billion dollars worth of foreign exchange reserves and a balance of payments surplus of over two billion dollars a year? What if savings are rising faster than investment and now exceed it by two per cent of the national income? Is there any conceivable reason for not stepping up investment either by allowing the banking system to increase its advances, or resorting to deficit financing? This was the situation which prevailed during the first year of the Janata government's rule. The country's total foreign exchange reserves amounted to Rs 4547 crores on March 31, 1978. And this figure did not include some Rs 1000 to Rs 1500 crores worth of gold and contingency reserves held in various accounts. The annual balance of payments surplus had been exceeding two billion for the previous two years and was likely to continue. There were nearly twenty million tonnes of grain in the government buffer and operational stocks at the end of 1977. A bumper harvest of 125 million tonnes was expected in 1977–78 and procurement for the entire year was expected to be of the order of 14 million tonnes, which meant that the buffer stock would rise still further. The government was keen to step up investment, but was mortally afraid that once it commits itself to an expanded programme of investment by drawing more heavily on the private savings held with the banks a poor monsoon could easily cause a run on these private savings by people trying to maintain their consumption in the face of higher prices. This could result in a sharp increase in food and raw materials prices which even the existing reserves of food and foreign exchange might not suffice to contain. So great was the government's fear of such an eventuality that it was not willing to allow any expansion of bank advances, and wished to raise investment only out of its own savings. For this purpose, it resorted to savage taxation in the budget for 1978–79 without realizing that financing additional investment out of new savings would not close the deflationary gap and might not therefore end the recession in industry. What is more, since the scope for additional taxation was inevitably limited when the ratio of taxes to the national income already exceeded 17 per cent the government has been forced to cut back its plans to expand investment. The annual plan for 1978–79 is only 16 per cent larger than that for 1977–78. Since only 10 per cent of the proposed expenditures are earmarked for new projects, very little of the plan funds will find their way into the much-vaunted rural development programmes!

It does not seem to have occurred to the government that its fear is irrational. Increased investment now, when the country has enough food and foreign exchange reserves to weather even two poor monsoons can easily put the country in a position where the supply of wage goods is sufficient to cope with future adversities without needing to hold very large reserves. But if the industrial stagnation continues, sooner or later, a succession of poor monsoons will wipe out the food and foreign exchange reserves and abort any remaining possibility of accelerated growth. Only minds conditioned by more than a decade of stagnation could have worked out such an elaborate rationale for stagnation.

The tragedy of the Janata is that, unlike Mrs Gandhi's Congress, it did have an inkling of the forces behind the upsurge which swept it into power. When its leaders talked of a second revolution, they were expressing not just rhetoric but a vague awareness of a historical process. In its heady first weeks of power the Janata responded strongly to the call of the electorate. The talk of the need for a Gandhian model of development, for channelling funds into rural development, and for revitalizing the cottage industries of India in order to attack the roots of poverty did not reflect a retreat from modernization (an attempt to 'go back to the days of the bullock cart' as it was contemptuously labelled by both the left and the right). It was born of the awareness that the party had been put in power mainly by people who had not benefited from the type of development which had taken place in the previous thirty years. But while promises are easy to make their implementation is slow, unspectacular and politically unrewarding. It was when the time came to find ways of implementing these brave new resolves that the beneficiaries of this "development" struck back. They have now succeeded in burying the "Gandhian" model under a heap of scorn. All that is left of it today is a yet to be developed "tiny" sector, a never-to-be-developed cottage-sector, and a token rural development programme which, like Mrs Gandhi's 20-point programme, is not much more than a re-grouping of existing agricultural development schemes under a new heading.[1]

The crowning irony is that the very people who put the Janata into power are beginning to switch their allegiance back to Mrs Gandhi, the person who did the most to legitimize the rise of their oppressors. In Karnataka and Maharashtra, the new Congress ministries are packed with members of the lower castes, a sure indication of where Mrs Gandhi has drawn, and hopes to draw, her support. While the caste antagonisms which have played a part in the political rebirth of Mrs Gandhi have been extensively commented upon, the class connotations have, as usual, been overlooked. But the clearest indication of the strong class bias in the emerging strategy of the Congress is given by C. Subramaniam, former minister for finance, industry and planning in Mrs Gandhi's government in his attack on the budget (*Economic Times* March 14). In it Mr Subramaniam attributed the Janata's failure to keep down retail prices (which rose by 5.8 per cent even though wholesale prices went up by only 1.2 per cent in 1977–78) to the strength of the traders' lobby in the party. He said that the beneficiary of the much trumpeted freedoms which it had restored was the trader 'who can now hoard, profiteer and indulge in blackmarketing with impunity'. He pointed out that the restoration of the 8.33 per cent compulsory bonus and cash payments of impounded dearness allowances benefited the **organized** sector, which accounted for five per cent of the population and would push up prices, and thus reduce the consumption of the remaining 95 per cent. An even more significant admission was made the next day during the same debate by T. A. Pai, former minister for industries who said 'I'm afraid politics in this country has developed a vested interest in poverty' (*Times of India*, March 15, 1978).

Both Pai and Subramaniam are with the official Congress, and therefore opposed to Mrs Gandhi's Congress. But their speeches indicate the growing realization in the official Congress also, that to retain political relevance it must make a decisive break with the intermediate class and seek new alliances. More significantly, it highlights their awareness that this opportunity has arisen only because the Janata has failed to cement its alliance with the groups which have suffered at the hands of the intermediate classes, and has instead fallen steadily more under their sway.

March 1978 thus marks the end of an all-too-brief spell of hope— indeed of what some writers have disdainfully but correctly described as a period of political romanticism. In that month, the Janata presented its budget and unveiled the sixth plan, and dashed all lingering hopes that it would still make a significant departure from the policies followed in the previous decade. In that month also, the elections in Andhra, Maharashtra and Assam showed that its share of the vote had begun to slip.

March 1978 also marks the beginning of a new and even more destructive phase of political conflict in the country. In Karnataka the Congress (I) ministry of Devaraj Urs moved legislation to reserve 58 per cent of all seats in educational institutions and of government jobs for members of the backward classes, while in Bihar a Janata government under Karpoori Thakur has proposed the reservation of 26 per cent of all such positions for the backward classes in addition to the 24 per cent already reserved for the scheduled castes and tribes. Predictably, the moves have touched off angry protests in both states and a spate of violence against the Janata government in Bihar.

It is not easy to see how a stagnant economy will be able to absorb the conflict which is about to be unleashed so gratuitously within it. The tragedy here too is that the move stems from a misinterpretation of the conflict between the intermediate classes and the other groups in society. What is really a conflict between the gainers and losers from policies directed towards the perpetuation of economic stagnation, has been misinterpreted as a conflict between the more and less privileged castes in society. Given the close historical relationship between ritual status denoted by caste and economic status denoted by the ownership of land or the exercise of military/bureaucratic power, the confusion is perhaps understandable. But its consequences for the country are nevertheless likely to be tragic.

NOTES

1. The actual allocation for agriculture and rural development programmes of all types comes to 37.8 per cent of the 6th plan as against 42 per cent of the 4th plan.

PART III

9 / Redefining the Objectives of Economic Growth

THE CAUSES OF INDIA'S economic stagnation in the past ten years are at least as much political as economic. The economic causes described in Chapters 1 to 4 are now fairly common knowledge. It has long been clear that the basic assumption underlying the adoption of a capital-intensive strategy of growth—that it would enable the country to maximize the rate of reinvestment of savings and therefore the accumulation of capital—was unfounded. The capital-intensive growth model failed to take account of the ability of organized labour to raise its wages through collective bargaining, and what is more important, of the inability of a democratically elected government to resist the demand to create more jobs, even if these are only sinecures in a bloated bureaucracy. The two pressures have diverted more and more of the surplus available for reinvestment, into consumption, to the point where the country is now hard put to find the funds even to maintain its existing stock of capital.

However, the specifically political constraint on growth imposed by the rise of the intermeditate class is not yet fully perceived, let alone understood. This is why critiques of the Indian economy tend to over-emphasize the role of the capital-intensive growth strategy in frustrating the achievement of self-sustaining growth.

Any programme for reviving the Indian economy and tackling the problems of poverty and unemployment must therefore have both an economic and a political component. On the economic front it must aim at undoing some of the harm that has been done by the excessively capital-intensive pattern of investment in the past. On the political front an attempt needs to be made to contain the growing power of the intermediate class and to end the anti-growth bias which its rise has imparted to economic legislation during the past decade.

The dual character of the problem also imposes serious constraints on the kind of programme that a future government can hope to push through. There is absolutely no point, for instance, in advocating programmes of collectivization, or the total expropriation of all landowners and the redistribution of their land on some 'equitable' basis, because such a radical attack on property will be resisted tooth and nail not only by the rich farmers but also by the entire property-conscious intermediate class, both in town and country. By contrast a programme of moderate reform involving the consolidation of holdings, the elimination of absentee land ownership, and greater security of tenure for tenants, is likely to prove more effective if only because it will isolate the hard core of the rural land-owners from the rest of the intermediate class. (This is the reverse of the argument that orthodox 'leftist' writers on Indian agricultura have put forward, viz. that moderate land reform is bound to be frustrated by the *kulak* lobby and therefore only drastic reforms brought about through revolutionary upheavals in the countryside, can improve the lot of the rural poor. Yet it follows logically, using Marxist methods of analysis, once social classes have been redefined to take cognizance of the intermediate class.)

It may be tempting to argue that since there are both political and economic constraints on further development, the removal of either one or the other set of constraints may be sufficient to restart the engine of growth. In other words, either a change in growth strategy, or a decisive move to reduce the political power of the intermediate class may suffice. This is not so. To begin with India already has a sizable modern industry, requiring modern inputs and producing sophisticated products. This cannot be abandoned overnight. Thus, (as is argued in Chapter 11) change has to be gradual and at the margin of investment. Secondly, while cutting down the size of the bureaucracy, and repealing the restrictive economic legislation which has inhibited the growth of large scale industry and aided the rise of the intermediate class will almost certainly boost the rate of investment and industrial growth in the near future. It too is not likely to provide a panacea for India's social and economic problems in the long run.

The experience of other developing countries in Latin America, Africa and South East Asia has shown that even in countries with a high rate of growth of the national product, capital-intensive growth has created 'dual' economies, with small enclaves of prosperity surrounded by hinterlands of poverty. The impulse to growth which these high income enclaves have imparted to the economy has been weak and fitful. This is no accident, but a logical outcome of such a pattern of development. The relatively high wages in the industrial enclaves have ushered in radically different consumption patterns modelled on those of the affluent nations, in which consumer durables, luxury housing and fancy foods have found an increasingly important place. To meet this demand a whole range of secondary processing and packaging industries (which are also fairly capital intensive) have sprung up. These have preempted scarce resources that should have been spent on producing basic consumer goods and on improving health, housing, and education. The diversion of capital, skilled labour and scarce managerial skills from essential consumer goods to luxuries has made the economy more vulnerable to inflationary pressures, and endemic inflation in turn has caused a further shift of income from the poor to the rich. This has not only reinforced the demand for home made 'foreign' consumption goods, but also triggered demands for higher wages in the organized modern sector of the economy. This has further increased the profitability of replacing labour with capital, and reinforced the trend toward dualism. In theory the capital-intensive growth strategy is supposed to spread prosperity by sucking in more and more people from the stagnant countryside into the high-income industrial enclaves. As the absolute numbers of people living off the land diminishes, it permits the introduction of labour-saving machinery to raise productivity in agriculture also.

But with the growth of dualism, the capital intensive strategy of development dooms itself to failure. The adoption of an alien capital-intensive pattern of consumption on the one hand and the steady rise in wage rates within the advanced enclaves on the other, force a steady rise in the capital to labour ratio. (This is the main reason why firms tend to keep going back to their foreign collaborators for constantly updating their technology and for entering into new collaboration agreements to diversify their production.) The rise in the capital-labour ratio means that *even if a country is able to maintain a constant rate of capital accumulation, the rate of growth of employment falls.* In turn this means that the growth of demand even within the modernized enclaves is bound to slow down over time, and with it the growth of the import-substituting consumer goods industries will also slacken. Domestic entrepreneurs respond initially to this slackening of demand by going back along the chain of production and producing more and more of the capital goods needed to sustain the given level of consumption. But this only postpones the day of reckoning by a few years for it causes a further, and this time a much sharper rise in the capital to labour and capital to output ratios, a further slowing down in the growth of employment and consequently an even steeper decline in the rate of growth of consumption. Finally, as more and more concerns go into the red, the rate of capital accumulation also tapers off.

The only course left open to entrepreneurs in these circumstances is to rely ever more heavily on the world market to make good the deficiencies of domestic demand. Modern industry in a poor nation then comes more and more to serve the interests of buyers in the affluent countries and less and less those of the poor and the destitute at home.

Few people who have studied the performance of the developing nations will fail to notice that in most cases it has conformed closely to the pattern described above. The study of the unemployment problems of Columbia, with which the International Labour Office initiated its wide ranging reassessment of the objectives and strategies of economic development, began by pointing out that even in those Latin American countries whose national incomes have grown rapidly, unemployment, the gap in living standards between the rich and the poor, and that in life styles between town and country, has grown even faster. This has speeded the migration to the cities and the mushroom growth of shanty colonies in them. The ILO's subsequent studies of Ceylon, Iran, Kenya and the Philippines have only confirmed the universality of this pattern.

That the Indian experience has conformed uncomfortably closely to this model hardly needs to be stressed. The capital to output ratio has risen not only between the first plan and the second, when it could have been ascribed to a change in the strategy of planning, but also in each subsequent Plan, even though the strategy and the broad sectoral allocations have remained more or less unchanged after 1956. The marked shift in the pattern of private investment from consumer to intermediate and capital goods in the second and third Plans has already been noted by R. K. Hazari.

The decline in the rate of growth of factory employment in the organized private sector during the 'sixties can be attributed to the growing capital intensity of investment, although it manifested itself only after the beginning of the absolute decline in investment initiated the Plan holiday. By the same token, the sluggishness of demand not only for capital goods but also for manufactured consumer goods (except during the three inflationary years from 1972 to 1974) can be traced to the exhaustion of the impetus given by import substitution to the growth process. Finally, the rise in the country's exports after 1967, after domestic demand began to slacken, and the advice given by the World Bank to the Indian government in its annual report for 1974 to look to the world market for making good the deficiency of domestic demand, speak for themselves.

The exhaustion of the stimulus to growth given by import substitution has been commented on very widely. One of the clearest descriptions is given in the ILO's study of the Philippines. The report shows that the impetus provided by import substitution is weak, as it stems from the demand of a small minority. Very soon therefore, the focus of industrialization begins to shift from producing consumer goods to making the machines that produce these goods. However, this raises the capital output ratio and correspondingly the need to generate ever increasing surpluses in some other sector of the economy to finance continued industrialization.

In orthodox growth theory, the report points out, the surpluses are supposed to come from agriculture. Indeed it is one of its fundamental premises that rapid increases in productivity and income can come about only from industrialization and that the main function of agriculture is to generate the surpluses needed to finance the growth of industry. The Philippines report goes a long way towards refuting this belief.

It points out that this premise holds true only so long as a country has a favourable man-land ratio and the necessary surplus can be generated by the extension of traditional agriculture to new areas.

However, agricultural surpluses start dwindling when the 'land frontier' is reached, usually as a result of a rise in population. This tends not only to choke the supply of capital to industry but also to slow down the growth of the rural market for manufactured goods.

In other words, the strategy of spreading prosperity through a steady expansion of industrial enclaves until they embrace the bulk of the population, and of relying on the percolation over time of the benefits of a high rate of growth of GNP to all strata of society is as unsound in theory as it has proved unworkable in practice.

The starting point of any viable alternative strategy of growth must therefore be an abandonment of urban-centered industrialization fuelled by import substitution. While this much is clear, the alternatives put forward so far have been far from satisfactory. For instance, the ILO report on the Philippines suggests the adoption of a strategy of 'balanced rural mobilization'. This concept itself represents a gradual crystallization of ideas contained in its report on Columbia and Kenya. In the first study the team had laid great stress on the need for land reform, and for the initiation of energetic health, education and welfare programmes in the villages to close the gap in the availability of these facilities between town and country. The Kenya report had implicitly admitted that the hope of closing the town-country gap in this way was Utopian and proposed instead that the government should nourish the growth of what it called the 'informal sector' of small craftsmen meeting a variety of newly emerging needs both in the towns and the villages. All these proposals have one thing in common: they aim at widening the base of demand by maximizing the creation of productive employment.

But what if those who grow rich in the informal sector in their turn demand the products of the import-substitution based 'formal' sector: if the mechanic wants to buy a car, and the children of the village cobbler want to wear only factory made shoes? If this happens—and even the most superficial view of contemporary India will confirm that it is happening—the informal sector will never remain more than an industrial fringe under constant threat of extinction from the superior competitive power of the organized formal sector. It has been glibly assumed in the past that this superior competitiveness stems from greater efficiency. But this is not always so. (To cite two examples: a lady in Mysore taught villagers around Srirangapatnam to make soap at home. Using edible oils only they produce soap for no more than 40 paise per hundred grammes! The cheapest factory made soap cost 95 paise for 85 grams. Similarly in 1974, small bakeries provided a loaf of bread for Rs 1.50, as against Rs 1.35 for an equal sized loaf from a public sector mechanical bakery.[1] But while the baker bought his wheat from the open market, the public sector bakery got it from the government at the subsidized price of the ration shops!)

The superior competitive power of the large-scale sector stems at least as often, and perhaps more often, from the greater strength of demand for its 'western', 'modern' and 'superior' products. So long as this strong consumer perference remains, dualism will be at best mildly diluted and the pyramid of prosperity will be only slightly more broadbased than before.

The truth is that the prime cause of 'dualism' is not the adoption of capital-intensive techniques of production but the adoption of an alien pattern of consumption. So long as a country defines prosperity in terms borrowed from advanced countries, dualism is inevitable. Merely adopting labour intensive techniques of making consumer goods which form a part of the life style of countries with a lot of capital and a shortage of labour, will make at best a marginal difference to the capital intensity of production. To really generate millions of more jobs one must not only produce hand-printed cotton textiles, but also be able to persuade people that these are not only usable but actually in many instances preferable to mill-made cloth, synthetic fabrics and screen prints. By contrast if television sets and cars remain symbols of affluence one may employ the most labour-intensive techniques for assembling them but there will be no escape from having to mass-produce their components.

The implicit premise behind the ILO's encouragement of the small scale sector, and its plea for a 'balanced rural mobilization', is that the beneficiaries of such development will be less likely to adopt a radically different life style when they become richer. If with their extra incomes people only demand more of what they already know and use, then the local carpenters, cobblers, potters, tailors, printers, bakers, and masons will be the first beneficiaries of development. The change in life style which characterizes dualism will then either not take place or will be much less marked. But this is at best a pious hope, and there is little in the experience of the developing countries to sustain it.

The prime objective of growth which the ILO recommends to developing nations—to create more productive employment rather than more goods and services therefore turns out to be a pseudo-objective. If the GNP was a veil that the first generation of development economists chose to throw over the ugly process of economic transformation, then employment is only another, somewhat more diaphanous veil. To create more productive jobs is a more important and tangible goal than to create more goods and services, but to those who wish to control or hasten the process of economic transformation, neither can be a final objective.

The ultimate aim of development planners in the poor countries must be to prevent the fracture in life styles and values which lies at the root of 'dualism'. By the same token in countries like India which have been colonies of the affluent nations, the first task must be to heal the inherited rift in values and perceptions between the colonized 'elite' and the relatively untouched masses of the country.

In concrete terms this involves a prolonged and even painful reappraisal of almost every one of the ideas that govern our lives today. We have not only to question whether steel plants are the temples of modern India, as Pandit Nehru asserted so emphatically, but even simple every day notions such as whether eating with a knife and fork off a dining table, and wearing a lounge suit represent advances over eating with our hands, sitting on the floor, and wearing a *dhoti* or a *pyjama* and *kurtha*. We have to ask ourselves whether houses with mosaic floors, RCC roof slabs and air-conditioners are really more comfortable and make for more elegant living than those with floors of hard-packed clay and roofs of baked country tiles, cooled by the wind blowing through damp 'khuskhus' screens. In the same vein we need to question ourselves whether patent leather shoes, stainless steel cooking pots and mechanically baked bread, make for better living than say hand-made Kolhapuri sandals, ceramic cooking utensils and home-baked bread. Indeed we must ask ourselves whether even such universally derided institutions as the caste system are really as bad as they are made out to be. The exercise is invaluable not so much because one expects to arrive at a different conclusion from the accepted one, but because it is important for us to arrive at even the same answers on the basis of our own independent appraisals instead of unquestioningly accepting someone else's opinion. The aim of such a reappraisal must be nothing less than to reject many of the underlying 'western' values on which we base our notions of prosperity and welfare for without this it will be impossible to prevent the birth and growth of dualism.

The vehicle for this reappraisal is of course education. But as Schumacher has pointed out in his book *Small is Beautiful* it is not the kind of education which teaches us how to cope with specific problems but that which transmits 'ideas of value, of what to do with our lives'. Without such education we have no means of choosing between different ways of achieving the same ends. Needless to say the transmission of values is not the same as the transmission of scientific or engineering know-how. Values are the tools with which we order our perception of the world. In other words, they make up the intellectual tool-box with which we assess the worth of other ideas, notably those which we employ to get things done.

A change in these basic 'ideas of value' is nothing short of a mental earthquake 'for it shifts the perspective from which we view life itself'. Schumacher gives a vivid illustration of such a shift in perspective in a chapter on what he calls Buddhist economies.

Contrasting it with 'modern' economics Schumacher has this to say about the value of human labour:

'Now, the modern economist has been brought up to consider "labour" or work as little more than a necessary evil. From the point of view of the employer, it is in any case simply an item of cost, to be reduced to a minimum if it cannot be eliminated altogether, say, by automation. From the point of view of the workman, it is a "disutility"; To work is to make a sacrifice of one's leisure and comfort, and wages are a kind of compensation for the sacrifice. Hence the ideal from the point of view of the employer is to have output without employees, and the ideal from the point of view of the employee is to have income without employment.

'The consequences of these attitudes, both in theory and in practice are, of course, extremely far-reaching. If the ideal with regard to work is to get rid of it, every method that 'reduces the work load' is a good thing. The most potent method, short of automation, is the so-called 'division of labour' and the classical example is the pin factory eulogised in Adam Smith's *Wealth of Nations*. Here it is not a matter of ordinary specialisation, which mankind has practised from time immemorial, but of dividing up every complete process of production into minute parts, so that the final product can be produced at great speed without anyone having had to contribute more than a totally insignificant and, in most cases, unskilled movement of his limbs. . . .

'The Buddhist point of view takes the function of work to be at least three-fold: to give a man a chance to utilize and develop his faculties; to enable him to overcome his egocentredness by joining with other people in a common task; and to bring forth the goods and services needed for a becoming existence. Again, the consequences that flow from this view are endless. To organize work in such a manner that it becomes meaningless, boring, stultifying, or nerve-racking for the worker would be little short of criminal; it would indicate a greater concern with goods than with people, an evil lack of compassion and a soul-destroying degree of attachment to the most primitive side of this wordly existence. Equally, to strive for leisure as an alternative to work would be considered a complete misunderstanding of one of the basic truths of human existence, namely that work and leisure are complementary parts of the same living process and cannot be separated without destroying the joy of work and the bliss of leisure.

'From the Buddhist point of view, there are therefore two types of mechanization which must be clearly distinguished; one that enhances a man's skill and power and one that turns the work of man over to a mechanical slave, leaving man in a position of having to serve the slave. How to tell the one from the other? The craftsman himself, says Ananda Coomaraswamy, a man equally competent to talk about the modern west as the ancient east, can always, if allowed to, draw the delicate distinction between the machine and the tool. The carpet loom is a tool, a contrivance for holding warp threads at a stretch for the pile to be woven round them by the craftsmen's fingers; but the power loom is a machine, and its significance as a destroyer of culture lies in the fact that it does the essentially human part of the work.'

Talking about the aims of economic activity Schumacher has the following observations:

'...the modern economist...is used to measuring the standard of living by the amount of annual consumption, assuming all the time that a man who consumes more is "better off" than a man who consumes less. A Buddhist economist would consider this approach excessively irrational: since consumption is merely a means to human well-being, the aim should be to obtain the maximum of well-being with the minimum of consumption. Thus, if the purpose of clothing is a certain amount of temperature comfort and an attractive appearance, the task is to attain this purpose with the smallest possible effort, that is, with the smallest annual destruction of cloth and with the help of designs that involve the smallest possible of input of toil....

'The ownership and the consumption of goods is a means to an end, and Buddhist economics is the systematic study of how to attain given ends with the minimum means.

'Modern economics, on the other hand, considers consumption to be the sole factor and purpose of all economic activity, taking the factors of production—land, labour, and capital—as the means. The former, in short, tries to maximize human satisfactions by the optimal pattern of consumption, while the latter tries to maximize consumption by the optimal pattern of productive effort. It is easy to see that the effort needed to sustain a way of life which seeks to attain the optimal pattern of consumption is likely to be smaller than the effort needed to sustain a drive for maximum consumption. We need not be surprised, therefore, that the pressure and strain of living is very much less in say, Burma than it is in the United States, in spite of the fact that the amount of labour saving-machinery used in the former country is only a minute fraction of the amount used in the latter.'[3]

And on the use of natural resources Schumacher has this to say: 'Another striking difference between modern economics and Buddhist economics arises over the use of natural resources. Bertrand de Jouvenel, the eminent French political philosopher, has characterized "western man" in words which may be taken as a fair description of the modern economist:

'He tends to count nothing as an expenditure, other than human effort; he does not seem to mind how much mineral matter he wastes, and, far worse, how much living matter he destroys. He does not seem to realize at all that human life is a dependent part of an ecosystem of many different forms of life. As the world is ruled from the towns where men are cut off from any form of life other than human, the feeling of belonging to an ecosystem is not revived. This results in a harsh and improvident treatment of things upon which we ultimately depend, such as water and trees.'

'The teaching of the Buddha, on the other hand,' Schumacher goes on to say, 'enjoins a reverent and non-violent attitude not only to all sentient beings but also, with great emphasis, to trees. Every follower of the Buddha ought to plant a tree every few years and look after it until it is safely established, and the Buddhist economist can demonstrate without difficulty that the universal observation of this rule would result in a high rate of genuine economic development independent of any foreign aid. Much of the economic decay of south-east Asia (as of any other parts of the world) is undoubtedly due to a heedless and shameful neglect of trees.

'Modern economics does not distinguish between renewable and non-renewable materials, as its very method is to equalize and quantify everything by means of a money price. Thus, taking various alternative fuels, like coal, oil, wood, or water-power; the only difference between them recognized by modern economics is relative cost per equivalent unit.

'The cheapest is automatically the one to be preferred, as to do otherwise would be irrational and "uneconomic". From a Buddhist point of view, of course, this will not do; the essential difference between non-renewable fuels like coal and oil on the one hand and renewable fuels like wood and water-power on the other cannot be simply overlooked. Non-renewable goods must be used only if they are indispensable, and then only with the greatest care and the most meticulous concern for conservation. To use them heedlessly or extravagantly is an act of violence, and while complete non-violence may not be attainable on this earth, there is nonetheless an ineluctable duty on man to aim at the ideal of non-violence in all he does.

'Just as a modern European economist would not consider it a great economic achievement if all European art treasures were sold to America at attractive prices, so the Buddhist economist would insist that a population basing its economic life on non-renewable fuels is living parasitically, on capital instead of income. Such a way of life could have no permanence and could therefore be justified only as a purely temporary expedient. As the world's resources of non-renewable fuels—coal, oil, and natural gas—are exceedingly unevenly distributed over the globe and undoubtedly limited in quanity, it is clear that their exploitation at an ever-increasing rate is an act of violence against nature which must almost inevitably lead to violence between men.'[4]

To extol 'Buddhist Economics' is not to pretend that Buddhist
countries are doing a better job of managing their economies than
say Christian ones. Schumacher points out that the Burmese for
example extol 'Buddhist economics' but they call in a 'modern
economist' from the west to frame their five year plans. But his
illustrations show how the beliefs that have fuelled two centuries
of economic activity in the west are not absolute truths about
human nature, as the modern economists so fondly imagine, but
metaphysical propositions whose only real sanction is the high
degree of acceptance that they have gained so far.

In India, the most striking example of the distorted vision which
is born of imported second-hand values and perceptions is the
tolerant contempt with which the middle-class city dweller views
the villages and their people. This contempt for the '*dhotiwala*'
the '*bhaiya*', the '*gawaar*', the *ghati*, which impregnates films,
radio programmes, novels and short stories and even finds expression in the left intellectuals' antipathy to the rural *kulak*, is
at root based on nothing more than an unquestioning admiration
of the British colonists and their ways. Even a moment's thought
would show to anyone whose mental tool-box is not already filled
to the brim with such second-hand perceptions that while rural
India may be poor, except in the areas where capitalist farming
has come to stay (such as Punjab and Haryana), its life styles and
economic system have not been fractured by the impact of western
technology and the craving for a western style of living. In fact for
those who have not yet come to believe that whiskey after sun-
set is the acme of good living, the most striking feature of village
life is its remarkable efficiency and economy, and the sturdy independence of the values on which it is founded.

Mahatma Gandhi was one of the few in our time who did. He
never ceased to extol the self-sufficiency of the villages before the
advent of industry disrupted their economy. In a letter to a cor-
respondent in 1934 he wrote: 'There is hardly anything of daily
use which the villagers have not made before and cannot make
now' (Tendulkar D.G., *Mahatma*, vol. 4 p. 2) and in an article
in *Harijan* of November 6, 1934:

'The idea of forming the (village industries) association took a
definite shape during the Harijan tour as early as when I entered

Malabar. A casual talk with a khadi worker showed to me how necessary it was to have a body that would make an honest attempt to return to the villagers what has been cruelly and thoughtlessly snatched away from them by the city dwellers. The hardest hit among the villagers are the Harijans. They have but a limited choice of the industries that are open to the villagers in general. Therefore, when their industries slip away from their hands, they become like the beasts of burden with whom their lot is cast.

'But the villagers in general are not much better off today. Bit by bit they are being confined only to the hand-to-mouth business of scratching the earth.... Extinction of the village industries would complete the ruin of the 7,00,000 villages of India.'

Out of this profoundly human perception came a distinct philosophy of growth:

'I have seen in the daily press criticism of the proposals I have adumbrated. Advice has been given to me that I must look for salvation in the direction of using the powers of nature that the inventive brain of man has brought under subjection. The critics say that water, air, oil, and electricity should be fully utilized, as they are being utilized in the go-ahead West. They say that the control over these hidden powers of nature enables every American to have thirty-three slaves. Repeat the process in India and I dare say that it will thirty-three times enslave every inhabitant of this land.....'

'Mechanization is good when the hands are too few for the work intended to be accomplished. It is an evil when there are more hands than required for the work, as is the case in India....

'...Strange as it may appear, every mill generally is a menace to the villagers. I have not worked out the figures, but I am quite safe in saying that every mill-hand does the work of at least ten labourers doing the same work in their villages. In other words, he earns more than he did in his village at the expense of ten fellow villagers. Thus spinning and weaving mills have deprived the villagers of a substantial means of livelihood. It is no answer in reply to say that they turn out cheaper better cloth, if they do so at all. For, if they have displaced thousands of workers, the cheapest mill cloth is dearer than the dearest khadi woven in the village.'

Many modern cost-benefit analysts would enthusiastically endorse the above proposition. But Gandhi saw far deeper in 1934 than most of them do even today. For he saw clearly that the roots of the problem lay in mechanization and that mechanization had come in to serve a radically different way of life.

Where Gandhi failed was in convincing even his closest collea-gues in Congress that the self-sufficiency of the village economy was not a product of necessity but of choice. It was not a regression from an earlier golden age, forced on rural India by the disruption of political life and the growing insecurity of transport and travel, but the product of centuries of unconscious choice, designed to produce a life style which made the optimum use of the resources available to the community. Thus even today the villager consumes the cereals, pulses and vegetables that he grows, feeds the husk and most of the straw which is a byproduct to his cattle, uses the rest of the straw for roofing his home. He builds the walls of his house of clay and chopped straw on bamboo or timber frames, collects nearly all the dung produced by the cattle, uses four-fifths for fuel and the balance as a manure. He relies on his cows for milk and ghee (animal proteins) and on his bullocks, for plough-ing and transport.

Even today, poor families cook in clay pots and until not long ago, most villagers wore homespun and hand-printed cloth, as they still do in the more remote areas of the country. The economy in the use of resources, and the almost complete recycling of all materials is breathtaking. If the goal of good economic manage-ment is to get the maximum benefit from a minimal use of resources, village India had come very near to achieving it, given the state of technology at the time when its distinctive life style emerged. Today, therefore, the task before the social planner should not be to set up industries or develop transport systems which destroy this economy and cohesion but to inject technology in such a manner as to raise the entire system to a higher level of efficiency without altering its basic self-sufficiency and economy. Hence he can encourage farmers to use high yielding seeds in place of the traditional varieties, to grow two or three crops in place of one, and to set up *gobar* gas plants providing both fuel and fertilizers instead of using dry cowdung cakes which can be used for fuel alone. The aim of science must be to develop say an improved bullock cart with ball bearings, lighter wheels, rubber tyres and a simple braking system, hybrid cows to replace the degenerate pure-bred strains and pure drinking water in place of shallow open wells.

Economic development on these lines would raise living standards steadily while continuing to conform to the 'Buddhist' maxim of getting the most by way of benefits for the smallest consumption of natural resources and the minimum additional use of labour. What is more important, it would be almost free of the violent social conflicts that are generated by the invasion of an alien system of values, and which economists are willing to dismiss, albeit rather uneasily, as the 'revolution of rising expectations.' Most important of all, the continuity of change would avoid the perils of 'dualism.' Consumption patterns and standards would change only gradually, and the resulting change in modes of production and social and economic relationships would take place more smoothly over a period of time.

Notwithstanding the shaky metaphysical foundations of the western work-ethic, so powerful is its hold on our minds, and so overwhelming its apparent benefits, that breaking it would have been well-nigh impossible if serious doubts had not begun to arise in the minds of leading western thinkers about the direction in which their societies are evolving. It is not necessary to embark here on a detailed discussion of these misgivings, which have been and will continue to dominate debate in the advanced countries for decades to come. It is sufficient for our purpose to point out that these misgivings arise from two sources, firstly the growing realization that at the current rate of growth of exploitation the exhaustion of all known natural resources is only a few decades away.

E.J. Mishan has summed up the prospect for the next decades as follows:

'Whether or not they believe these conclusions realistic, all the people debating this issue recognize that we inhabit all too tiny a planet. Most of them are alarmed at current population trends; the prospect of some fifteen billion human beings swarming over the planet in fifty or sixty years' time is not an inviting one. With the existing population of about four billion souls, we are already getting in each other's way and stepping on each other's toes. Assuming the mobility indices continue to rise— car ownership in Western Europe increasing at about 8 per cent per annum, air travel at about 10 per cent— the mounting frustrations of travellers and the resentments of indigenous populations may break out in civil disturbances.

'Apart from population growth, though aggravated by it, there are the familiar problems of pollution, food supplies, and the depletion of natural resources. Although there have been some local improvements over the last quarter of a century—there is, for example, less sulphur dioxide (though much more carbon dioxide) in the air of London than there was twenty years ago, and some (possibly mutant) species of fish have recently been discovered in the murky waters of the Thames—nobody seriously challenges the fact that air and water pollution exist on a larger scale today than ever before in man's history. The global scale of pollution not only destroys flora and fauna but spoils the foods we eat. Chemical pesticides enter our bloodstream either directly through our consumption of chemically sprayed plants or indirectly through our consumption of cattle that ingest them. The poisoning of rivers destroys fish in estuaries and renders the flesh of the survivors increasingly toxic to humans.

'Turning to material resources, in particular fossil fuels and metals, a common estimate is that, if present consumption trends persist, we shall run out of oil by about the end of the century even allowing for the discovery of new reserves, and of all but a few of today's 'essential' metals within about fifty years. Indeed, at the current rates of usage, all known reserves of silver, gold, copper, lead, platinum, tin, and zinc will have been used up within a couple of decades.'

Mishans' forecast is almost certainly too pessimistic, but to pin our hopes for the survival of industrial man on an unprovable assumption that endless technological substitution is possible is a monstrous gamble, which Kenneth Boulding, a 'renegade' economist has summed up in his now celebrated phrase 'anyone who believes that infinite growth is possible on a finite planet is either a mad man or an economist.'

But the more serious ground for misgiving is the growing realization that rising levels of material affluence have demonstrably *not* made people happier. On the contrary every indicator of human well-being shows exactly the opposite to be the case. Thus divorce, mental illness, crime, juvenile delinquency and addiction to narcotics, have all increased sharply with the growth of affluence.[5]

The immediate causes of this visibly growing alienation have been summed up succinctly by Mishan who points out that the obsession with increasing the national product has caused modern industrial societies to view man solely in his role as a producer and to neglect man in his role as a consumer. Thus automation and the division of labour have increased his productivity, but steadily restricted and finally robbed him of all opportunity for creativity in his work. Similarly, industrial society encourages the *worker* to be mobile but chooses to ignore the immense strain of dislocation that such mobility imposes on the *man* and his family (new schools, a new neighbourhood, loss of the old friends, and uncertainty about making new ones to name only a few).

Industrial society fetters a man to his machine but tries to compensate him for the loss of his freedom by showering him with consumer goods. Upto a point it succeeds. When a man is genuinely poor, he may willingly forfeit some of his freedom for more food, better clothes, and a more comfortable home. But the statistics on the growing alienation of industrial man from his own society show that the point of optimum satisfaction has long been passed. Except possibly in a few "depressed" areas the extra consumer goods that further growth makes available to the average man in the affluent countries have long since ceased to compensate him for growing mental stress and an increasingly polluted environment. In other words the basic tenet of "modern" economics that an increase in material possessions denotes an increase in welfare has broken down.

Today western man is worse off even than the squirrel in a cage. Every year he spends larger and larger sums on an increasingly unsuccessful attempt, through advertising, glossy packaging, rapid changes in models and inconsequential improvements in product, to persuade *himself* that by purchasing more, newer, and shinier products he is actually becoming happier, and every available indicator of the human condition shows that he is failing.

How has industrial man fallen into this trap? The basic cause as Schumacher points out is that the whole of industrial society is based on a faulty premise that the market price of goods and services reflects their value. And for this he holds the science of economics to blame. Economics has glorified the market mechanism, as the best instrument available to man for securing the most efficient allocation of resources. But 'in the market place for practical reasons, innumerable qualitative distinctions which are of vital importance for man and society are suppressed' they are not allowed to surface. Thus the reign of quantity celebrates its greatest triumphs in 'The Market'. Everything is equated with everything else. To equate things means to give them a price and thus to make them exchangeable. To the extent that economic thinking is based on the market, it takes the sacredness out of life, because there can be nothing sacred in something that has a price. Not surprisingly, therefore, if economic thinking pervades the whole of society, even simple non-economic values like beatuy, health or cleanliness can survive only if they prove to be 'economic'. . . .

'Economics deals with a virtually limitless variety of goods and services, produced and consumed by an equally limitless variety of people. It would obviously be impossible to develop any economic theory at all, unless one were prepared to disregard a vast array of qualitative distinctions. But it should be just as obvious that the total suppression of qualitative distinctions, while it makes theorising easy, at the same time makes it totally sterile. Most of the 'conspicuous developments of economics in the last quarter of a century' (referred to by Professor Phelphs Brown) are in the direction of quantification, at the expense of the understanding of qualitative differences. Indeed, one might say that economics has become increasingly intolerant of the latter, because they do not fit into its method and make demands on the practical understanding and the power of insight of economists, which they are unwilling or unable to fulfill. For example, having established by his purely quantitative methods that the Gross National Product of a country has risen by, say, five per cent the economist-turned-econometrician is unwilling, and generally unable, to face the question of whether this is to be taken as a good thing or a bad thing. He would lose all his certainties if he even entertained such a question: growth of GNP must be a good thing, irrespective of what has grown and who, if anyone, has benefited. The idea that there could be pathological growth, unhealthy growth, disruptive or destructive growth is to him a perverse idea which must not be allowed to surface.'[6]

The reduction of everything to the common currency of the market place obscures two sets of fundamental distinctions: between natural and man-made goods and between renewable and non-renewable natural resources. Thus the road to environmental pollution, forced obsolescence, and the rapid exhaustion of natural resources lies in the valuation of coal, petroleum, metals and so on not on the basis of the millions of years of immense heat and pressure it took to make them, but the paltry cost of scratching the earth's surface—and the roots of alienation lie buried in the equation of the value of labour (a factor of production) with a machine (a man-made good). The market place serves one and only one function and that too only moderately well: that of making the best use of scarce resources. A price mechanism is therefore an essential tool for tackling the problems of poverty. But it is worse than useless as a tool for resolving the problems of affluence.

Today industrial man is in a pitiable plight. He has gone too far along one road. He sees that it is leading him over a cliff, but does not know how to turn back. He cannot even stop moving forward, for he is chained to the juggernaut of technological 'progress' and competition. Either one by itself could be a blessing. But in tandem they spell disaster, for the first will inexorably keep finding newer and cheaper ways of using our 'factors of production' while the second will force the discoverers to exploit these ways for fear of being overtaken by their competitors.

However, most developing countries can still exercise the option of not following in the footsteps of the industrialized countries. The great engines of technology and competition have not yet run amok. But for this they must first learn to shun the path to affluence followed by the west. They must see and believe that western levels of material prosperity may not only be un-attainable (for India and China to attain the present level of per capita steel consumption in Europe, for instance, is unthinkable) but totally undesirable. For chalking out a different route to greater welfare the shift in perspective from 'modern' to 'Buddhist' economics, commended by Schumacher is the first essential requirement.

In India, Buddhist economics has two fundamental implications. The first is that the planners must redefine the meaning of prosperity and consequently the goals which the country must aim at, to bring them in line with the natural endowments and traditional life styles of this country. Secondly, based on such an exercise they must set concrete targets for the provision of food, clothing and shelter. The debate on whether to aim for more material prosperity at the risk of a further degree of alienation can be reopened after these have been attained.

The first need in developing a new concept of prosperity is to realize that this country is extremely lucky in enjoying a warm climate. The bulk of its basic energy needs are met by the sun: energy to grow three crops a year, to dispense with all but a minimum of clothing, and to spend most of the day in the open air instead of in buildings with 'skins' to keep out a hostile climate. An Indian can therefore attain the same level of material well-being as a European at perhaps one-tenth of his per capita income (at current exchange rates). For instance, if the European can live reasonably on a diet which is equivalent to the calory value of say 500 kg of cereals a year, the Indian may be able to live moderately well while consuming around half as much. The cost of cheap housing in the U.K. in 1975 was £18 a square foot. A man can be equally comfortable in a single storey brick or tile house in India costing 18 to 20 rupees a square foot to build. The Hindu of ancient India who went around bare bodied and warded off the chill of the evening with a single shawl was no less well clad than the European wearing three layers of 'woolies' today. The sun therefore is our greatest ally. Yet so powerful is the hold of western India on our minds that even so perceptive a writer as Nirad Chaudhuri has deemed it a curse. A reappraisal of the meaning of prosperity on these lines will lead us straight back to the life style of traditional India, and that is the base from which all attempts at economic development must begin. Any attempt to find a short-cut to western prosperity using 'the fruits of two centuries of scientific advance to bridge the gap between the rich and the poor nations' will lead us straight into the trap of economic dualism.

After the preceding remarks it is perhaps belabouring the obvious to say that no such exercises have ever been attempted in India. On the contrary, the planners' uncritical acceptance of the need to follow the growth trajectory traced by the West is reflected most clearly in their addiction to expressing the objectives of the five-year plans in terms of growth rates of the national product. While successive plan documents have contained any number of rhetorical flourishes about the need to reduce inequalities of income, check the concentration of economic power, develop the backward areas and so on, the kernel of the government's objectives has been stated invariably in just two or three sentences specifying target rates of growth in agriculture and industry, and consequently in the gross national product.

In twenty-five years it seems to have occurred to no one that gross national product is like Santa Claus' sack. The larger it is the more presents it contains, but the size of the sack gives no indication of its content. To plan in terms of a growth of GNP alone is to express an indifference to what is actually produced. In effect this amounts to an endorsement of the existing composition of output, and therefore of income distribution and prices. In other words, such planning takes as constants precisely those things which it should be the government's aim to change. To plan for an increase in GNP alone is therefore to plan without concrete goals.

The main needs of a poor society are obvious—food, clothing, shelter, health and gainful employment. This may be precisely the reason why they are so often ignored. One has only to turn the pages of the successive Plan documents to notice the stepmotherly treatment which the planners have given to these basic goals. Eighty per cent of the population lives off the land, yet the share of agriculture in successive plans has dwindled from 31.4 per cent in the first plan to 20.7 per cent in the fourth. It has been slashed further in the annual plan for 1974-75 in order to save its so-called 'core'.

To house the present population, the country needs to build at least 60 million more dwelling units. In addition, it needs to build two and a half million houses every year to cope with the annual increase in population. Yet the total number of houses being built, judging from the figures for the urban sector alone, does not exceed half a million a year. In the same manner, eighty per cent of the country's all too few doctors and nurses serve twenty per cent of the population living in the towns. And as for unemployment, the government seems to have decided that it has only to stop thinking of the problem to make it disappear.

Had there been any coherent thinking about the objectives of planning, the government would have first spelt out clearly what it considered an acceptable standard of living for the population in terms of individual and family needs, and then proceeded to convert this into aggregate requirements of food, fertilizers, cloth, medicines, dwelling units and so on. After taking into account the growth of population, it would have specified a time period—say twenty or twenty-five years—for the achievement of these objectives. Only then would it have begun to compute the annual investment required for the achievement of these goals.

Had it proceeded in this manner, the Planning Commission would soon have found that using conventional—that is to say western—norms of nutrition, clothing, housing, medical facilities and so on, the annual investment needed would be far beyond the country's means. It might then have begun to look for cheaper ways of achieving the same ends, for instance by putting more emphasis on the consolidation of holdings, proper crop rotation practices and the use of organic manures instead of chemical fertilizers to increase agricultural production, by altering the building code in the cities to permit houses to put up at a cost of of Rs 2,000 to Rs 3,000 each, and by training more basic doctors conversant with social hygiene, and fewer specialists.

In spite of the resources crisis it is not too late even now for the government to reorient its economic planning. The problems that the country faces look forbidding only so long as one looks at them through the prism of western values.

For instance, assuming a marginal decline in the rate of growth of population, it should be possible to raise the average consumption of foodgrains to 200 kg a year in twenty years, if the annual output can be pushed up by a little over three million tonnes a year. This is most certainly not beyond the country's capacity. But it will remain so if the planners continue to rely on a package of practices which requires so much capital investment to start with that it cannot possibly be adopted by more than ten per cent of the farmers in the country.

Similarly, once the government decides to change the building code in the towns in order to permit cheap, low-rise, high density housing it will be possible to make housing schemes pay for themselves. If this happens, the state governments will suddenly rediscover their enthusiasm for housing projects. It will even be possible to entrust the implementation of such schemes in urban areas to private entrepreneurs, while the government reserves its own funds for more urgently needed projects.

The growing transport needs of the cities can also be met to a large extent by licensing millions of cycle rickshaws and pedicabs. These will cater to the need for local transport in each sector of a city, and free the available buses for meeting inter-sector transport needs.

All these schemes have one feature in common: they do not need money to implement but only a fresh approach combined with a much greater organizational effort. In short, whatever investment is called for is in building human, and not physical capital. Once this investment is made, all kinds of new departures will become possible. For instance, a good part of the fuel needs of a city like Bombay can be met by methane obtained from the hundreds of millions of gallons of sewage and urban waste which is now discharged into the sea. In the same way, a revitalized khadi and village industries (KVIC) programme will go a long way towards reducing underemployment in the rural areas.

It is a measure of the enslavement of the policy makers to pseudo-western values, that today none of these schemes is being considered seriously. On the contrary, municipal authorities in many cities are phasing out the use of cycle rickshaws and pedicabs by not issuing fresh licences; the Life Insurance Corporation demands construction in reinforced cement concrete, with teak fittings and mosaic tiled flooring as a precondition for giving building loans; the KVIC programme is being starved out of existence in deference to the urban lobby; and the setting up of *gobar* gas plants has been left in the frail hands of this ailing organization, while the government blithely spends up to Rs 560 crores in order to set up a single fertilizer plant that will employ no more than 1,800 people.

In recent years it has become increasingly fashionable to assume implied conflict between the dictates of economic rationality and political expedience and to ascribe every economic failure of the government to its unwillingness to court political unpopularity by taking hard decisions. The implicit assumption behind such reasoning is that economic rationality dictates one and only one course of action—the one that is politically unpopular. It is high time planners began to challenge this cozy assumption.

A course of action can be judged to be rational or irrational only in relation to the goals it is designed to serve. If 'economically rational' policies are proving unpopular it is because the goals they are designed to promote are not subscribed to implicitly or explicitly by the majority of the people.

The real failure of planning in India has been that its prime objective, the promotion of self-reliance, in pursuit of which it has asked people to postpone the satisfaction of their immediate needs and build heavy industries instead has not enjoyed popular support. The immediate and pressing needs of people are for food, clothing and shelter. The per capita availability of foodgrains is about the lowest in the world. In this context only people who have never felt the real pangs of hunger and deprivation can continue to talk blithely about giving priority to "building the sinews of the economy."

Under the steadily mounting pressure of peoples' demands many Central and state leaders began to entertain doubts about the strategy of capital intensive growth at least a decade ago. They were unable to articulate this growing distrust clearly, and most certainly not in the jargon of the economists. But it was obvious in their lack of enthusiasm for many of the projects included in the Central and state plans, and the ever more presistent demands during the fourth plan period to include a variety of 'crash' employment schemes in the plan itself, in preference to a variety of other more capital-intensive schemes.

Mrs Gandhi's own doubts were reflected first in her many abrupt changes in the membership of the commission and the most notably in her choice of the late Prof. D.N. Gadgil, as its chairman and his equally abrupt dismissal in 1971. Prof. Gadgil was the forerunner of the present generation of welfare economists who are applying notions of social costs and benefits to the theory of economic development. One of his earliest, and most important contributions was a study of the social costs and benefits of two canal systems in Maharashtra. He spent most of his academic life in studying various aspects of the problem of poverty and was one of the main sources of ideas and information to Gunnar Myrdal while he was working on his monumental book, *The Asian Drama*.

When Mrs Gandhi chose him to head the Planning Commission it was in the obvious hope that he would be able to change the strategy of planning to make it more responsive to the needs of the poor. But Mr Gadgil found out soon enough that any investment strategy, once adopted, tended to acquire a momentum of its own, and that a shift to a different strategy was by no means easy. With a large number of incomplete projects, with many others which were complementary to those already completed or under implementation, and with a shrinking resource base, he was forced to choose in effect between allocating the limited amount of money that was available to these projects, thus creating a plan that was little different from its predecessors, or allowing a number of projects to lapse or to be rendered infructuous for lack of complementary investment.

Today, both economic and political rationality demand a shift in the strategy of planning. The erosion of investible resources has reached a point where there is simply no money available for locking up in capital-intensive long-gestation projects. In real terms the net investment in the first year of the fifth plan was barely equal to what it was during the last year of the third plan. At the same time the mounting shortages of food, edible oils, cheap cloth and jobs has completed the disenchantment of leaders of all political hues with the goal of self-reliance which the capital-intensive strategy was designed to subserve.

This disenchantment has also been fuelled by the growing realization that the goal itself is a will-o'-the-wisp. The country is not much less dependent now on foreign know-how than it was twenty years ago: on an average thirty per cent of the components of its heavy engineering products have still to be imported. As for living within a slender foreign exchange budget, the reduction in its consumption of foreign exchange has been secured at least partly at the cost of inhibiting the growth of exports.

An Intermediate Technology for Agriculture

When there are too many hands doing too little work and when four out of five people live in the villages, any viable growth strategy must aim first of all at reviving the rural economy, and turning the villages into dynamic centres of growth.

This chapter is devoted to.outlining what could be a viable intermediate technology for agriculture. In Chapter 2 it was shown that the wheat revolution petered out prematurely in 1972 only because there were severe institutional hurdles in areas other than the northern wheat belt, which sapped the farmers' desire and ability to switch to intensive high-risk cultivation. What the removal of such hurdles can do to raise yields, without a single rupee of investment, is shown spectacularly by a comparison of the progress of agriculture in Indian and Pakistani Punjab, made by Manohar Singh Gill, a member of the Indian Administrative Service who spent some time at the centre of South Asian studies in Cambridge, U.K.[7] This is what he has to say:

'The two Punjabs are eminently suited for comparison. Part of a single agro-climatic zone and sharing a common culture, they were, till 1947, a single unit of agricultural production... In the division of assets of the old province, West Punjab came off much better and consequently started with an advantage. The major development of the fifty years prior to Partition had gone into the western half of the State, for that is where the open lands and the lazy water-filled rivers lay.

'The great British effort of canal irrigation lay entirely in the West. At the time of Partition, West Punjab inherited all that. Dr M.S. Randhawa in his book, *Out of The Ashes*, estimates that West Punjab inherited 55 per cent of the population of the joint Punjab, 62 per cent of the area, 69.9 per cent of the income and more than 70 per cent of the canal irrigation. The real wealth of the province lay in the cultivated lands and the irrigation.

'In the division of these, the East lost heavily. Sikhs and Hindus abandoned 67 lakh acres of land in the West, of which 43 lakhs were irrigated, 22 perennially; but there were only 47 lakh acres to offer to them in the East, of which only 13 lakh acres were irrigated, and barely 4 lakh acres perennially'. Thus in 1947 East Punjab was the poorer of the two new States and was even deficit in foodgrains by 35,000 tonnes. However, the subsequent 25 years have seen an agricultural explosion in Indian Punjab. The total production of cereals has trebled in 20 years, with the output of rice having gone up by over four times while that of wheat has increased almost three-fold (See Tables 9.1, 9.2 and 9.3)

Table 9.1

	Rice (000 tonnes)	Wheat (000 tonnes)	Total Cereals (000 tonnes)
1960–61	229	1974	2453
1972–73	955	5368	7399

As this table below shows, more than half of this increase in total production has come from increases in per hect*are yields*.

Table 9.2

	Rice	Wheat
	(in kg. per hectare)	
1950–51	956	1042
1972–73	2007	2233

However in spite of its superior endowments, there has been no such revolution in West Punjab. The following table shows the increase in per acre yields for the two Punjabs:

Table 9.3
Production in the two Punjabs
(Average yield per acre in maunds)

	1950–51		1971–72	
	W. Punjab	E. Punjab	W. Punjab	E. Punjab
Wheat	11.00	9.8	13.6	26.2
Rice	9.3	9.7	15.6	22.2
Cotton	2.1	2.2	3.5	3.9
Maize	9.9	6.1	12.8	17.0
Gram	8.0	6.5	5.7	9.1
Sugarcane	31.5	30.6	38.2	42.4

The reasons for the change in relative fortunes of the two Punjabs are given succinctly by Gill as follows:

'Partition gave both halves the opportunity to restructure the ownership of land so essential to productive agriculture. Randhawa describes how a graded cut was imposed on the claims of the refugees (from Pakistan) varying from a minimum 25 per cent to as much as 95 per cent on the biggest claimants.

The shortage of land in the East and a relatively more progressive outlook encouraged this policy of levelling down.

'The really big landlords—those with thousands of acres, so common in the West, were (thus) absent in the East. Even those who got relatively more land did not retain it for long. The new ceiling laws and the rights conferred on tenants made absentee landlordism an expensive hobby. One either stayed on the land and cultivated it, or sold out and moved away. Even though the land laws may not have been perfectly implemented, the insecurity created by them was sufficient to have pushed out the parasites and to have broken up the large holdings. So East Punjab became a land of peasant proprietors who cultivated the land themselves with a stake in making improvements.

'By contrast as the years passed, the hold of the feudal owners strengthened all the more in West Pakistan. Leslie Nulty in her book on the green revolution has shown the farcical nature of the Ayub reforms. The measures introduced by Bhutto also leave each man something like 300 acres of irrigated land, with opportunities to put the rest in his relations' names.

'The ownership pattern has not changed one bit in the West. In East Punjab a farmer with 25 acres is well-to-do today; in the West he is still a petty farmer, a nobody. Such is the difference. It shows in the cultivation pattern. Each Punjab has less than ten per cent tenants—nearer six in fact. In the West, more than 50 per cent of the land is tenant-farmed. What is more, they (the tenants) have next to no security. How then can they have an interest in higher production and how can they find the means for better inputs? It seems that the rich and absentee landowner is still to be seen dotting the flat West Punjab landscape. In the East, such weeds have been pulled out.

'Consolidation of land holdings, so essential to productive agriculture, had been started in a small way by the co-operatives in the Punjab in 1920. By the time of Partition, a million acres had been consolidated. East Punjab, under the dynamic leadership of Sardar Partap Singh Kairon, pushed this programme with all the zeal at its command. By 1969 all the land had been remapped and consolidated—an achievement not equalled by any other State.

'West Punjab was also not able to produce the political will and administrative capability to push through this vital programme. Between 1969-71 and 1971-72, 12.86 million acres had been consolidated out of a cultivated area of 27.20 million acres. They still have a long way to go. This may be one factor partly explaining the comparative lack of tube-wells—for such investment cannot be made if the land is fragmented. 'The green revolution technology is based on a package of practises and a package of inputs, namely fertilizer and water. Both need credit to buy them with. In East Punjab the co-operatives put in a great effort ((to supply the necessary funds). The following figures speak for the themselves:

	1960–61	1972–73
Total cereals produced	24.5 lakh tonnes	73.9 lakh tonnes
Short-term loans disbursed by Co-ops.	Rs 11.7 crores	Rs 62.0 crores
Long-term loans disbursed by Co-cps.	Rs 31 lakhs	Rs 16.2 crores
Fertilizers distributed		

'Most of the short-term loans are given in the shape of ferti-lizers and the long-term ones in the shape of tube-wells. In West Pakistan, by contrast the co-op structure has almost been allowed to wither away and nothing has really replaced it. Thus, as against an annual distribution of about Rs 80 crores of credit in East Punjab, in the West only Rs 14.8 crores were given for a much larger cultivated area in 1971-72.'

The Punjabi road to agricultural prosperity is not necessarily open to other parts of the country. Bihar and Uttar Pradesh for instance did not undergo the convulsion that occurred in Punjab and cannot simply wipe the slate clean and redistribute land afresh to all claimants. What is more, even if they could, there simply wouldn't be enough land to go around. As mentioned earlier, the operational holdings in Punjab are many times the operational holdings in Bihar because the pressure on the land is much less. Secondly, Punjab solved the problem of security of tenure, by simply eliminating tenants, turning most of them into agricultural labourers. This was possible without causing a social upheaval because peasant proprietorship was already the dominant mode of cultivation and tenant farming covered only a minor part of the land. In Bihar and eastern Uttar Pradesh however, even under the first round of land reforms millions of tenants were reduced overnight to the status of agricultural labourers as the land they tilled was resumed for personal cultivation. Tenant farming is still the dominant mode in Pakistani Punjab and absentee landownership is common. What is more even today tenants enjoy next to no security of tenure.

Thus the most urgently needed land reform is to give security of tenure to the tenant. This can only be attained by making the tenant virtually irremovable. What is more, he can only be made creditworthy if the present system of crop-sharing is replaced by a fixed land rent that allows the tenant to keep the entire increase in produce that results from his adoption of more efficient agricultural practices.

These are the moderate land reforms which along with the consolidation of holdings, Gunnar Myrdal has championed so strongly in his *Asian Drama* and *Challenge of World Poverty*. As he has pointed out, they run less risk of coming into headlong clash with the interests of the dominant farm lobby, than the ceiling on land holdings which the government has been pursuing so ineffectually since 1969. Yet even these are bound to come up against opposition, and if imposed from the top, their effects are bound to be diluted by the exploitation of legal loopholes and the non-co-operation of the rural government officials who keep the land and revenue records, and are nearly always to be found hand in glove with the village notables. In particular, tenants can be given security of tenure only if they have easy access to the law courts. This in turn requires a complete revamping of the judicial system, a mammoth task which is bound to take time.

Unfortunately, time is just what the country has run out of. The food situation in the country is so precarious today, that it has no option but to find means of raising agricultural production *immediately*. What is more there is a good deal of evidence to show that even the most urgently needed institutional social changes will only come after an initial technological breakthrough which increases the bargaining power of the landless labourers and tenants in relation to the rich farmers. Indeed it is more than likely that, security of tenure, the fixation of money rentals, the elimination of absentee landownership, and the consolidation of holdings, may only come when the bargaining power of the tenants and the poorest of the landowners has been increased by technological change.

On both counts therefore, it is imperative to find a technology that permits an immediate rise in agricultural productivity. What is more, in order to be accessible to tenant farmers and owner cultivators with fragmented holdings, it must be one that does not require a great deal of initial investment. In other words, what the country urgently needs is an intermediate technology for agriculture that is between traditional cultivation and the high-yielding varieties programmes.

While the inputs that make up such an intermediate technology may vary from one part of the country to the next and from one crop to another, its basic features are not likely to differ greatly. The crucial requirement is that it must be capable of raising farm yields without significantly increasing the risks of cultivation. Only then will it be within the reach of the millions of small farmers in the country. In effect this means that the country needs a technology capable of giving significantly higher yields in rain-fed and dry farming conditions using a minimum of chemical fertilizers.

What is more, farmers should be able to adopt it without the government having first to make far-reaching institutional changes such as a reform of the tenurial system and the consolidation of holdings.

The elements of such a technology have been in existence for several years. It is only the government's preoccupation with obtaining quick results from the high-yielding varieties programme that prevented it from putting together into an alternative agricultural strategy. For instance, agricultural scientists have pointed out repeatedly that many high-yielding varieties give better yields not only with concentrated doses of chemical fertilizers, but also when little or no fertilizer is used. It is only now, when the country is faced with an acute shortage of chemical fertilizers that the government is beginning to heed their advice.

The truth is that most high-yielding varieties give substantially better yields even when no fertilizers are used because they have a much better grain-to-dry matter ratio than the traditional varieties. For instance, whereas the traditional tall varieties of wheat yield

250 to 300 kg of grain for every tonne of dry matter, the high-yielding varieties yield up to 500 kg. of grain. Since the total amount of dry matter produced is closely related to the nutrition supplied to the crop, irrespective of whether it is a traditional or a high-yielding strain, the latter gives a higher yield of grain under identical conditions.

While the government has continued to promote high-risk cultivation based on an optimum package of inputs, a number of farmers have been finding out the virtues of high-yielding varieties used with a bare minimum of inputs on their own. In north Bihar, for instance, many farmers are growing the new rice varieties under rain-fed conditions, with little and often no application of fertilizers. Even so, they are getting 20 to 50 per cent higher yields than from the traditional varieties. What is more the shorter duration of the new varieties, makes it possible for them to grow a wheat crop on the same land—which was not possible before.

If the new seed varieties are capable of giving higher yields without fertilizers, they will perform even better when nourished with organic manures. Thus the second element of a viable intermediate technology consists of promoting the extensive use of organic fertilizer, green manuring, and scientific crop rotation. The key role of the bio-gas plant in this context hardly needs to be emphasized. Since three-quarters of the dung produced in the country today is used by villagers as a domestic fuel, the bio-gas plant provides the only way of meeting the need for fuel while simultaneously producing enriched manure for the fields.

The use of organic manure has so many other advantages that it remains a mystery why the Central and state governments have done so little to promote their use so far. The obvious one is that it is extremely cheap and therefore accessible to a host of small farmers who either cannot obtain or cannot afford to use chemical fertilizers. But of greater importance is the fact that organic manure contains not only nitrogen but also phosphates and potash as well as a number of micronutrients like zinc, sulphur and iron. Its use does not impoverish the soil. On the contrary, its prolonged use maintains and even builds up the fertility of the soil.

The most important advantage of organic fertilizers, however is that it does not mortgage the farmer's future to the availability of scientific back-up facilities. The way in which this has happened under the HYVP is best illustrated by the experience of farmers in Punjab. Two to three years after switching to the HYVP many of them found that the crop was not responding to the fertilizers they were using and rushed to the Punjab Agricultural University for help. When the PAU found that excessive reliance on nitrogenous fertilizers had exhausted the phosphates in the soil. The composition of the fertilizer was changed accordingly, but after another couple of seasons the farmers were once again confronted by a dramatic decline in the health of their crop. Further tests revealed that the soil was now deficient in potash and the fertilizer mix had to be changed once again. Today there is growing evidence that the soil in Punjab is in acute need of micronutrients like zinc and sulphur.

This dependence on the agricultural scientists has not hurt the Punjabi farmer only because of the pioneering role which the PAU has played in building a sophisticated extension service with a rapid feedback of information from the farmers. The state government has also helped by making the PAU solely responisble for meeting the farmers' need for know-how and relegating its own agricultural department to a subordinate role.

The university now has mobile laboratories manned by teams of scientists who can go anywhere in the state and make on-the-spot diagnosis of a soil deficiency, or the outbreak of a new plant disease, within hours of receiving a request for help. What is more, its findings are broadcast over the radio, usually within the next 24 hours. However, one has only to describe this elaborate system to appreciate how far other states are from developing anything that can compare with it in efficiency and reliability. In these circumstances to make farmers rely solely on chemical fertilizers is fraught with the risk of a major backlash when the initial spurt in production is over and the soil begins to show signs of exhaustion.

The HYVP makes the farmer dependent on factors which he cannot control in other ways as well. Once he switches to high-risk cultivation and installs a tube-well, he is dependent on others for the supply of electricity or diesel in addition to chemical fertilizers and pesticides. As the number of imponderables surrounding cultivation grows larger the risk of things going wrong also increases. By contrast the use of organic fertilizers involves no danger of a backlash and no need for a sophisticated infrastructure of power, transport and scientific facilities. Since in any case these are in short supply and likely to remain so for a long time, there is no escape from adapting agricultural technology to do without them as far as possible.

An intermediate technology along these lines, will not be a substitute for more scientific agriculture. In the long run, as the demand for food grows, there is no escape from making sweeping institutional reforms, extending assured irrigation wherever this is possible, using higher inputs of fertilizers and placing ever greater reliance on the agricultural scientist to maintain the health of the soil.

However, it will give the country the breathing space in which to prepare for the next phase of agricultural development. What is more, a rise in yields, and an increase in cropping intensity will also raise farm incomes and make more farmers in each village capable of making the initial investments needed to switch to a high risk, high-yield agricultural technology.

The prime requirements for an intermediate technology are therefore a reservoir of high-yielding seeds, an all-out effort to set up *gobar* gas plants throughout the country, a sustained attempt to educate farmers in the use of organic fertilizers and a renewed emphasis on crop rotation, green manuring and other improved agricultural practices. Such programmes do not need very much money to implement, but they will call for a major effort to strengthen the agricultural extension services and a drive to re-educate extension workers so that they themselves recognize the need for such an intermediate technology for agriculture. The lynchpin of an intermediate technology for agriculture is obviously the *gobar* gas plant. But this is the one innovation which has been systematically neglected so far. It is true that in the immediate aftermath of the rise in oil prices, Fakhruddin Ali Ahmed and some other Central ministers made brave statements that the country would make do with cattle-dung. But these were obviously for the voters' consumption and not meant to be taken seriously. How else does one explain the fact that not a single feasibility study or cost-benefit analysis has been carried out in order to reassess the economics of *gobar* gas plants in the vastly altered circumstances which obtain today?

A part of the answer for the neglect of organic manure is that chemical fertilizers were extremely cheap, during the days of hectic competition between the oil companies in the 'fifties and 'sixties. Even as recently as four years ago they cost $46 a tonne in the world market. Today, however, it costs nearly $400 per tonne, and the economic viability of the *gobar* gas is no longer in doubt. The credit for this goes to the Khadi and Village Industries Commission, the frail and often sneered at successor to Mahatma Gandhi's Khadi and Village Industries Association.

Over the years the KVIC has done an enormous amount of work in developing various sizes of gas-cum-manure plants and by 1973, had set up around 6,500 of them all over the country. The results that it has obtained demonstrate, beyond a shadow of a doubt, their enormous potential for meeting the fuel and fertilizer needs of the countryside.

Today three-quarters of the cattle-dung in the country is being dried and burnt as a fuel and less than ten per cent is being converted into compost for manure. The *gobar* gas plant produces both more heat and more manure from the same dung. The methane generated by the fermentation of cattle-dung (and any other organic waste) generates twenty per cent more heat than cowdung cakes. At the same time, the residual sludge provides 43 per cent more fertilizer than the manure made in a compost pit. It is also richer in humus, which improves the binding and water-retaining properties of the soil.

While the potential benefits from the *gobar* gas plant are enormous, the KVIC has not so far been able to make much headway with their installation. This is because it has concentrated so far on designing small plants for individual families or farms. As a result capital costs are rather high. The smallest plant, which uses about 45 kg of dung a day, obtained from four to five head of cattle, and yields two to three cubic metres of gas, costs around Rs. 2,500 (in 1975). As a result it is beyond the reach of most of the small farmers whom it is meant to benefit.

But capital costs decline sharply as the size of the plant increases. A 180-kg plant costs a little more than twice as much as the 45-kg. plant. The well-to-do farmer for whom it is designed, however, has not shown much interest in it so far because of the very low price of chemical fertilizers (until 1972, urea cost round Rs 700 a tonne).

In fact since *gobar* manure contains one-thirtieth as much nitrogen as urea, its economic price in 1971 was no more than Rs 13 a tonne. Even after allowing for its other advantages, its value to the farmer could not have been placed at much higher than Rs 16-18 per tonne. It is hardly surprising therefore that the KVIC preferred to stress the advantages of the *gobar* gas plant as a source of fuel and not fertilizer.

The fuel crisis has changed all this. The domestic price of urea has increased to around Rs 2,000 per tonne and the world price is almost twice as high as around Rs 3,500 per tonne. *Gobar* gas manure is now worth at least Rs 70 per tonne to the farmer. To the nation its social value is a minimum of Rs 90 per tonne, and in view of its other advantages is more likely to be Rs 100 per tonne.

This has made the *gobar* gas plant a highly profitable proposition not only in terms of private rates of return to the farmer but even more so in terms of the social benefit accruing to the nation.

To take private costs and returns first: the largest size of *gobar* gas plant developed by the KVIC will cost around Rs 5,000 to install and has a capacity of around 50 tonnes of fertilizers a year. In addition it will yield around 10 cubic metres of gas per day. If the gas is priced around 30 paise a cubic metre, and the fertilizer at Rs 70 per tonne, the imputed revenues of the plant when working at 80 per cent of its capacity will be Rs 2,800 for the fertilizer and another Rs 900 for the gas. This gives a capital-to-turnover ratio of 1.3 to 1.0, which is lower than for a chemical fertilizer plant.

In terms of social costs and benefits the *gobar* fertilizer plant is even more profitable. To begin with, at a social price' of Rs 100 per tonne, the social value of the fertilizer alone is Rs 4,000. Since 10 cubic metres of gas are equivalent to 6 litres of kerosene, the social price of *gobar* gas is actually around 60 paise per cubic metre. The social yield in terms of fuel of the 10-cubic-metre-a-day plant is another Rs 2,000 a year.

But this is only the beginning of the story. If *gobar* gas plants are set up on a commercial scale the dung that is fed into the plants and the labour that goes into its collection must be paid for. A good part of the first and the whole of the second payment will go to the poorest people in the village, most of whom are usually Harijans. Some idea of what this will mean can be had from the example of a typical village with a population of 1,000, owning 400 head of cattle. If 80 per cent of the dung is recycled, the annual value at market prices of the fertilizer and gas obtained will be in the neighbourhood of Rs 80,000. If only 20 per cent of this is earmarked towards paying the cost of collection and this task is performed by members of the fifty poorest families in the village each family will earn on an average an extra Rs 320 a year or enough to buy over two quintals of additional grain.

Though *gobar* fertilizer may not eliminate the need for chemical fertilizers, it will cut it down very drastically. For the village described above the total output will amount at a conservative estimate to 1,000 tonnes a year, which is equivalent in terms of nitrogen to 50 tonnes of urea. If the village owns approximately 400 acres, (the average in areas with a reasonably assured rain-fall) this is equivalent to 125 kg. of urea per acre. In view of the fact that organic fertilizers are far more efficient than chemical fertilizers this will meet a large part of the requirements of even farmers who grow two crops a year.[8]

It will be no exaggeration to say therefore that the *gobar* gas-cum-fertilizer plant can become the lynchpin of a gigantic movement for rural regeneration. However, to cover 550,000 villages with such plants poses a staggering managerial problem. Apart from persuading the villagers that they really stand to gain from the new arrangements for recycling dung and other waste products. It involves problems of plant design, standardization, supply of materials, disposal of fertilizers and pricing. Quite obviously the first need is to scale up the household plant so that an entire village is served by half a dozen large plants. This may also help to further reduce capital costs per tonne of fertilizer.

The disposal of the fertilizer will also pose several problems as it must be done in the vicinity of the village and within the block, close coordination between the programme to set up such plants and other agricultural extension schemes. Thirdly, pricing will pose several ticklish problems. For instance, a family with five head of cattle, which previously used all the dung that they obtained as fuel, must be paid enough to cover at least the cost of the gas it must buy in return.

These problems are not insuperable, but their resolution is well beyond the capabilities of either the KVIC or the present block level administrative staff. One way to tackle them may be to ask the largest 2,000 business firms in the public and private sectors to delegate one middle-rung manager each, in order to form managerial teams of seven to ten persons for each district. These teams can work in close collaboration with the technicians and agronomists of the state government, in a programme designed to cover say 15 villages in each district every year.

In this way, most of the country can be covered in as little as ten years. To bring social and private rates of return in line, the central and state governments will do well to give a cash subsidy of 40 per cent on the cost of the plant. The idea is not new. The Planning Commission made a similar proposal in 1972 in order to tempt the private sector into setting up coal-based fertilizer plants.

NOTES

1 These prices prevailed in 1975 and 1976.
2 E.F. Schumacher, *Small is Beautiful*, Sphere Books Ltd, London p. 45.
3 Ibid. pp. 47–8.
4 Ibid. pp. 49–50.
5 Two easily accessible books which summarize these findings are *Blueprint for Survival* and *Rethink* by Gordon Rattray Taylor, Pelican, London.
6 Ibid., pp. 37, 39–40
7 'Pakistani Punjab vs. Indian Punjab', *Illustrated Weekly of India*, August 10, 1975.
8 While this is broadly true, a good deal more research is needed to establish the best way to use the slurry manure which is produced by the *gobar* plant. Some

studies by the Indian Agricultural Research Institute, for instance, indicate that while direct slurry is not a particularly efficient fertilizer, when composted with green leaves or cereal stalks or when mixed with judicious amounts of chemical fertilizers, it yields a fertilizer that is more efficient per gramme of nutrient than chemical fertilizers alone. One recommended way of using slurry is to dry it on a bed of green leaves or cereal stalks, use the mixture for the starter for a compost pit and mix the manure obtained in this way with a small amount of nitrogenous and phosphoric fertilizer. This is both simple and cheap, yielding a far more efficient fertilizer per weight of nutrient.

10 / An Alternative Strategy for Industrialization

CHANGING THE PATTERN of industrial growth to avoid the trap of dualism presents far more complex problems than proposing an intermediate technology for agriculture. The reason is that whereas only a few small areas of the countryside have been touched by capitalist agriculture and the accompanying changes in the style of life in the urban areas, industrialization is already far advanced.

Nearly all the industrial growth in the last thirty years has involved importing sophisticated technology either for the production of export goods or for import substitution. For instance, the entire development of the public sector in this country has been inspired by the latter. Nor is the pattern of investment in the private sector very different. Even the consumer goods manufactured by it are mainly for the consumption of the well-to-do city dwellers who have already adopted the life-style of the affluent countries.

Changing the strategy of industrial growth therefore involves making a break with the existing pattern of industrialization, which is not unlike moving a train bodily off one set of tracks and setting it down on another. In practice there are three major constraints to the speed and the extent to which this can be done. Firstly, there is the problem of complementarity. Certain types of investment necessitate others to make them fruitful. A steel plant must be complemented by coal and iron mines, a rail transport system and a range of steel-using industries. A petrochemicals complex requires the import of crude oil and complementary investment in oil refineries, chemicals and synthetic materials industries. Taking the economy as a whole, once it has adopted a particular pattern of industrialization complementarity tends to perpetuate this pattern, as well as the income distribution which gave birth to it. A change in direction can only be made gradually, phasing out one group of plants and industries and pouring money into another. The process is almost as long drawn out as rectifying the mistakes made in planning a city without knocking large parts of it down.

The second major constraint is the need to export a part of the country's product to meet the cost of imports. Here the developing countries are at the mercy of the tastes which prevail, and the specifications which are acceptable to consumers in the buying countries. The domination of world trade by the affluent nations ensures that it is their tastes and quality requirements which rule the world market. The need to meet them forces the poor nations to import the most sophisticated and therefore capital intensive technology (98% of the total research in the world is carried out in advanced countries, and nearly all of it is designed to replace men with machines). The only solution to this problem is to minimize imports and exports, and this, as discussed earlier, cannot be done without first renouncing the goal of attaining specifically western levels and patterns of prosperity. Obviously this too takes a long time and is itself dependent on a profound change in the objectives and strategy of economic growth. In the meantime, there is no escape from foreign trade and the limits it imposes on the adoption of an intermediate technology for industry.

The third constraint, which reinforces the first two, is the need to build a modern army, navy and air force. No large country can escape from having either to manufacture or import the arms it needs. And as experience has shown, there is little scope for making do with anything but the most sophisticated and modern armaments.

Any change of direction in industrialization must therefore necessarily be gradual. What is more, it will also be incomplete for no matter what happens the country will always need a modern capital intensive sector of industry for the production, at the very least, of armaments and export goods, for the generation of power and the provision of mass transport. Willy-nilly, therefore, any viable model of industrialization will have to contain two sectors. What is more, the new strategy must contain measures to ensure that neither sector swallows the other.

The mere mention of a multisector growth model, raises the question of where the line must be drawn between the sectors. This is a question to which mathematical economists have paid a good deal of attention in the last two decades. But questions which concern the precise line of division are distinctly premature and in the final analysis sterile, for there are too many imponderables affecting the division to permit any pat solutions. What is more, their importance is subject to sudden and drastic changes. Thus there is no way in which a model can take into account changes in international relations and the possibility of discovering hitherto unknown natural resources, to name only two. Both of them obviously have a vital bearing on the future size of the modern sector, but neither can be predicted or controlled. Thus it is more important to concentrate on the direction in which the pattern of industrialization must change, and the means of bringing about this change, without causing a severe dislocation of the present economy and without wasting the investment that has already been made. The problem is therefore two-fold: firstly how to free as large a proportion of current resources as possible for the new investment, and secondly, deciding which areas to put the money into.

Raising the rate of saving in the economy

Far from having enough money to start new projects, the Central government is finding it difficult to complete the projects it already has in hand. Exercises carried out in the first half of 1975 by the Central ministry for energy showed that even with the special efforts the government was making to finance the power generation programmes contained in the fifth plan, not more than half the funds that would be needed were actually in sight. Similarly the irrigation ministry had calculated that it would need at least Rs 700 crores more than the Rs 2,400 crores it was allocated to meet the targets set for it.[1] These are only two examples drawn from important areas of investment. In the same way departmental undertakings are so short of funds that they are unable to replace even worn out capital equipment, let alone start new projects. The railways for instance, have been cutting back on their replacement needs to the point where not only is the bulk of their rolling stock hopelessly over-aged, but they cannot keep their own locomotive and passenger-coach factories fully occupied. In 1975, The Chitta-ranjan Locomotive Works was therefore looking for orders in African countries and the Integral Coach Factory at Perambur had been allocated only Rs 27 crores, or enough to turn out no more than 500 coaches even though its proven capacity is over 720 coaches a year.[2]

Even the premier public sector undertaking in India, Hindustan Steel, has been forced to dip into a special fund that was created by the Steel Authority of India, the parent holding company in November 1973 for expanding productive capacity in the steel industry to replace worn out equipment instead. It has been forced to do this because the depreciation funds of the enterprise, as of all public enterprises, have been appropriated year after year by the Central government towards meeting its current expenditures![3]

What is more, as the annual surveys by the *Economic Times* show clearly, real private investment in industry has also declined continuously since the last years of the Third Plan, to the point where process industries like cement, rubber tyres, and aluminium are unable to replace worn out plants from internal resources. The country has therefore to find *both* the money needed to safe-guard the investments that it has already made, *and* to finance a radical shift in the pattern of new investment.

On the face of it, the two imperatives are not easily reconciled. The conflict between them is, however, more apparent than real. By initiating major reforms in its pricing and tax policies the government can generate enough funds even today to finance essential investment in projects that build up the economic infra-structure, and yet have enough left over to make a start on a net-work of bio-gas plants and on low-cost housing and other pro-grammes which will answer the most pressing needs of the people.

The first step in such reform is to lift price controls on all com-modities (except a few essentials like foodgrains and sugar which should be subjected to dual-pricing through a rationing system) and in particular on all products manufactured in the core sector. The second must be to reduce the excise duty levied on these items to the absolute minimum. The effect of such reform will depend on the state of the economy, but will in every case be beneficial.

Under inflationary conditions such as those which existed till October 1974, since the controlled prices of items like steel, cement, aluminium and copper are scarcely ever adhered to outside the government sector, the lifting of price controls will lead to a large increase in the sales revenues of both public and private plants in the core sectors without pushing up their actual market prices. Nor will the government lose much revenue by drastically cutting down excise duties. Around two-thirds to three-quarters of the rise in companies' sales revenues will in any case come back to it in the form of corporate and dividend taxes. The balance will stay with the enterprises, make them more self-reliant and thus reduce the demands they make on the public exchequer and the banking systems.

What this means in concrete terms can be seen from the fact that the ex-factory price of steel in 1974 was no more than Rs 900—1200 per tonne, while its market price (for non-priority uses like housing) was Rs 1600—2200 per tonne. Even this was a good deal below the black market price which was as high as Rs 2,400—2,600 per tonne in the middle of 1974. However, the c.i.f. price of steel imported from Japan in 1974 was around Rs 2,800 per tonne. By letting the plants charge Rs 1800 per tonne of steel and reducing the excise duties sharply the government could have added up to Rs 450 crores a year to the net profits of the steel industry. A part of this increase could have been passed on to the power generation industries. This would have enabled them, in turn, to finance a much larger part of their own expansion. Of the remainder, around Rs 300 crores would have come back to the government in the form of direct taxes, while at least Rs 100 crores a year would have been retained for reinvestment by the two companies. This would have been sufficient to finance the setting up of another 1.5 million tonnes worth of steel making capacity during every five year plan period.

In the same way, the ex-factory price of aluminium ingots of Rs 5000 per tonne in mid-1974 was around Rs 1000 below the American and Canadian export prices (c.i.f.). Even though the government levied an excise duty of approximately 40 per cent, there was a thriving black market in this metal. An increase in the ex-factory price of Rs 2000 per tonne, and a reduction of

duty to Rs 1000 per tonne would not therefore have added significantly to the existing inflationary pressures, but would have virtually
made the industry self-financing.

The proposal to lift price controls is usually opposed on two
grounds: firstly, that it will raise the cost of living and secondly,
that since the government is itself a major consumer of many of
the commodities whose prices are subjected to control, its
own expenditure will rise. Neither will stand a close examination.
The cost of living is influenced mainly by the prices of foodgrains.
It goes without saying that in this and other essential commodities
such as sugar, edible oils, and even life saving drugs, some form
of dual pricing is the only way of ensuring that the poor can buy
enough to survive. But in other industries the lifting of price controls
will have little or no effect on the cost of living. This is because
wherever a black market exists today, the lifting of price controls
will yield a free market price which is a weighted average of the
previous controlled and black market prices. Thus while some
consumers will pay more, others will pay less.

The problem is complicated by the fact that over the years the
government has acquired a huge vested interest in these controls,
for it uses them to meet its own needs cheaply, leaving the hapless
private consumers to meet a part of theirs in the black market.
Officials therefore fear that the lifting of controls may benefit
the private consumer but will hurt the government. But this fear
also is entirely groundless. Even when the government buys half
the total output of a commodity, the lifting of price controls will
raise its expense by half of the total extra income earned by the
manufacturer, but corporate and dividend taxes will bring back
two-thirds of the manufacturer's extra income by way of taxes.
The public exchequer will therefore remain a net gainer to the tune
of one-sixth of the rise in the manufacturer's pre-tax sales revenue.

This can be illustrated by taking the example of the cement
industry which is almost entirely in the private sector. The black
market price of cement in 1974 was around Rs 30 per bag as against
the controlled price of Rs 17. If price controls had been lifted the
free market price would have stabilized at anything between Rs 20
and Rs 25 per bag and the sales revenue of the cement industry
would have increased by nearly 15 to 55 per cent. The government,

which buys roughly half of the total output of cement would have contributed half of this increase in revenue. However, it would have got back two-thirds of it by way of direct taxes on croporate profits and dividends. In other words it would have been a net gainer of up to Re 1.33 per bag or Rs 27 per tonne. Since the country has a production capacity of around 18 million tonnes, this would have meant added revenues of up to Rs 48 crores a year!

Lifting price controls is only one aspect of the more fundamental need to restructure prices, at least of basic and intermediate goods so that they reflect the social costs of producing them. If the social cost of power today is around 20 paise a unit, and if pricing it at something approaching this figure will push up the price of aluminium ingots from Rs 5,000 to Rs 10,000 per tonne, is there any reason to sell aluminium more cheaply? In 1975 the government did push up aluminium prices sharply, but it did so by introducing a two-tier system of pricing based on the end use for which the aluminium was destined. Needless to say, this creates other problems. In the same way, if the ex-factory price of steel is barely 40 per cent of world prices, not because labour is cheap but because coal is being priced at around Rs 100 (instead of the social value of Rs 250) and iron ore at only little more, then who is the gainer? When energy, whether coal or electricity, is scarce, to provide it at less than its social cost is to deny to the country the much higher benefits it could give in an alternative use. Thus, there is a strong case for pushing up the price of key products of the core sector, which consume huge amounts of scarce resources to prices that fully reflect this scarcity, irrespective of whether the domestic market can absorb the entire output of the industry concerned. Till October 1974, when signs of an incipient recession appeared in the Indian economy, the pull of demand was sufficiently strong to sustain a price of say Rs 2,500 for steel and Rs 10,000 for aluminium. Since then, demand has slackened, even as the domestic production of both has increased. But this is at best a reason for combining higher prices with vigorous measures to revitalize the economy and not for shelving such reform altogether.

It may also be argued that to put up prices in the absence of a buoyant demand, will push up the price level in the economy.

This is true up to a point, but since higher prices will cause a decline in the purchase of these metals, the impact on the overall consumer's budget will be reduced. Higher prices will, in particular, end a host of wasteful uses, such as the use of steel and aluminium for the construction of houses and the manufacture of office furniture, cooking utensils, and venetian blinds, and the use of aluminium foil for the packaging of biscuits, cigarettes and the like. Furthermore the decline in home demand will eliminate the need to import such scarce materials and even permit the country to export them in a modest way.

The resistance among the policy-makers to any suggestion that excise duties should be drastically reduced, if not removed altogether, is even greater. Over the years the Union ministry of finance has come to lean so heavily on this simple, direct way of raising money that asking it to dispense with it is like asking a cripple to throw away his crutch. And yet here too a closer look will show that the government will lose money only in the very few industries, such as those wholly in the public sector, where, the manufacturer is in no position to hide a part of his output from the tax authorities. However, if the manufacturers who are subject to excise levies are concealing even ten per cent, of their output on an average, then the removal of the duty will not cause any loss of revenue to the government.

A simple example will help to prove this. If a firm produces 100 units of the product costing Rs 10 each and the government levies a 40 per cent excise duty the tax will yield Rs 400 by way of revenue. But if the duty is lifted, and the firm now declares the 11 additional units of output that it has been concealing, the increase in its declared gross profits will amount to Rs 400 *plus* the revenue from the scale of 11 extra units (156) less at most the direct materials cost of their manufacture. In other words the increase in gross profits will amount to around Rs 500. Since two-thirds or more of this (Rs 333) will come to the government by way of taxes, the real loss in revenue will be at most Rs 67. And even this marginal decline in tax revenues must be balanced against the far larger increase in the retained profits of the firm, the reduction of its dependence on external capital for financing further expansion, and the consequent release of resources elsewhere in the economy for financing new projects.

The above exercise is hypothetical. But in actual practice since the government has tended to impose price controls and levy heavy excise duties on the same industries, the removal of both is likely to increase the government's tax revenues and the sums available with the industries for financing their future growth at the same time. In the example of the steel industry quoted earlier the sales revenue will go up by Rs 400 crores of extra revenue. The government will receive around Rs 250 crores by way of corporate taxes. This is far more than it receives today in the form of excise duties. And even after paying this the steel industry will be left with enough reserves to finance the setting up of one steel plant every five years.

The question may well be asked that if the lifting of price controls on the products of core sector industries does not have any significant inflationary impact (because the resulting free market price will only be a weighted average of the controlled and the black market prices) and if both the government and the enterprises gain added revenues, where will the extra money come from? The answer is from the parallel economy. The lifting of price controls will stamp out black marketing by the trading community. A drastic reduction of excise duties will also more or less put an end to the evasion of these taxes and the consequent diversion of a part of the output to the black market by the manufacturers.

The examples of the soap and vanaspati industries given in Chapter III show how much black money can in fact be siphoned back into the legitimate economy, and the revivifying effect these added funds will have on it.

Reform of direct taxation

Price controls and heavy excise duties are only one, albeit the main source of funds for the parallel economy. The evasion of direct taxes is the other.

The government took its first hesitant step towards a reform of the tax system when it lowered income tax rates from a maximum of 97 to 77 per cent. Yet it is obvious from what its spokesmen have said in recent months that it has no clear idea of what this measure is intended to achieve. Mr Y.B. Chavan, the Union finance minister till October 1974, expressed the hope (as did the Wanchoo Committee two years earlier) that it would actually increase the yield of the income tax.

In the present context, this is not an important objective, and it would be folly to judge the appropriateness of any proposed reform on this ground alone. The touchstone of any tax reform today must be its ability to block the flow of funds into the parallel economy. A measure may be worth adopting even if it reduces the tax revenues of the government, provided it causes a much larger diversion of funds from the parallel economy back into legitimate channels of saving such as the banks and the share market. Beyond this, any proposed reform should also conform to the principle of equity in taxation (which means that the well-to-do must pay more than the poor, and be simple to administer.) to administer.)

There is, in fact, a simple way of achieving all three objectives. This is to stop taxing incomes and to tax expenditure instead. The idea is by no means new. It was put forward first by Nicholas Kaldor in a book entitled *An Expenditure Tax* in 1956. Kaldor argued in favour of taxing expenditure alone, mainly on the grounds of equity. He pointed out that a man should be taxed on what he withdraws from the community's pool of scarce resources—in short his consumption—and not on what he earns, which is really a rough and ready measure of the value society places on his services. He also brought out the fact that the taxation of income was only on the assumption that the taxpayer spends every penny that he earns, and what is more, does so within a year of earning it. Both assumptions are patently unfounded.

Kaldor's proposal for five inter-locking taxes—a lower income tax, a wealth tax, a capital gains tax, a gift tax, and a small expenditure tax, which he submitted to the Indian government in 1957 was conceived of as a substiture for the single all-embracing expenditure tax which he had proposed earlier in his book. The reason why his original proposal did not find favour with any government was his insistence that expenditure should be computed directly with the aid of a complicated system of vouchers and a computer to keep records straight.

A much simpler way of calculating expenditure is to treat it as a residue after deducting savings from income. Savings, particularly those held in approved forms, such as bank deposits, shares and securities are far easier to keep track of than consumption. Indeed, with nearly the whole of the banking system already in government hands, and the transactions in share market closely supervised, this would be a relatively simple task.

The government has only to ask the taxpayer to declare his income and the change in his bank deposits and holdings of approved shares and securities, and to give full particulars of the latter. An increase in these assets should be counted as savings and deducted from his income for tax purposes, while a decline can be treated as expenditure and added to his income for taxation.

A consumption tax on these lines is not proof against evasion— a man can still conceal his income if he wishes to. But it is proof against manipulation. For instance, no man can evade it by putting a lot of money into the bank a week before the end of the financial year and taking it out a fortnight later. While this will reduce his assessable income for the current financial year, it will increase it for the next year. The exemption of savings from taxation will also weaken one other important motive for tax evasion—the desire to provide a cushion against old age, disablement or a business failure, and to build up an enterprise as quickly as possible by reinvesting all of one's profits in it. These motives hardly affect the salaried classes, whose members run no entrepreneurial risks, enjoy security of employment and get a pension, gratuity and provident fund on retirement. But they are of cardinal importance to the self-employed. A fire in a retailer's shop can reduce him from riches to rags overnight. A car accident will cost a lawyer or a doctor not only his medical expenses but also the income he could have earned in the time that he is convalescing in the hospital.

A dressmaker or a carpenter, the demand for whose products increases, often finds that under the current tax laws the only way in which he can reinvest in his own enterprise is to conceal a part of his profit. Authors, film artists, musicians and painters live even more insecure lives, and the current tax laws which allow them to average their incomes over three years only, is particularly hard on them.

The exemption of saving from taxation will allow all these people to hold openly, at least that part of their incomes which they treat as a reserve against contingencies. Since, according to one set of estimates given in the Wanchoo Committee report, the self-employed are responsible for three-fifths of all tax evasion in this country, the impact of exempting savings from taxation on the flow of funds into the parallel economy will be quite substantial.

In several of its tax laws the government has already conceded the desirability of encouraging savings by granting tax exemptions. Dividends up to Rs 3,000 a year are exempted, as are a part of the contributions to the provident fund and the premia paid on life insurance policies. But there is absolutely no economic justification for distinguishing between one form of saving and another. In fact, the very nature of these exemptions gives rise to the suspicion that they have been conceived of by salary earning bureaucrats, to benefit mainly themselves.

The decision to shift the base of direct taxation from income to consumption may not even lead to a fall in tax yields. This is because saving by some taxpayers will be offset by dissaving by others. But even if it does, the fact remains that the fall in tax yields will be more than compensated for by a much larger rise in savings held openly.

New Directions for investment

Left to itself, money tends to flow automatically into those industries where the money return on investment is highest. What is more, the lure of money profits is precisely what has led to the lopsided growth that characterizes the dual economy, for it has subordinated the pattern of investment to the dictates of money demand and not to the needs of the really poor, who should be the first beneficiaries of development. To the extent that the standard of living of the poorest section does rise under *laissez faire* investment policies, it is an accidental byproduct of industrialization.

Thus the common starting point of all attempts to change the pattern of industrialization and make it responsive to the real needs of the poor, is the rejection of market prices as the determinant of investment.

The search for alternative criteria has led directly to the development of social cost-benefit analysis, which is becoming an increasingly important tool in appraising investment proposals all over the world. Cost-benefit analysis attempts to remedy the shortcomings of market prices, interest, and wage rates as determinants of investment decisions, by 'adjusting' them to bring them more in line with the real cost of goods and services, of capital, and labour, to a poor country.

Though there are two major schools of cost-benefit analysis, developed respectively by IMD Little and James Mirrlees for the Organization for Economic Cooperation & Development and Sen, Marglin and Dasgupta for the United Nations Industrial Development Organization, both in their essentials subscribe to the same set of principles. These are, to value all goods and services that enter into international trade at their world prices instead of their domestic prices thus eliminating the effect of domestic tariffs and taxes on their prices and costs: to value capital and power, which are both scarce in relation to the overall needs of the country at prices well above their market values, and correspondingly to value unskilled labour at a lower social value than the market wage rate, on the grounds that the social cost of employing an unskilled worker is not equal to his entire wage but the difference between it and the amount he was consuming when he was sitting idle at home.

In addition to these basic adjustments the UNIDO guidelines also enable other objectives to be included in the appraisal such as whether an industrial project serves to develop a backward region, promote a fairer distribution of income (by making a mass consumption good avilable more abundantly and therefore cheaper, and so on).

A discussion of the finer points of social cost-benefit analysis would take us very far afield and is in any case not relevant to the main arguments of this chapter. Let it be conceded straightaway, that a systematic application of cost-benefit analysis will greatly improve the use of scarce resources like power or capital and, by biasing all choices towards making greater use of unskilled labour will, over a period of time, increase the growth of employment in the economy. But cost-benefit analysis cannot by itself yield a radically different strategy of growth, for the simple reason that while it provides a method for choosing between alternative means, it is a poor guide at best to the choice between alternative ends.

To take a concrete illustration, cost-benefit analysis may help one to choose between a bus service and a train service to meet the transport needs of a growing city, but it will not in the normal way help one to choose between buses and cycle-rickshaws. The reason is not that the analysis cannot be extended to apply to cycle rickshaws also, but that normally no city authority would consider cycle rickshaws as an alternative to trains and buses, and would not even submit a project based on their use for the consideration of the Central planning authorities. For it to do this, it must first break completely with accepted ways of thinking, and accepted norms: It must ask not which form of transport is best suited to the city, but what kind of city is best for those who use bicycles, cycle-rickshaws or prefer to walk. The decision to go in for cycle-rickshaws would involve completely revising all our notions of urban planning, and setting up a new objective before the town planners: of creating urban modules in which people seldom have to move more than a mile to get to their place of work or shopping or to an entertainment centre. Cost-benefit analysis by itself gives no hint of when such a complete shift of focus is either necessary or possible.

Or take another example: a cost-benefit study may reveal a high social rate of return for a stainless steel plant and recommend its inclusion in any package of new projects whose choice is based solely on social rates of return. But what if most of the stainless steel is destined for the kitchen utensils industry? And what if increased production by this industry will throw out of employment thousands of potters all over the country by making it possible for families to replace earthenware pots with stainless steel ones? In theory it is possible to allow for the employment displacing potential of the project in making the estimate of its social returns, but only *after* the danger has been clearly perceived. And once again this is possible only when people stop regarding the use of metal pots and pans as a *necessary* requirement of increased prosperity and begin asking themselves whether they would indeed be any better off with steel utensils than with earthenware or ceramic vessels (ironically the use of ceramic cooking and serving dishes is just as much of a status symbol in the affluent west as stainless steel or aluminium utensils are in India). Cost-benefit analysis therefore becomes a powerful tool only if society has first defined the content of the prosperity that it hopes to achieve, and then looks for ways of achieving it with the maximum efficiency.

The manner in which this can be done in the agricultural sector has already been discussed in the previous chapter. In industry the basic aims must be to make the least possible departure from the existing pattern of consumption and to meet these basic consumption needs (1) by making the least possible demands on the community's non-reproducible resources, and by using as much as possible of its most abundant asset, unskilled labour.

It is impossible to give an exhaustive catalogue of all the ways in which these aims can be fulfilled in different areas of human want, for the simple reason that the wants themselves keep changing. But here are a few simple prescriptions which will create millions of jobs in the country, within as little as a decade. These are banning the manufacture of cooking utensils, whether of steel, aluminium, or ceramic in large and small factories and reserving this industry for the cottage industries, imposing a ceiling on the output of cloth by both the textile mills and the powerloom sector, except in so far as they are able to increase their exports; similarly banning the use of screen printing machines in the textile industry, banning the use of steel in housing or office buildings, discouraging the use of cement by greatly raising its domestic price, and reorganizing urban transport to enable a part of the need to be met by cycle rickshaws.

The example of cooking vessels has been referred to already. Before metal pots and pans came into widespread use, every one of the half million villages in this country had at least one potter, often several. Pottery was also a lucrative profession in the towns. A good deal of cooking was done in hand baked pots of various kinds and these are still used for cooking by the rural poor, and for making curds by nearly all families in India. This is not to say that metal dishes were not used at all, but that these were used by the more well to do and only for certain types of cooking. The switch to using stainless steel and aluminium vessels has caused the number of village potters to dwindle sharply. There are no estimates of how many families have lost their livelihood in this way over the last two decades, but it is a fact that until as late as 1960, around 80 per cent of the demand of stainless steel was for cooking vessels, and that even today, this remains by far the largest stainless steel using industry in the country, accounting for over 30 per cent of the demand.

What is true of the village potter is true of the basket weaver, the shoemaker, and a number of other traditional craftsmen. Nor are village artisans the only ones who have lost their livelihood through the expansion of power operated industry. The shoemaker in the cities is another vanishing breed. Thirty years ago, each city teemed with highly skilled cobblers, and most people wore made-to-order shoes of excellent quality as the rule rather than the exception. Today, the only remnant of this tribe is the occasional Chinese shoemaker. Their place has been taken by the mass manufacturer of shoes, whose product ironically is not one bit cheaper than his used to be, and is often of a far poorer quality. There is hardly a single specialized hand made product whose makers are not being squeezed out remorselessly by power operated industry. In the last five years, as Kolhapuri sandals (which are made by the cobblers of Kolhapur, a district in Maharashtra) have come into vogue both in India and abroad, every major shoemaker has come out with mass produced imitations. Sooner or later the Kolhapuri sandal makers will go the way of the other artisans of India. Indeed, the supreme irony today is that hand-made shoes are rapidly acquiring the same snob value among the elite in a country with perhaps 30 million unemployed persons as they enjoy in the labour-starved west.

Another example of the mindless encouragement to employment displacing industries, is the government's decision not only to allow a chain of privately owned mechanized bakeries to be set up in the larger cities, but also to set up five such bakeries in the public sector. What is more, it plans to set up many more. Over the last ten years, these have snuffed out the livelihoods of thousands of bakers. A few have survived by baking cakes and

pastries for the urban market. But the majority have been reduced
to destitution. Nor has the government rested content with this.
In 1974, when it officially introduced dual pricing for wheat by
restoring open market sales in the major cities, it forced all privately
owned bakeries to buy wheat in the open market, but supplied it
to the state-owned bakeries at the controlled price, which was
between half and three quarters of the open market price. Even
so, the small private bakeries in Bombay are still able to sell bread
at barely 10 per cent above the price charged by the mechanized-
bakeries.

The case for putting a ceiling on the production of cloth in the
organized sector hardly needs to be elaborated. The government
did actually put a ceiling on the output of the large mills in 1957,
which has not been formally lifted even today, although it is virtually inoperative. But it placed no such ceiling on the small scale
powerloom sector, with the result that a move aimed at assisting the
khadi industry ended by causing the phenomenal growth of small
scale industry which also uses power, employs full time workers,
creates an industrial proletariat, causes all the problems of urbanization associated with large scale industry, but does far less to resolve
them by building housing colonies and so on. In addition it pays
its workers more poorly, and indulges in every kind of violation
of the industrial safety, dearness allowance and other rules. Today,
fully half the cloth produced in the organized sector comes from
the powerloom industry.

The damage done by the growth of the organized sector could
have been mitigated if the government had at least not permitted
textile printing also to be mechanized. A single screen-printing
machine deprives literally scores of printers of their jobs. Yet it
has never occurred to the government to ban the import or installation of such machines.

Nor can it claim that no one has drawn its attention to the
threat. Under the chairmanship of Mrs Kamaladevi Chattopadh-
yaya, a veteran member of the pre-Independence Congress party,
and a staunch Gandhian, the All India Handicrafts Board had
pleaded repeatedly for a ban on the production of printed cloth.
The Board had urged the government to permit mills to produce
plain cloth and to reserve printing for the hand block printers.

This plea fell on deaf ears. The results are visible for all those who have eyes to see. As recently as eight years ago, travellers in Rajasthan would see women in the villages and working in the fields dressed exclusively in clothes with the famous 'tie-and-dye' prints of that state. Today, the Rajasthani 'bandini' as given place almost everywhere to the *polka* dot patterns produced by the mills, and the traditional red, saffron yellow, and green vegetable dyes have given place to improbable shades of purple, blue and green that only synthetic dyes can give. More recently the mills also invaded another preserve of the artisan by beginning to duplicate the exquisite floral patterns of Saurashtrian applique work with such skill that from as little as five yards away it is difficult to tell the difference. Sooner or later this too will be driven out of the villages and will join handmade shoes, handprinted cotton sarees, and genuine 'tie-and-dye' prints in the snobbish *boutiques* of the larger cities.

In an earlier chapter, the bias of economic legislation against large scale enterprise, whether privately or publicly owned and in favour of small scale industry, has been described in some detail. The government has justified this on the grounds that it creates more employment and prevents the concentration of economic power. But it is significant that it has not carried this logic any further, and set up a similar bias in favour of cottage industry, although this would have generated even more productive employment and further widened the spread of prosperity and diffused the ownership of productive assets. Indeed the history of the Khadi and Village Industries Commission shows how the attempt to rejuvenate the artisans of India has slowly fizzled out. Thus, the funds allocated to the KVIC rose from 0·6 per cent of the first plan to 1·7 per cent of the second plan, but thereafter declined steadily to 0·7 per cent of the outlays during the first three years of the fourth Plan.

The emphasis in the objectives of the government also shifted subtly and disastrously over the years. In the first plan it was placed correctly on increasing the prosperity of the rural poor, mainly by giving them work during the agricultural lean periods. In the second plan, these industries were expected to supply consumer goods at a lower capital cost to take the edge off the inflationary pressures that would be generated in the heavy investment sector of the plan.

In later years, the demand grew more insistent that subsidies should be done away with, and a government committee under Ashoka Mehta, a former socialist, endorsed this demand in the late 'sixties. Although the committee made a lot of sympathetic noises about the value of these industries an generating employment, its insistence on the khadi and village industries becoming self-reliant virtually amounted to a death sentence on the handloom industry, for it meant that henceforth the artisan could survive only by producing expensive items for urban boutiques and for export, but not by meeting the needs of even the rural let alone the urban masses. By relegating cottage industries to satisfying this tiny segment of the market, the government destroyed, once and for all, their capacity to generate employment and spread prosperity in the rural areas.

Ironically, even a rudimentary cost-benefit analysis would have shown that the social cost of handloom cloth is much less than their market cost, and therefore, that these products can be subsidized without any loss to the nation. Alternatively, it could be argued that since the part-time weavers who produce the cloth have to feed themselves during the agricultural lean season irrespective of whether they are gainfully employed or not. There is no need to pay them minimum wages of the kind paid to factory workers, for any increase in their incomes during the lean season makes the entire family better off than it was before. Thus handloom and other village products could have been safely priced at only a little above the cost of the raw materials of which they were made. But such cost-benefit notions, were, significantly, never deployed in defence of the rural artisan. As Mahatma Gandhi's ideals faded, and the Gandhians were steadily pushed out of the Congress party, the village industries programme was also allowed to waste away.

The examples given above are of human wants that can be satisfied by modern industry, but where it must be eschewed in order to achieve other goals—the even spread of prosperity, the growth of productive employment, and the prevention of the uncontrolled urbanization.

Housing however, falls into a somewhat different category. Investment in it also meets one of the most basic needs, and therefore is powerfully conducive to greater well-being. But what is more, the *only* way to meet this need effectively is through labour intensive techniques that create as many jobs as all the other cottage industries combined. One has only to drive through the sprawling acres of shanty towns, and to witness the neglect, and squalor of the typical Indian village to see that this most vital human need has also been the most neglected so far. Estimates of the number of dwelling units that are needed to provide a minimum of shelter for every family in the country vary considerably, but the one most often cited is around 60 million dwelling units, of which 12 to 14 million are urgently needed in the towns. Since around two and a half million additional houses are needed every year to cope with the annual increase in population, even a twenty-five year programme to provide adequate housing to the population requires the construction of between five and six million homes every year. No one knows how many houses of clay and thatch, country bricks and tiles are being put up in the villages, but in the cities, which need at least a million dwelling units a year, not even a quarter of this number are being put up. The backlog is thus growing steadily larger.

Yet housing is one of those problems that should simply not exist. To make a home is one of the strongest urges in man, being part and parcel of the drive to marry and raise a family. Left to themselves, human beings will sooner or later build or buy their own homes. Thus a housing problem only arises when something frustrates this urge. In the villages, there are few such impediments. Thus houses do get built all the time and nearly everyone, barring the very poorest people with absolutely no secure claim to any piece of land, has a house of sorts to live in. The problem there, is mainly of providing cheap improved materials, such as locally made brick in place of clay, tiles in place of thatch, and so on, and of meeting basic needs such as for clean drinking water and covered drains. Beyond this, for anyone to impose either radically new kinds of housing, or urban notions of town planning on the villagers and ask them to use building materials such as concrete is both an intellectual presumption and an economic folly.

In the towns the problem is entirely different. Here the hurdles which prevent the expression of the urge to build are (1) the semi-seasonal working population, whose members leave their families behind in the villages and do not wish to put down their roots in a city, (2) the physical lack of space, or where this is available, the need to travel a very long distance to one's place of work and (3) the high cost of construction.

A discussion of the nature of the industrial working class in India would be out of place here. That a large part of it is still rural in origin, and that many workers go back to their villages every year at harvest time, if not oftener, is beyond dispute. Indeed the leave facilities enjoyed by the working class, which are generous to a fault and permit the compounding of different kinds of leave are at least partly the result of the desire among employers to turn a blind eye to a practice that they cannot condone but equally cannot prevent (many employees habitually take their annual leave, then fall conveniently sick during the last week, and stay away for another six weeks). Thus it is hardly surprising to find that even a century after the beginning of industrialization absenteeism among the workers in many of the public sector enterprises still runs as high as 19 per cent of the working year.

So far as the second and third hurdles are concerned, these have been created by the housing policies followed by the city authorities all over the country. These policies have been based on a number of fallacies which have long since been exposed. The first is that land is expensive and the use must be economized. The second, which follows from the first, is that the best way to economize in the use of land is to build high-rise buildings. Since high rise construction requires large quantities of steel and cement, and are therefore expensive, it leads directly to the third and last heresy—that low-income housing must be subsidized, and that the rich must somehow be made to pay for housing the poor. Unfortunately since the rich are also nearly always powerful, the predictable result is a complete neglect of low income housing.

Bombay once again provides an excellent example of how these fallacies have blocked investment in all but the most luxurious types of housing. Till 1971, when the prevailing cost of construction by the public works department was around Rs 25 to Rs 30 per square foot even a 200-square foot tenement cost Rs 5,000–6,000 to build. After taking the provision of water, electricity, roads and drains into account, the meanest dwelling calls for an investment of Rs 7,000 to 8,000. This is what the Maharashtra government was actually spending per unit on one of its housing schemes, but the expenditure on some other schemes came to much more. For instance, the Maharashtra government's scheme to clear the slums along the road to Bombay's airport was expected to cost Rs 10,000 to Rs 12,000 per house. Indeed some of the public sector corporations have been unforgivably extravagant. In Rourkela, for instance, the average cost per dwelling unit turned out to be Rs 13,000 fifteen years ago!

The failure to bring down the cost of construction has proven doubly unfortunate. It has prevented private builders from putting up houses for low-income groups, and has made house-building by the government a heavy drain on the public exchequer. To get a ten to twelve per cent return on a house that costs Rs 10,000 a builder has to charge a rent of Rs 80 to 100 a month. Since people who earn Rs 150 or Rs 200 a month can seldom afford to pay more than Rs 20 to Rs 30, no private entrepreneur in his senses is prepared to build houses for the low-income groups. The government and the public undertakings which build for their employees in effect give a concealed subsidy of between Rs 40 and Rs 80 per month to each family.

This accounts for the reluctance of most State governments to make use of even such meagre grants as they receive for housing from the Central government.

In the last seven years, the minimum cost of construction for multi-storeyed buildings, even those intended for low income groups, has risen from around Rs 25 to Rs 30, to Rs 50 or more per square foot, and a one-room, 200 – square foot flat, now costs over Rs 10,000. At current rates of interest, therefore, even if a man is prepared to spend 15 per cent of his salary on housing, he had to earn Rs 700 to Rs 800 a month to afford even such a miserable tenement. In other words not even five per cent of the families in the country can afford to live in a 200-square foot flat!

The housing problem cannot therefore be eased unless ways are found of building houses so cheaply that a man who earns no more than Rs 200 a month is able to pay for his house in 10 to 15 years. This means that the overall cost of building a house for him and providing the basic amenities must be brought down to between three and four thousand rupees. Only then will the government be able to 'revolve' the funds which are invested in its low-cost housing programmes. The first step in this direction is to abandon the notion that urban land is expensive. This may be so for an individual, but is not for the state. The social, as opposed to the private, cost of land is not more than the value of what it could have produced in its best alternative use. For instance, when a town is built on what used to be agricultural land, the social cost is the present discounted value of all its harvests. When it is built on rocky hills or on reclaimed land, the social cost is at most the cost of land reclamation or of levelling and developing the site.

Many municipal authorities, including those of Bombay defend imputing a high value to land on the grounds that in leasing it to the low-income groups they are foregoing the income that they would have obtained by selling or leasing it to a private builder of luxury residential or office buildings. Such an attitude may be condoned in a private landowner but is inexcusable in a public authority which has by definition more of a responsibility to the urban poor than to the rich. What is more, the argument itself is wholly fallacious. If we assume that the total amount of land to be set aside for urban development has already been decided, the decision to further set aside a part of this land for low-income housing will automatically restrict the supply of land available for sale to the rich and push up its price. The government will thus get back in the form of higher sales or lease values and higher taxes, a good part if not all of the money it loses on the plots reserved for low-income housing.

Once the government realizes that it is not incurring any real loss in leasing land at nominal rents to low income earners, much of the temptation to build multi-storeyed apartment blocks will vanish. The little that remains will also disappear when it realizes that putting up high rise buildings does not save much land either. This is because as buildings grow taller it becomes necessary to leave more open space around them to let in a minimum of light and fresh air. What is more since this space must be left on all sides, the minimum open area is the *square* of the minimum distance between any two buildings. As a result, the densities obtained by putting up towers of six and ten stories, can be obtained just as easily with various configurations of single or at most two-storeyed houses.

In fact in a low-cost housing competition organized by the Housing and Urban Development Corporation in 1975, one of the prize winning entries envisaged the setting up of single-storey, two and three-room houses, to attain a gross urban density of 240 per acre!

Once the government takes a firm decision to encourage no more than one or two-storeyed housing, it becomes possible to do away with steel, cement, mortar and concrete, deep foundations, and elevators, and go back to simple construction, using lime or even mud mortar, tiled or asbestos sheet roofs, and thus bring the cost of a two hundred square foot dwelling down to Rs 4,000 or thereabouts. In fact, by using the self-help principle, giving people developed sites with a basic minimum of facilities and some cheap mass-produced fixtures it. is possible to bring costs down still further, while giving full reign to man's home-building urge.

How powerful and constructive this urge can be was revealed to this writer during a visit to one of Bombay's three experimental 'slum improvement' schemes in 1972. A typical beneficiary of the scheme was a handcart puller named Kashinath, one of the million or more persons in Bombay who had never lived in a *pucca* house. Until three years before, his home was a miserable hut, ten feet by eight feet, with walls made of worm-eaten planks taken from broken crates, a roof of rusting tin and burlap, and a sloping 'floor' which could never be kept dry during the monsoon.

His wife washed the family's clothes and bathed the children in foul water in a nearby hollow and queued for drinking water at a public tap half a mile away in the dead of night. For the privilege of living in this festering hole, Kashinath had to pay a 'pugree' (illicit transfer price) of Rs 400 to the previous owner, and a 'rent' of Rs 15 a month to the camp bosses who 'squared' the municipal authorities.

His luck turned in 1969 when the police razed the colony to the ground and, instead of leaving him to his devices, moved him and his neighbours to a site prepared by the Bombay Municipal Corporation under its 'slum improvement' scheme in Deonar, an outlying suburb of the city.

The new colony, set up by the Corporation consists of units of eight dwellings, each 15 feet by 10 feet, with common lateral walls, all built on a cement plinth, 80 feet long and 30 feet wide. Between adjoining plinths there is an open, cemented drain, fed by smaller ones from each home. There are common washing and toilet complexes for every four such plinths which means for every 32 families. The colony also has a school and a market place. When I met him, Kashinath lived in a house he had built for himself.

By conventional standards it was not much of a house. It had four foot high brick walls, topped by another five feet of corrugated tin sheets, laid over a wooden frame. But the floor was clean and dry. There was an eight-foot-wide pavement on either side of his house to sit on in the evenings, and a *pucca* drain in place of a stinking cesspool into which to discharge waste from his kitchen.

In 1972, Deonar already had 5,100 such houses. It had cost the municipality Rs 10 lakhs to provide the basic amenities, or just under Rs 200 per dwelling unit. Beyond that Kashinath and the other residents had spent Rs 700 to Rs 1,200 on each dwelling. Thus for a total expenditure of between Rs 1,000 and Rs 1,500, some slum people had taken their first big step towards owning a home.

The experiment at Deonar goes a long way towards proving that the cost of a dwelling unit can be brought down to Rs 3,000 or even less if the state governments give up constructing multi-storeyed tenements and take to developing proper sites where families with modest incomes can build their own one or two-storeyed homes. But, since it has been conceived of only as a slum improvement scheme and not as a full fledged self-help housing colony, it has failed to demonstrate its full potential.

It is true that people in the new Deonar colony live in far greater comfort now than they did in their tin-burlap shanties. But, hampered by a host of municipal bye-laws, they have not been able the most out of the money they have spent.

For instance, the municipal authorities have reserved the option to move the 23,000 people in Deonar to still another site, in case they decide to put the land in the new colony to another use. They have therefore allowed the construction of only 'temporary structures'. This means that the people are not allowed to put up brick walls higher than four feet. All construction above this height, including the roof, has to be of easily removable materials such as corrugated tin or asbestos sheets, or of wood. As a result, these shacks are not only ugly and flimsy, but have often cost more to build than similar structures of brick and tile.

Even so anyone visiting these modest homes can see how keen the people are to improve their living conditions. Defying the municipal laws, many have tiled their roofs. The tiles cost 40 p. each in 1972 and the entire roof, including the framework of light, wooden struts on which they were laid, cost approximately Rs 250.

One also saw a window with glass panes here, a gaily painted doorway or a colourful mosaic-floor there.

The better-off had even added a second storey to their homes, thus doubling their living space to 300 square feet. This was true of most of the shopkeepers, who had been allotted corner sites where they can set up a stall facing the main strut.

But the best example of what could be achieved with a little bit of rational planning and effort was the home of a Bengali furniture-maker. Tucked away in one corner of the colony his attractive two-room bungalow had brick walls plastered and painted a light green, and white painted doors and windows. The floors were of mosaic tiles, and the area around the tap which served as a kitchen had glazed white tiles. The cost per room, according to its proud owner, had come to no more than Rs 2,500.

NOTES

1　*Financial Express*, September 20, 1975.

2   *Financial Express*, September 2, 1975.
3   This conclusion is based on an estimate of Central and State tax and non-tax revenue *including* the gross surpluses of the public enterprises (i.e. depreciation fund less actual replacement which is as yet small as the plants are new) given in the annual *Economic Survey*, and on the sum of the non-plan development and non-development expenditure which can be obtained from the Reserve Bank of India's *Currency and Finance Report*.
4   T.S. Bharde, *Khadi and Village Industries, A Perspective*, p. 11. Published by the Khadi & Village Industries Commission, Bombay 56.

11 / The Political Dimensions of Economic Reform

FEW READERS are likely to have missed the seeming contradiction between the strategy of growth which has been proposed in the last three chapters and the package of economic reforms that have been suggested for financing its adoption. While the first aims to encourage the increased use of not even small but cottage-scale technology which makes the least possible use of concentrated sources energy, the second aims at raising the revenues of large scale industry and thereby encouraging its further growth. This amounts to supporting the growth of both the 'primitive' and the modern sectors of industry at the same time, or, put in another way, to advocating simultaneously a strategy of growth which diffuses employment opportunities as widely as possible, while proposing fiscal and monetary policies which will further increase the population and the concentration of income in the cities.

The contradiction, however, is more apparent than real. Both types of technology are not intended for the same industries. And the aim of generating surpluses from currently established industry is not so much to finance their growth, as to generate resources for ploughing into new programmes of labour-intensive, cottage scale investment. This could be done by using excise duties, tax rebates and subsidies selectively to discourage fresh investment in power-driven industry and encourage its diversion to cottage industry, and by banning the production of some basic consumer goods in the modern sector. (The fact that in 1976 the Central government lifted certain excise duties and restrictions designed to inhibit the setting up of garment making factories, in the name of export promotion, shows how insensitive it is to the need for employment generation and how susceptible to the blandishments of the urban industrial lobby.)

Secondly, for a large country like India which cannot do without a sizable armaments industry, and cannot wholly cut itself off from the world market, there is no escape from building a modern industrial sector. But the change of strategy proposed in the last three chapters requires that modern industry should no longer be cast as the star in the drama of economic growth, but be given the role of an indispensable supporting actor.

Many of the needs of human beings in their roles both as producers and consumers can only be met by industry. A steel instead of a wooden plough, cobblers' tools, potters' wheels, galvanized iron pipes for a piped drinking water system, steel and cement for certain kinds of construction, improved seeds, chemical fertilizers to supplement organic manure, medicines, and a thousand other products of industry, will continue to be needed by ordinary consumers. This primary demand will lead in turn to a demand for complex machinery. Thus, in any circumstances, the need for complementary investment will ensure the creation of a pyramidal structure of industry. The only difference is that the pyramid envisaged here will have a much broader base of demand emanating from millions of reasonably prosperous artisans and farmers spread throughout the country, instead of the narrow base provided by a high-income predominantly urban elite, serviced by a few thousand firms producing consumer goods designed to sustain a 'western' standard of life. Generating more resources by unfettering industry and particularly heavy industry is a necessary precondition to this change. As these resources are poured into modernizing agriculture and rehabilitating the artisan, the increase in employment and consequent rise in income and demand in the rural and urban areas will exert its own influence on the production pattern of the heavy industries which have been built up so far. And this will ensure that the present base of heavy industry will eventually sustain a much higher level of production of consumer goods and consequently a far higher level of income.

The emphasis on promoting cottage industry on the one hand and large scale industry on the other, does not also mean that there is no role for small scale enterprises. There exists a symbiotic relationship between small and large scale enterprise. This is particularly so in the engineering goods industries which usually find it profitable to delegate the manufacture of some components to small ancillary units.

The right policy towards the small scale sector is therefore to let it grow naturally so that it can fill its own assigned niche in the industrial structure. It should neither be encouraged to expand into areas where the larger units can work more efficiently, nor into those which are better left to cottage industry.

It must also be faced that over time as the level of economic activity rises, some small units will grow into large enterprises, while others will be driven out by competition or by their own poor management. This will be no loss, for in sociological terms small-scale industry is almost indistinguishable from large scale enterprise. It too requires a wholetime labour force, with a powerful interest in collective bargaining to secure higher wages and better working conditions, and therefore in limiting the spread of employment. It too leads to a concentration of labour in small areas. Finally, it raises the wages of the worker by enough to permit the adoption of 'western' styles of living, and hence enhances the dualism which has been the bane of the poor nations during the last half a century.

By contrast, cottage industry can be a part time occupation for the agricultural lean season, and can be carried on at home. It thus creates no industrial proletariat and no problem of urbanization. It neither raises issues of minimum wages and living and working conditions, thereby restricting employment growth, nor does it cause a quantum jump in productivity and incomes, thereby encouraging a change in consumption habits. Most important of all, cottage industry eliminates the two root causes of the growing alienation that besets the advanced countries—the growing 'round-aboutness' of industrial production and its corollary—the fragmentation of the creative process, and the displacement of men by machines. The real watershed therefore lies not between small and large industry, but between modern and cottage industry. The crucial jump in technology occurs with the use of concentrated fossil fuels or hydroelectric power to drive machines, in place of human, animal, wind or water power.

The seeming contradiction between the proposed strategy of growth and the suggested reforms of economic policies disappears entirely when one examines their political implication. For both are designed in different ways to cut down the political and economic power of the intermediate class.

While the alternative growth strategy aims at widening the base of economic power in the country beyond the twenty million or so families which account for the bulk of the intermediate class today, the proposed economic reforms are intended to close the channels for making money illegally which the intermediate class has taken advantage of to increase its economic power at the expense of the other classes in society. Thus, without price controls black marketing will cease to be a serious problem and much of the income that goes to the wholesale and retail traders will go to producers instead. Similarly, the reduction of excise duties to reasonable levels (except where these are designed expressly to discourage new investment in a particular industry) will greatly reduce, if not altogether eliminate the concealment of production by owner-managed enterprises. In the same way there is evidence that the reduction of income tax rates in the budgets for 1974–75 and 1976–77 has led to a small reduction in tax evasion, but its more important effect has been to increase the retained earnings of the upper salaried classes, notably the professional managers in industry.

The overall result of these and other measures of economic liberalization will be to strengthen the manufacturer in relation to the trader, large scale enterprise in relation to small units, and the professional managerial and other salaried classes in relation to the owner-managers. Most important of all, these measures will deprive the intermediate class in the cities of a good part of the funds which it has been able to convert into political power.

The effect of the growth strategy proposed in the previous chapters will mainly be on the classes which fall below the intermediate class on the income scale. To the extent that it promotes cottage industry, it will both increase the supply of goods in the economy (thereby reducing the conditions of chronic scarcity in which the intermediate class has prospered) and, by increasing the incomes of artisans, small farmers and landless workers, increase the political power of these classes. To the extent that small farmers, tenant cultivators and landless labourers for instance, can go in for dairying, growing vegetables or for cottage industry, their bargaining power in their dealings with the larger land-owners will increase and they will be in a better position to secure higher wages during the seasons when the demand for labour attains a peak in the rural areas.[1]

In the same way a large and thriving unorganized sector in the towns producing a wide range of goods and services will offer a greater variety of choice to the urban consumer, and curb the monopolistic tendencies which are only too apparent in the organized sector.

Some readers may object that the creation of more self-employment is a strange way of trying to reduce the power of the self-employed classes. The answer is that the objection is not to self-employment as a mode of production, but to a specific situation in a coalition of self-employed groups has been able to seize political power to create monopolistic conditions through the perpetuation of economic stagnation, swell its profits and income and plough back a part of these into further strengthening its hold on political power.

One of the dominant characteristics of the unorganized sector in the cities, even today, is that in sharp contrast to the organized sector it is highly competitive.[2] This is even more true of cottage industry than of the lower fringes of small scale industry in which most of the unorganized sector falls today. Competition is likely to ensure that the benefits of a rise in the supply of consumer goods is passed on to the consumer in the form of lower prices and a larger output.

In the villages, the immediate proximity of consumers and producers will tend to keep prices down by cutting out the middle-men (who are members of the intermediate classes). In overall terms, the success of the proposed growth strategy in reducing the power of the middle classes is likely to be reflected in a decline in the share of the tertiary sector in the national product. However, to complete this process, the economic reforms proposed above need to be supplemented by one specifically political reform. This is to break the link between black money and political power. The best way of doing this is to set up a state fund to finance the electoral and the normal expenses of the recognized political parties in this country. Prior to the declaration of an 'emergency', and the curtailment of democratic process as in India in June, 1975, the demand for electoral reform on these lines had grown steadily stronger as more and more people had become aware of the political parties' dependence on holders of black money.

As elections grew more and more costly, and as the role of money in gathering votes became more important, the government came more and more to resemble a bargain basement, where a rise in sugar prices, an increase in export subsidies, an import licence for a scarce material, would be exchanged for cash donations to the party.

The stench of this corruption finally began to offend even the members of the Congress parliamentary party, particularly after electoral corruption became the main plank of attack by the student dissidents in Gujarat and Mr Jaya Prakash Narayan's movement in Bihar. The resulting demand for electoral reform took two forms: while some Congressmen argued forcefully for repealing the ban on company donations that the party had enacted in 1967, others proposed the setting up of a state fund along the lines of some of the Scandinavian countries, which would be divided among the recognized parties on the basis of a statutory formula.

Of the two, the second course is infinitely the more preferable. Repealing the ban on company donations will break the nexus between the political parties and black money, but only at the cost of making them excessively susceptible to pressure from big business. While this may be an improvement on the present situation, it is bound to invite precisely the kind of political backlash from populist elements in the country, which led to the initial ban on company donations and the sustained campaign against 'big business' which followed.

Thus repealing the ban on company donations will not restore long term health to the polity. For this the electoral system needs to be put beyond the reach of any organized group in the country. The only way to do this is to set up a standing fund to finance elections, and what is more, make it so large that political parties no longer need to rely on private donations. According to some intra-party estimates made by leaders of the Congress party, the cost of fighting a general election, for all the parties amounts to no less than Rs 200 crores. If this figure is accepted, the state would need to set aside Rs 40 crores a year for the special election fund. This would seem a small price to pay for achieving so major a purpose, but human nature being what it is, the proposal has also been opposed vigorously on a variety of grounds. Ironically, some of these objections have come from the very opposition parties that stand to gain most from the reform. Thus it has been argued that financing elections on this scale would be too expensive; that the creation of a state fund will not ensure that corrupt politicians do not continue to take money from businessmen in return for specific favours, and most important of all, that no just system for sharing the funds can be evolved.

None of these arguments stands up to a close examination. The concept of 'expense' is necessarily subjective, but it is worth remembering that Rs 40 crores a year represents less than 0.4 per cent of the annual revenues of the Central and State governments, which now exceed Rs 10,000 crores a year. It is also no more than one third of what the Central and State governments have been giving away every time there is an increase in the dearness allowance of their employees.

But will such a reform cleanse the political system? The answer to this question depends on how much one hopes to achieve. Quite obviously there will always be people in every party, who will not be able to resist the temptation to feather their own nests. But a state fund will remove the *compulsion* on individual politicians, and on the political parties, to exchange favours for funds. Over a period of time, the party as a whole and hopefully most of its legislators will become honest. This will in turn make it possible for the party to isolate and expel members who are irredeemably corrupt, and to induct more honest and dedicated people into their ranks. The change will be slow, to begin with (while the 'old guard' still hold positions of power within each party), but will gather momentum with the passage of time. Eventually a new breed of politicians and a more responsible politics will replace what the country has today.

Many people who accept the need for state financing of elections tend to draw the line however at subsidizing the day to day activities of the political parties. This at least, they say, should be met from membership dues and donations, if for no other reason than because the need to raise the money will force political parties to build up a mass base, and maintain closer links with the people whom they purport to represent. What is more, they argue that the provision of funds on such a liberal scale may actually tempt them to organize more agitations and other disruptive activities in order to attract support.

Both these fears are groundless. The compulsion on political parties to build up some kind of mass base, and to keep in constant touch with the populace, comes from the need to fight and win elections. Compared with this, the stimulus provided by the need to collect dues from 'four-anna' or 'eight-anna' members, is of relatively little importance. On the other hand, as 25 years of experience of the Congress party has shown us,[3] moneyed people can easily prepare bogus lists of members, pay their dues and use their voting rights to lever themselves into power within the party organization. Thus, such membership drives can easily become the means by which a caucus of powerful individuals takes control of what remains in appearance a mass-based party.

The truth is that in a country as poor as India, a party system consisting of mass-based parties modelled on the British Labour and Conservative parties, with strong constituency units funded and supported by voluntary donations of money and services, is an impossibly remote idea. The people are too poor, the constituencies much too large and national and even state issues too complex to evoke much voluntary support. Politics, therefore, becomes a profession (witness the rising proportion of legislators who describe themselves as 'professional politicians')[4] and money to sustain the profession has necessarily to come from either an impartially administered state fund, or from the urban and rural rich. The scope for reform is therefore necessarily limited, and the state fund emerges clearly as the best of the available alternatives.

As for the fear that providing political parties with more money will encourage them to whip up more agitations, the reverse is more likely to be the case. The shortage of funds to finance even day to day party work has debilitated both the right and the left in this country, although in different ways. On the right it has prevented the building up of strong party organizations, staffed by reasonably well paid full-time professional politicians. On the left the Communist parties have been able to build and maintain reasonably strong organizations only by continually whipping up an ideological fervour among the rank and file. This is why splinter groups have emerged among the Communists always on the left of the official party line. But a strong ideology necessarily limits the appeal of a party. Thus the ultimate price that the left has paid for maintaining a reasonably cohesive organization has been to forego all opportunities to widen its popular base.

The agitational politics which became the bane of government in the late '60's and early '70's was both a symptom and a product of this gradual debilitation of the opposition. Parties serve either as an instrument for the capture of power or as a vehicle for an ideology—they can rarely if ever serve as both. In India the *raison d'etre* of all parties except the Communists has been to capture power and for this they have been only too willing to sacrifice any ideology, be it Gandhian, socialist, or Hindu revivalist. But to maintain their cohesion in non-election years such non-ideological parties need a strong organizational structure. And this in turn costs money to build and maintain. Starved of funds, the non-ideological parties have found their organizations withering away, and have failed progressively to attract young people to their ranks. As their own organizations have crumbled, the opposition parties have resorted increasingly to agitation, espousing no matter what cause, to keep themselves in the public eye.[5]

There is thus every reason to believe that far from encouraging agitational politics, the generous provision of funds to the political parties will help to curb it, and to channel their energies back towards building up a strong organizational base.

This is not the only benefit to be reaped from such generosity. The capacity to pay party workers more or less according to their market value in other occupations, will also raise the quality of persons whom the parties will attract to their ranks. In particular, it will permit them to set up investigative teams to enquire into social and economic abuses, and policy planning and research organizations to examine the impact of legislation, and to frame short as well as long term policies. Kochanek has pointed out that even the Congress party has never had such a planning body, and that for the research that must precede the framing of policy it is entirely dependent on the bureaucracy. In fact the desire of bureaucrats to defend all previous measures enacted by them, if for no other reason than to protect their own skins, is chiefly responsible for the absence of any real evaluation of social and economic policies among ruling circles, and the complete dearth of new ideas pertaining to the conduct of national affairs.

Can the distribution of state funds be made wholly just? Quite obviously, no system will satisfy everyone, but the nearest approach to a just division will be to divide the funds according to the proportion of the total vote received b; each party in the previous national or state election. To qualify for a subsidy each party must obtain a minimum of say three or five per cent of the national vote. Since this system will not exhaust all of the money in the election fund—a part of the vote having gone to independents and parties that fail to qualify for assistance—the residue can be divided according to some agreed formula among the smaller opposition parties. What is more to meet the objections of regional parties there is no reason why separate funds should not be established for financing the parliamentary and state elections.

By building in certain other safeguards such a method of distribution can both discourage defections from large parties and encourage small splinter groups and independents to come together to form stable opposition parties. Thus, the electoral laws could be made to stipulate that unless more than half of the members of a party defect from the current leadership, the funds will remain in its control. This means that when a group defects from say the Congress to the Jana Sangh, the latter will have to field a larger number of candidates with the same funds.

By the same token, the government can also stipulate that to qualify for funds a coalition of small parties or individuals must have been formed at least one year before the previous elections. The two laws together will inhibit both defections and opportunistic coalitions.

Can one expect a government that reflects the interests of a dominant intermediate class with a 'perimeter of influence' that embraces upwards of 200 million people, to take steps to reduce the political and economic power of this very class? Alternatively, where is the coalition of forces sufficiently strong to challenge the hegemony of such a large class, particularly within the democratic system?

In the Indian context the interests that oppose the intermediate classes are the urban working classes,[6] the urban fixed income groups, the professional managers and shareholders of widely owned joint stock companies, and the rural unprotected tenantry and agricultural labourers. But so far no party with the possible exception of the Naxalites, has made a determined bid to marshall these forces. Instead, as Rudra and Bardhan have pointed out, all of them, including the two major communist parties, have competed for the votes of the intermediate class, a competition that they could not hope to win against the Congress. This does not however mean that no alternative strategy is possible. The growing restiveness of the students and the urban educated unemployed, of some segments of the unorganized working class, such as the domestic servants and also among teachers, nurses, doctors, railway locomotive drivers and engineers (such as those of the state electricity boards), and the increasingly frequent revolts of the Harijans in various parts of the country, shows that the elements for the creations of an alternate base of power, or at least of limiting the dominance of the intermediate class, are all present in the country.

There are three other reasons why it may not prove too difficult to clip the wings of the intermediate class. The first is that as the economy continues to stagnate, more and more of its members are likely to become aware of the contradiction between their own short and long term ends. In other words, they may come to the conclusion that the very forces of economic stagnation which have increased their power and prosperity will eventually destroy them altogether.

Secondly, the reforms proposed above do not seek the annihilation of the intermediate class but merely the limitation of its power and wealth, in order to secure a more healthy balance of political and economic forces. There is likely to be less opposition to such moderate reforms than to a more fundamental restructuring of society (such as the nationalization of all trade and transport, the banning of private practice by doctors, lawyers and other professionals, and the complete discouragement of small scale enterprise).

Finally, the scope for reform is increased by the lack of homogeneity within the ranks of the government. While the Congress party is now made up almost entirely of members of the intermediate class, the senior officers in the bureaucracy, the police and the armed forces still belong to the fixed income groups. Not only has this class shared a common decline in fortunes during the last ten years, but it is tightly knit in a variety of other ways. For instance, its members move all over this country in search of jobs, they speak a common language—English—and share a more or less similar way of life. They are also drawn for the most part from the elite castes of the country, a fact whose significance should not be underestimated.

Thus, the decisions taken in 1974–1975 to lift price controls on a number of important consumer and capital goods, to charge economic prices for some basic products like aluminium and power, to arrest thousands of smugglers and wholesale and retail traders suspected of being corrupt, is probably the result of both the dawning awareness of its insecurity in the intermediate class, as well as the pressure of the old elite in the bureaucracy, which is at least getting some political support for action about whose necessity it has long been convinced.

NOTES

1 Proof of this, and of the resentment of the intermediate classes of the improvement in bargaining power of the poor was furnished when the government started minimum wage and employment guarantee programmes in the rural areas. Wherever such programmes were started, landless workers refused to work for the peasant proprietors for less than Rs 3 a day (the minimum guaranteed on government projects). This provoked violent attacks on them by the rich landowners, who often burnt their homes and murdered their relatives (See article by G.S. Bhatnagar, *Harijan Unrest in U.P.* in *Times of India*, 14 August 1972).
2 See Joshi and Joshi, op. cit.
3 See Kochanek, *Congress Party in India*, Princeton, 1969.

4 See article by the author on the Composition of the 5th Lok Sabha, in the *Times of India*'s Supplement on the general elections published on March 31st, 1972.

5 Angela Burger, op.cit. describes how this happened to the PSP and SSP in UP, contrasting it to the more dynamic Jana Sangh.

6 The alliance with this class which was forged by successive Congress governments through protective legislation and a liberal enactment of allowances, compulsory bonuses and so on finally broke down in May 1976, when the government crushed the railway workers strike, and adopted a tough policy towards all wage demands in the public sector. Under the emergency, strikes had been banned, and the compulsory 8.33% bonus to workers had been withdrawn.

Chapter 1: Appendix 1

Long term projections and assumptions underlying the choice of planning strategies for the second and successive Plans.

IT SEEMS IRONICAL in the light of what followed, that the planning strategy adopted in 1955 for the 20 year period 1956-1975, began by postulating goals not in terms of the rate of growth of product but of employment. This was based on estimates of the number of jobs that had to be created to absorb the backlog of unemployment and the new entrants into the rural and urban labour force, and to reduce somewhat the existing under-employment in agriculture and the small-scale enterprises. The planners' calculations were based on the expectation that the work force of the country would increase from 164 millions in 1960-61 to 235 millions in 1975-76, or by 43·2%.

To absorb this increase they proposed that programmes be formulated which would absorb 19.5 million people in agriculture, 24 millions in mining and manufacturing and 28 millions in services.

Of the 24 millions in the secondary sector, they expected 13 millions to be absorbed by small-scale industry (presumably including cottage industry) and 11 millions in the medium and large scale sector. In percentage terms this meant an increase of five per cent a year in the small scale, and fifteen per cent a year in the large scale sector.

Given the structure of the Indian economy and the nature of the industrialization process, the rates of employment growth postulated both for the entire economy and within the secondary sector, were reasonable. Although agriculture was the largest sector of the economy by far, it was accorded the least important role in fresh employment generation because of the already existing backlog of underemployment which had to be eliminated.

In the secondary sector, 80% of production was in the cottage and small scale sectors. Yet the expansion of modern industry, which was seen as the key to attaining higher levels of real income, tended to displace workers, particularly those employed in the household sector. Thus the emphasis in government policies was on the reservation of areas of industry for the small scale sector to ensure non-competitiveness between it and the large scale sector, and on imposing indirect levies on the latter to balance the lower cost of mass production. With this essentially defensive view of small industry the planners' choice of a mere 5% growth rate for employment in this sector was on the whole realistic. Thus the burden of expanding employment in the secondary sector of the economy was to fall on the large-scale sector. However, since the capital to labour ratio here was already high and was being pushed up further by the adoption of the goal of industrial self-reliance, this could be reconciled with the desired rate of employment growth only by aiming at and achieving a very high rate of growth of savings and investment. Since the planners also realized that in a very poor country extra savings could only come out of increased incomes, and not out of existing incomes, this led them to postulate a very high rate of growth of national and per capita output.

The planners therefore proposed a target growth rate of 7% per annum for 1960 to 1975, and a marginal rate of saving of 40 per cent. The average rate of saving was thus expected to increase from around 7 per cent of national income in 1955 to around 21% and to stablize at that level. With an assumed capital to output ratio of 3:1 this would give the required growth rate of 7% a year.

A high rate of growth of output was therefore absolutely necessary for the success of the above strategy, for slower growth in the face of a constant capital output ratio would force the government to push the marginal rate of saving up still higher. Achieving such a high growth rate involved a number of ancillary assumptions: that the foreign exchange constraint on domestic savings would be removed by foreign aid; and that agriculture would grow at $4\frac{1}{4}$ per cent a year-a rate calculated to be sufficient to feed the villages and the growing towns, and thus avoid the emergence of an inflationary barrier to higher investment.

All these projections involved major breaks with the existing trends. The actual growth rate of GNP in the 'fifties had been around 3.5 per cent and agriculture had grown by under 3 per cent during the first Plan. Thus, from the second Plan itself the Planning Commission wanted a steep rise in the growth rates in agriculture, industry and the services to meet the targets set down for 1960-1975.

On the assumption that a 21% rate of saving, a 7% rate of growth of national product, and a 4.25% rate of growth in agriculture were attainable, the planning model described above was consistent, and its employment targets seemed within reach. But the achievement of such high rates of growth presupposed a whole range of other favourable developments: a higher rate of agricultural growth required not only additional investment, but what is more important, the removal of institutional barriers to greater productivity. With agricultural growth at 4.25% a 7% growth rate of GNP required a much higher rate of growth of the secondary sector and this for the reasons outlined earlier, presupposed an even higher rate of growth in large-scale industry. In practice this meant that complex projects with long gestation periods had to be implemented fast and to work from the very start or near full capacity. This was essential if they were to generate profits and raise the rate of saving, while keeping down the capital to output ratio to the stipulated three to one.

The Planning Commission did foresee the possibility that the economy would fail to achieve the target growth rate of seven per cent. But it felt that while this would frustrate the employment goals of the Plans, it would not frustrate the process of industrialization, *provided* the volume of savings could be raised more or less as projected. It based this conclusion on the belief that industrial production tended to form a closed loop, with a large number of producer goods industries feeding each other and all of them being sustained by demand from the consumer goods industries. The final demand for the products of industry, however, was not expected to come from the whole market but from the large investment in new industries and in the giant infrastructure projects included in the Plans.

However as mentioned above, this 'second best' assumption implied a capacity to push up the marginal rate of savings even in the field of a slower than anticipated growth rate. Only thus could the required volume of domestic saving be attained. For this the planners proposed the adoption of stern fiscal measures to raise the share of government revenues in the national product; compulsory saving including deficit financing if this became necessary, and more foreign aid and to offset the slower growth of exports and the slower rise in domestic saving, which a slower growth of output might well entail.

The belief in self-sustaining growth in the *industrial* sector also required the planners to make two further assumptions: firstly that the government would exercise a firm control over its consumption expenditure (measured as a share of national product if not in absolute terms) so that the extra resources raised through taxation and forced saving would not be frittered away, and secondly that despite slower growth in agriculture there would be enough food available somehow to feed the growing population, above all in the towns and at the new industrial project sites.

Dr K.N. Raj and other economists have criticized the second of these assumptions as completely unrealistic and have condemned the planners' belief in the possibility of self-sustaining growth without rapid advances in agriculture.[1] They have pointed out that slower agricultural growth also means a slower growth of demand for consumer goods and, as proof of this, have cited the supposed tendency of industrial growth to spurt after a rise in agricultural production.

This criticism does not seem altogether valid, at least in the form presented above. To begin with, as Appendix II shows fairly conclusively, at least since 1960-61, changes in agricultural production have exercised no significant influence on industrial growth. The possible reason for this has also been touched upon in that Appendix.

Secondly, slow agricultural growth would act as a decisive brake on industrial growth by generating inflation only within the parameters of a closed economy. The Indian planning model has been a closed one only where industry was concerned. In agriculture the government has consistently imported large quantities of food. In fact throughout the 1960's, and till 1975, around five per cent of the total foodgrains consumed in the country was imported. This was a *quarter* of the consumption in the towns. What is more, till 1972, the world price of foodgrains was well below prices in India. imports therefore moderated local inflationary tendencies, and if anything facilitated a larger volume of investment than would have been possible if this food had been produced domestically. In fact the collapse of the fourth Plan after 1972 occurred precisely because without cheap food imports this cushion vanished and the deficit borrowing and financing which had sustained investment in the first three years (1967-72) had to be abandoned. The causes of a low rate of saving and investment particularly after 1965, must therefore be sought elsewhere.

Industrialization could not proceed without a sufficient *availability* of food. If this food could not be grown it had to be imported. Thus what India could not have with slow agricultural growth was economic autarky. In focussing on slow agricultural growth, most Indian economists have drawn attention away from the real cause of stagnation in the Indian economy. This is the utter failure of the Central and state governments to exercise any effective control on their consumption expenditures. Although the combined revenues of the central and state governments rose from around 7 per cent of national income in 1954-55 to 19·2 per cent in 1974-75, the ratio of public saving to the GNP has risen only from 1 per cent to just over 2 per cent. It is a sobering thought that if government consumption had remained pegged at six per cent of the national product, the rate of saving in the economy in 1974-75 would have been around 24 per cent, a good deal higher than the 21 per cent projected by the planners two decades ago. The reasons for this monumental failure are once again more political than economic, and have been explored in Chapters 4 to 6.

NOTES

1 K.N. Raj attached this assumption in his Radhakrishnan Memorial lectures, Oxford University, April-May 1975.

Chapter 1: Appendix 2

The Relationship between Agricultural Production and Industrial Growth

THIS ASSERTION runs contrary to a widely held belief among Indian economists that industrial growth is closely related to the size of the harvest, and that there tends to be a spurt in industrial production some time after a rise in agricultural production (this time lag is necessary to allow the extra demand in the rural areas to make itself felt). The table below shows however, that in the 1960s and 1970s at any rate, there is no such observable relationship. In it the industrial index figures have been lagged by nine months. This is the correct period to take because the crop from a *kharif* (winter) harvest in, say, 1960–61 begins to come to the market late in October 1960 and the maximum arrival of grain occurs in November and December. The increase in rural incomes therefore occurs from November onwards, and should begin to affect the sale of industrial products and therefore entrepreneurs' production plans by January at the very latest. Thus the agricultural production index for the fiscal year 1960–61 (i.e. April 1st 1960 to March 31st 1961), has been correlated with the industrial production index for the calandar year 1961. This makes it possible to read directly across the lines. (The figures are all taken from the *Economic Survey* and the *RBI Currency and Finance Reports* for various years).

Table I
Index of Agricultural and Industrial Output
(Agricultural average, 1959-61 = 100)

1	2	3	4	5
	Index of Food grains	NFC (Non-Food Crops)	Total Agriculture Production	Industry (lagged 9 months) (1960 = 100)
1960–61	102.1	103.8	102.7	109.2 (1961)
1961–62	104.5	104.7	104.6	118.9 (1962)
1962–63	97.1	103.3	99.3	128.4 (1963)

1	2	3	4	5
	Index of Food grains	NFC (Non-Food) Crops	Total Agricultural Production	Industry (lagged 9 months) (1960 = 100)
1963–64	101.2	106.2	103.0	138.1 (1964)
1964–65	111.0	119.0	113.8	153.8 (1965)
1965–66	89.9	107.8	95.8	152.6 (1966)
1966–67	92.2	105.3	95.0	151.4 (1967)
1967–68	117.1	115.6	116.6	161.1 (1968)
1968–69	115.7	113.2	114.8	172.5 (1969)
1969–70	123.5	120.5	122.5	180.8 (1970)
1970–71	133.9	126.6	131.4	186.1 (1971)
1971–72	132.0	128.9	130.9	199.4 (1972)
1972–73	121.2	118.9	120.4	200.6 (1973)
1973–74	131.5	137.1	133.4	201.8 (1974)
1974–75	125.6	136.5	129.3	210.2 (1975)

A purely visual examination of the above table shows little apparent correlation between agricultural and industrial growth. Although agricultural output stagnated from 1960–61 to 1963–64, industry grew at a steady and high rate of between 7.5 and 8.8 per cent per year. In 1964–65 there was a very sharp jump in agricultural output, and admittedly a further rise in the already healthy rate of industrial growth.

The orthodox view of the relationship between the harvest and industrial production is perhaps most valid for 1966 and 1967, when the sharp decline in agricultural production of almost 18 per cent did cause a halt in industrial growth. But in view of the unprecedented droughts and misery of 1966 and 1967, a mere halt in industrial growth is at best weak evidence of such a relationship. On the contrary it shows just how large the change must be in agriculture to make a perceptible impact on industry. This is confirmed by the figures for the next six years. For although the large agricultural recovery of 1967–68 is accompanied by a very moderate industrial recovery in 1968, the slight decline in agriculture the next year is accompanied by an acceleration of industrial growth in 1969. Finally, the sharp fluctuations of harvest after 1970–71 are in no way reflected in the index of industrial production. Instead, industry once again recorded its largest increase in 1972, after a fractional decline in the harvest in 1971–72.

Regression analysis

To test whether industrial production is related to change in the harvest, a regression analysis was carried out of the annual change in industrial production, against the change in the output of (1) foodgrains (2) agricultural products other than foodgrains i.e. mainly agricultural raw materials and (3) total agricultural production.

Since the end of the third Plan had seen a marked decline in the tempo of investment in the economy a dummy variable was also introduced in order to neutralize the effect of the change, equal to 1 from 1961–62 to 1965–66 and equal to 0 thereafter.

Since the results showed a significant correlation between the dummy variable and the independent variable in all three equations, (T factors were 3.486, 3.269, and 3.539 respectively), this was justified.

However, in spite of this the results show no significant correlation between any of the three independent variables and the dependent variable. The T factors were 1.632 for foodgrains, 1.305 for agricultural production other than foodgrains, and 1.710 for total agricultural production. (To be significant the T factor should be 2 or more). The analysis therefore confirmed the impression obtained by the visual examination of the true series.

Alternative hypothesis

One possible explanation for this lack of correlation could be that the demand for industrial products is not distributed evenly throughout the rural population, but is concentrated in certain strata, notably the well-to-do farmers who have a net marketable surplus to sell. Among these in turn it is likely to be concentrated still more in the new breed of commercially minded farmer, who has irrigated his land and switched to high yielding seeds. Furthermore, the demand generated by such farmers, who have clearly been responsible for most of the increase in production since 1967–68, and provide the bulk of the marketable surplus, depends not on their output, but on their cash incomes. Since the demand

Table II

Changes in Output of Foodgrains and Industrial Production
(lagged nine months over the previous year)

Year	Index of foodgrains output (1959-61 = 100)	Index of Industrial Production (1960 = 100)
1961-62	+ 2.3	+ 8.9
1962-63	− 9.3	+ 8.0
1963-64	+ 4.2	+ 7.6
1964-65	+ 9.7	+ 11.4
1965-66	− 19.0	− 0.8
1966-67	+ 2.6	− 0.8
1967-68	+ 27.0	+ 6.4
1968-69	− 1.2	+ 7.1
1969-70	+ 6.7	+ 4.8
1970-71	+ 8.4	+ 2.9
1971-72	− 1.4	+ 7.1
1972-73	− 8.2	− 0.6
1973-74	+ 8.5	+ 0.6
1974-75	− 4.5	+ 4.2

for fodgrains is notoriously inelastic, the price of foodgrains in particular tends to rise disproportionately to the decline in the marketed surplus. This means that the cash income in the hands of the farmers increases in years of poor harvests. Had the rich farmers been the only purchasers of industrial products, this would be reflected in a rise in industrial production after a good harvest and a decline after a poor one. However, demand from the poorer segments of the rural population must not be wholly ignored. While this may not be large, the sheer weight of numbers of the rural small farmers, peasants and labourers offsets to some extent their paucity of purchasing power. Since all these segments tend to suffer in poor years and their demand goes down, this no doubt tends to counterbalance the rise in demand from the rich farmers.

What is more, the total demand for industrial products will be affected by the decline in the purchases of city dwellers who will now have to spend more on food and will have correspondingly less left to spend on industrial goods. This affect may not however be very large because the rationing system which distributes between 30 and 40 per cent of the total marketed surplus of food grains, shields the working class to a very large extent from the rise in prices. (To the extent that the government meets the cost of the subsidy from current savings in the public sector, by resorting to deficit financing, or by borrowing from the banking system, there will be a decline in investment. But the effect of this will be spread over several time periods, and will be reflected in a long period stagnation of industry rather than in year to year fluctuations of output).

Taking the three influences together, it is reasonable to suppose that in poor years the overall effect of the harvest on the demand for industrial products is likely to be fairly small. However, what is more important, it could easily be in the opposite from the expected direction, i.e. a poor harvest can lead to a rise in demand for industrial products.

A re-examination of the data relating changes in foodgrains production with industrial output (Table II) reveals the significance of features whose meaning was previously obscure. In 1966, industrial production fell fractionally by 0.8 per cent in the face of a 19 per cent drop in the output of foodgrains in 1965–66, because the decline in demand of the urban and rural poor overwhelmed the rise in demand of the rural rich. In 1968 by contrast the increase in demand for industrial products from the rural and urban poor seems to have overwhelmed any decline in demand from the rural rich. In view of the fact that output rose by an unprecedented 27 per cent, this is not surprising. Another factor in the situation may have been the arrival of the first of the big wheat crops on the market in March 1968, and the huge price support operation the government launched to prevent a collapse of prices. This ensured that the incomes of the rich farmers declined less than such a large increase in marketed surplus would have merited.

Thirdly, the tendency for food output and industrial production to move in opposite directions seems to be growing stronger. In the table given above this occurred in 6 out of 14 years. Thse are 1963, 1967, 1969, 1972, 1973, and 1975. In two other years (1971, 1974) large increases in food output caused only fractional increases in industrial production, and as mentioned before, in 1966 a very large drop in food production caused a negligible drop in industrial output. Thus after the end of the Third Plan, contrary movements in industrial and foodgrains output seem to have occurred in every year except 1966-68 (agriculture) and 1968 (industry). One reason for this could be the rapid increase in the buying power of the rural rich with the onset of the 'green revolution', and the growing impoverishment of both the urban and rural poor with the increasing inequality of income distribution.

A graphic plot of the above changes in food and industrial output after 1966, when the steady rise in public investment came to an end shows that, with the single exception of 1968, all the remaining eight observations are bunched loosely together almost parallel with the X-axis. This tends to confirm the hypothesis given above.

The key to the above hypothesis is the inelasticity of demand for agricultural products. In the above analysis I have concentrated on food grains because these make up 62 per cent of total agricultural output, because the demand for foodgrains is probably even more inelastic than for cash crops and because the major break-throughs in the late sixties have occured in the production of cereals. The following table is designed to test the validity of the surmise that elasticity of demand for foodgrains is indeed less than 1. In constructing it I have assumed (1) that the price of foodgrains depends on the increase in supply of money and the change in the output in the *previous twelve months*. The reasons for giving a time lag of one year between changes in the supply of money and rises in prices, instead of a more realistic nine months, is that data for calendar years is not readily available. In the same way, the correct time lag for the effect of the harvest on food prices is perhaps even shorter—perhaps no more than seven to eight months. This is because by September in any given year the quality of the monsoon and its probable effect on the main *kharif* crop are known and prices begin reacting in anticipation of the harvest.

But once again foodgrains price data from September to August was not readily available to the author at the time of writing.

TABLE III

	Change in price of foodgrains %	Increase in supply of money in previous year %	Net change %(2-1)	Change in output of foodgrains in previous year%	Ratio 3 to 4
	(1)	(2)	(3)	(4)	(5)
1966-67	18.5	8	10.5	−19.0	0.6
1967-68	24.9	8	16.9	+ 2.6	NA
1968-69	− 12.0	8	−20	+27	0.7
1969-70	3.6	8	− 4.4	− 1.2	NA
1970-71	− 0.7	12	−12.7	+ 6.7	1.8
1971-72	3.9	14	−10.1	+ 8.4	1.2
1972-73	15.2	13	2.2	− 1.4	1.6
1973-74	19.6	15	4.6	− 8.2	0.6
1974-75	35.4	6.5	28.9	+ 8.5	NA
1975-76	− 10.7	11.7	−22.4	+ 4.5	5.0
1976-77	− 12.1	21	−33.1	+21.1	1.6

Average change in food prices as a ratio of changes on food output = 1.6

In the above table the change in food prices attributable to the factors other than the supply of money has been in the opposite direction to changes in the output of foodgrains in seven out of the last eleven years. In these years the average change in foodgrains prices was 1.6 times the average change in output. The difference is sufficiently great to confirm the view that the elasticity of demand for food grains is less than 1.

Chapter 1: Appendix 3

Causes of the rise in the share of income accruing to the tertiary sector.

THE FIGURES QUOTED for India in the main text need to be interpreted with great caution. To begin with since the comparison is between single years, and not averages of two or three years, it is possible that one or other of the years was abnormal. Since the main source of abnormality in Indian conditions is likely to be the monsoon, to test the validity of the conclusion that the share of the tertiary sector has risen, it is necessary to eliminate the cause of monsoons as far as possible. This has been done below by extending the series back to 1950–51, and choosing years in the 1960s when the monsoons were good, (as they were in 1960–61).

Table I
Shares in NDP at Factor Cost
(Upperline in constant prices of 1948-49.
Lower line in 1960-61 prices).

Year	1950-51	1955-56	1960-61	1964-65	1967-68	1974-75
Secondary Sector	65.6	64.7	62.6	59.7	. . .	. . .
	75.0	74.4	71.1	73.6	67.7	64.6
	(1951-52)					
Tertiary Sector	34.4	35.3	37.4	40.3	. . .	. . .
	25.0	25.6	28.9	26.4	32.3	35.4
	(1951-52)					

Source: (a) In 1948-49 Prices: Reserve Bank of India Currency & Finance Report 1965-66.

(b) In 1960-61 Prices: National Accounts Statistics, Disaggregated tables 1960-61 to 1974-75. Govt. of India, Central Statistical Organisation.

The table given above shows clearly that the rise in the share of the tertiary sector started with planned development in 1950–51. But since it is not easy to obtain reliable statistics for the services sector it is unwise to read too much into small differences. The lower line of estimates for the years 1950–57 to 1964–65 which were compiled later, when more data was presumably available, seems to show that there was no significant change in the share of the tertiary sector during the first thirteen to fourteen years of planned development from 1951 to 1965. This is precisely the period during which the country experienced a satisfactory rate of growth. The decline in the share of agriculture and industry seems to have taken place after 1964–65, and if we omit 1965–66 and 1966–67, on account of the unprecedented droughts in those years which reduced the share of the. primary sector abnormally, it seems to have been fairly rapid till 1974–75.

Thus in the Indian experience, the share of the tertiary sector in the national product seems to have been inversely correlated with growth.

This is in stark opposition to orthodox economic teaching, based on the work of Colin Clark, Chenery, Kuznets and others, all of whom have maintained that economic growth leads to a rise in the share of the national product originating in the tertiary sector. They attribute this to the growth of specialization in all fields of economic activity; the increasing 'roundabout', less of production which makes it necessary for the producer to reach the buyer through a chain of intermediaries, and the higher rate of technological progress in agriculture and industry than in trade and services. Conversely therefore it is often assumed that a higher level of tertiary activity is an index; however imperfect, of a rising level and differentiation of economic activity.

A look at the experience of a number of other developing as well as advanced countries shows that this relationship does not hold true for several of them also. The table below gives the share of agriculture and industry in the gross domestic product of the non-government sector of the economy. (GDP at factor cost *less* product originating in the government sector i.e. administration, and sometimes, import duties and subsidies) for a fourth of the countries, classified by per capita incomes.

These figures confirm that economic growth by itself does not lead to a rise in the share of the tertiary sector in the national product, irrespective of whether the country enjoys a low, medium

Table II
Share of Agriculture and Industry in GDP

Income group	Country	Per Capita Income 1972	Share of Ind. & Agriculture in GDP in %		Annual average rate of growth (simple)
			1960	1974	
Low	India *(b)	99	73.0	69.4	3.4
	Pakistan	82	66.4 (1963)	62.4	7.0
	Indonesia	71	71.3	66.4 (1973)	5.8
	Sri Lanka	169	64.3 (1963)	57.6	5.3
	Iran	470	67.8	70.3 (1970)	13.6
	Columbia	328	61.4 (1969)	59.0	6.2
	Turkey	378	68.3	62.7	9.4
Medium	Korea	274	62.0	62.5	18.0
	Philippines	195	62.2	61.1	7.2
	Argentina	1138	54.1	58.5	6.2
	Canada		52.6	50.3	5.9
	U.S.A.		48.4	48.9 (1973)	5.4
High	France		64.1	64.5 (1970)	7.8
	Germany		65.1	65.4	6.0

Source: UN Year Book of National Accounts Statistics.
Development Cooperation 1973 (OECD).

Notes: (a) Figures in brackets indicate years other than the terminal year given at the top of columns.

*(b) These results differ from ones given in the text, because the product orginating in the government sector, i.e. expenditure on administration is excluded from the UN figures on which these calculations are based.

or high income. (Turkey is the only exception to this rule in the Table).

More significantly, the low income group has actually experienced a sharp rise in the share of the tertiary sector, even though, the countries in this group have experienced slower growth than the members of the other groups. This reinforces the suspicion that the rise in the share of tertiary sector incomes is inversely correlated with the rate of growth of product.

Comparison with **Kuznets'** findings

A close look at the statistics on which Kuznets based his conclusions shows that the main support for the thesis that the share of the tertiary sector rises with economic growth, comes not from his time period studies in Chapter 4 (Economic Growth of Nations. Bellknap, Harvard 1971, pages 144 to 148), but from his cross-section studies of the division of the national product in 1958 (Chapter 3, page 102).

Kuznets admits that on the basis of even cross-section data, the correlation between growth and the share of the tertiary sector is weak (page 106), but seems to hold for countries with less than a mean income of $221 per capita (in his tables). The above table casts some doubt even on this finding as, apart from India and Indonesia, among the poorest, and Canada and USA, among the richest, all the remaining countries show a fairly similar distribution of the national product between the various sectors.

Kuznets' conclusions about changes in the share of the various sectors in the national product receive relatively little support from his time period data. In the majority of the advanced countries, such as Belgium, the United Kingdom, Netherlands, Germany, Norway, Sweden, Canada and Australia, the share of the tertiary sector has been declining ever since 1850, 1870 or 1900. The share of the tertiary sector rises clearly only in the case of the USA, and, in the UK between 1801 and 1907.

Kuznets' remarks on the trends in the handful of developing countries for which he could get some figures are of greater interest. Lumping together industry and services he found it 'intriguing' that the share of agriculture fell even though per capita national product had not risen by very much (pages 154–156). His conclusion that this may reflect a decline in product per worker in agriculture, probably as a result of overcrowding, with some rise in real product in the industry and services sector, is not inconsistent with the finding reported above. However, the rise in the share of the *services* sector alone revealed by the above table shows that the relationship is a far more complex one.

Interpretation of the above results

Taken in conjunction with the very sharp increase in employment in the tertiary sector which is described in the main body of this chapter, the Indian experience backed by the above table suggests that in poor countries, when the growth rate slackens there is both a rise in the share of the tertiary sector and a fall in the product per capita in this sector. This happens probably because the surplus of job seekers tends to gravitate to trade and transport, or government and domestic service, as these areas as a rule require no investment and few artisanal or technical skills (particularly in the lowest categories of government service where expansion has been greatest). Very often the resulting decline in productivity is not reflected in the statistics of GNP in constant prices because many governments simply use the increase in employment in this sector as the index of the rise in product. This would lead to an apparent rise in the share of the tertiary sector. But to the extent that the rise in the share of the tertiary sector is genuine, i.e. occurs despite slow growth, even after adjustments have been made for the decline in productivity, it means that income earners in this sector have been at least partially successful in preventing an erosion of their real incomes by appropriating the output of other sectors. The capacity of governments to do this by pushing up their taxes needs no elaboration. But this can also happen in trade and transport in conditions of all pervasive scarcity. Indeed the inflow of job seekers into these sectors would soon stop if those who are employed in these areas had not been able, through tacit collusion, to expropriate a part of the product of other sectors by charging higher distribution margins on the goods handled and sold by them.

The one structural change in an economy which makes this possible, is a rising inequality in the distribution of income. For any given volume of income a more unequal distribution of income makes it possible for those who are growing richer to pay a higher service margin, while those who are growing poorer have to forgo purchasing an ever-widening range of commodities. In time therefore the pattern of production itself changes away from mass consumption goods with low profit and distribution margins to fancy goods and boutique clothes, imported luxuries and so on, on which the margins are high. Inequality is bred by shortages. Thus the rising share of the real product going to the tertiary sector can be traced in the final analysis to the emergence and growth of shortages in the economy. These shortages are themselves the effect of slow growth.

Appendix to Chapter III

The Relationship of Gold Prices in India to the Nature of the Harvest.

THE FACT that Indian farmers tend to 'invest' a part of their additional income from a good crop in the purchase of gold (mainly in the form of ornaments) and to sell these ornaments when the crops fail in order to keep them going until after the next monsoon is common knowledge. The insatiable demand for gold in rural India has been a lament of two generations of economists. Very recently, however, it has come to be regarded somewhat erroneously as a windfall—a ready-made way of converting foreign exchange reserves which are piling up with the Reserve Bank into rupee resources. (The budget for 1978–79 actually made a provision for the sale of an unspecified amount of gold from the confiscated stocks held by the Reserve Bank of India, to raise investible funds). But no attempt has so far been made to integrate this vast ebb and flow of gold out of the rural sector into a model designed to explain the behaviour of prices in the Indian economy.

To a large extent this is because a good part of the trading in gold takes place in the unorganized market, and is of a clandestine nature. Since economists often lapse into the belief that what they cannot see or measure does not exist, this trade and its impact on prices, has remained largely unexplored. But its importance should not be underestimated. As suggested in the text of Chapter 3, the trade in gold probably has a quite disproportionate effect on prices because nearly all of the annual increase in the demand for gold in the country is met from imports—smuggled no doubt, but imports nonetheless. Since the net additional demand for gold should be larger after a good harvest, and smaller after a poor one, a good harvest is deflationary not only because of the increased availability of food but also because the recipients of the additional

income transfer a not inconsiderable part of it abroad as payment
for smuggled gold.

.   In theory it should be possible to trace the surge of demand after
a good harvest and its decline after a poor one in the behaviour of
spot prices of gold in Bombay. However the actual task is bedevilled
by the existence of a large number of pitfalls. To begin with gold
is demanded not only by the farmers, but by the city dwellers and
by industry. The demand from the latter two sources not to be
seasonal. Again gold is demanded for a variety of purposes—as
an industrial input, as a store of wealth, or purely for ornamenta-
tion. Thus the effect of a good harvest on the demand for gold
may easily be masked by changes in demand on other counts.

On the supply side, the domestic price of gold is bound to be
affected by its international price. While this was virtually constant
till 1968, it has risen sharply after the breakdown of convertibility
at fixed exchange rates and has been subject to very sharp fluctuations particularly after 1971. Again, even under the system of fixed
exchange rates, the availability of gold for the 'free' market and
hence its price seems to have been related to the general price
level of other primary products. The reasons for this are not altogether clear to the writer, but the underlying trend in spot prices
in Bombay in the 'fifties and for most of the 'sixties has been similar
to the trend in world primary product prices.

Finally, and perhaps most important of all, no commodity is
as sensitive to political changes as gold. If a country goes to war,
the demand for gold is bound to shoot up. This seems to have
happened in India after the Indo-Pak war of 1965. Nor will the
price of gold be affected by wars in India alone. A major war
anywhere, or a spate of political unrest can send the demand for
gold up in the affected area and restrict the clandestine flow to
India. This seems to have happened after the Suez war in 1966,
and also after the June 1967 Arab-Israeli conflict. What is more,
since these occurred in an area that falls in the direct supply route
from Europe to Dubai (whence gold is smuggled to the Indian
subcontinent), there may also have been a disruption of supply.

The task of comparison is complicated further by a series of
discontinuities in the annual series of gold prices published by the
Reserve Bank of India. Till September 30, 1960, the price of gold

was quoted per tola (11.6638 grams). From October 1, it was quoted for ten grammes. From August 28, 1963 trading in gold above 14 carats was officially closed till November 9, 1966, and spot prices therefore related to 14 carat gold only. Small discontinuities also arise from quotations having been for Mysore gold till July 13, 1958, Abyssinian gold till July 1959, and gold bullion thereafter. The import duty on gold was also raised by a small amount in May 1957.

In addition to the above discontinuities the somewhat arbitary choice of a time lag of one financial year between the rise in agricultural production and the rise in spot prices of gold (the annual average of daily quotations has been taken) is also likely to blur the result to some extent. Since the *kharif* (autumn) harvest begins to come to the market between October and December, the farmers should start spending their incomes by January at the latest. This means that ideally the harvest data for a particular *crop year* (say April 1965 to March 1966) should be correlated with the average gold price in the succeeding calendar year (January to December 1966). But since the Reserve Bank publishes gold prices only for each fiscal year (April to March) there is no option but to take a time lag of one year instead of nine months.

To construct a continuous index for Bombay gold prices, two expedients were used. All prices per tola were converted to prices per 10 grammes by dividing them by 1.16638. For the years 1963–64 to 1966–67, the price of 14 carat gold was converted to the price for gold bullion by multiplying it with the ratio of the two prices in 1963–64 given by the Reserve Bank itself. This is somewhat arbitrary, but the best I could think of doing under the circumstances. The fact is that the gold control order was largely ineffective. Trading in gold bullion and the smuggling of gold bricks continued. Jewellers continued to make ornaments of higher than 14 carat gold, because there was a loophole conveniently left by the government which permitted such ornaments to be made provided the gold was obtained by melting down old ornaments. Thus transactions involving 14 carat gold represented only a small part of the total transactions in gold. Nonetheless it is assumed here that trends in this price relfected trends in the gold market as a whole.

Two sets of regressions were tried out with the available data. The first was a multivariate regression relating the annual change in the average spot price of gold in Bombay to (i) the international price of gold, (ii) the index of world prices of primary products, and (iii) the changes in the harvest in India in the previous year. This analysis was carried out for 1951–52 in 1974–75 with a dummy variable from 1968–69 to allow for the unfreezing of international prices in 1968. The analysis yielded a significant correlation with the international price of gold and primary products, but not with the size of the harvest, or with the dummy variable.

It was then decided to try a linear regression of the change in Bombay gold prices with the change in the harvest in the previous year from 1951–52 to 1971–72 (year ending 31st March 1972). The results with a T factor of 0.3806 showed that there was no significant correlation here either.

However a close look at the graphic plot of the observations (see chart below) revealed certain significant features: to begin with 13 out of eighteen readings (two observations could not be made because of the breaks in RBI gold data) were bunched together fairly tightly along a clearly defined slope which was easily visible to the naked eye. Four out of the remaining five for 1956–57, 1958–59, 1964–65 and 1969–70 were in an almost straight line of a very similar slope at gold prices around 15 per cent above those involved in the main group. The sole reading which lay completely outside these two groups was for 1967–68, in which a 11.98 per cent drop in harvest in the previous year was associated with a 7.8 per cent *rise* in gold prices.

To take the second group first, the nature of these observations leads one to ask whether any exogenous factor could have been operating on gold prices in these years, to push them up by such a sizeable amount.

A close look shows that one of these observations is of gold prices for 1956–57, while two others are for 1964–65 and 1969–70. The relationship between the first of these and the Suez crisis of 1956 seems fairly clear. The end of 1964–65 saw the beginning of the Indo-Pak war of 1965, with the Pakistani occupation of the Rann of Kutch in February 1965. The fact that gold prices rose by a further 12.99 per cent in 1965–66 inspite of a good harvest in 1964–65 seems to bear out the belief that the 1964–65, and 1965–66 prices reflect the effect of the Indo-Pak war. Thus one can tentatively ascribe two of these four observations to the effects of war and the disruption of contraband supplies of gold.

The third observation on the upper 'line' is for 1958-59. The only plausible explanation for this is the severe foreign exchange crisis of October 1957, a crisis that led to the imposition of a complete ban on the import of consumer goods and the tightening of controls on all other types of imports. Prior to 1957, in the last year of the First Plan (1955–56) the government had issued a very large number of import licences. These goods arrived in 1956–57 and 1957–58 and large inventories of luxury goods, intermediate goods and components were built up within the country. These were sold at a fantastic profit after the imposition of controls and it is more than likely that a fair portion of these vast specultive profits were converted into gold during 1958–59. Thus the rise in urban demand for gold may have completely overwhelmed the effect of the fall in the harvest.

Before looking at the fourth observation on the upper line, for 1969-70 we must examine two 'wild' observations. These for 1966–67 and 1968–69. Despite a 11.99 per cent fall in agricultural production in 1965–66, gold prices *rose* by 7.80 per cent in 1966–67. On the other hand an increase in the harvest of 15.81 per cent in 1967–68 caused a relatively small increase of 2.48 per cent in gold prices. The explanation of the first increase is almost certainly the devaluation of the rupee in June 1966.

In 1968–69 on the other hand the rise in gold prices was small but if we look at the next year we find that prices rose by 11.95 per cent although agricultural production increased by only 0.97 per cent. This is in fact the fourth observation on the "upper" line mentioned earlier, and it seems possible that for some reason a part of the effect of the bumper harvest of 1967–68 was carried over to 1969–70. However this alone is not sufficient to explain the rise in price in that year. The more important cause was no doubt the unfreezing of international gold prices and the resulting 16 per cent rise in international prices in the calendar year 1969.

In view of the strong evidence of exogenous factors at work—a war in 1956–57, 1964–65 and 1965–66, devaluation in 1966–67

and the rise in international gold prices in 1969–70, these observations were omitted and a second linear regression analysis was
carried out. (The observation for 1958–59 was not eliminated
because of the conjectural value of the explanation). The analysis
showed that there was a significant direct correlation between
gold prices and the size of the harvest. The coefficient of correlation
was 0.5077 and the T factor was 2.077.

TABLE I

Prices of Gold, International Price of Raw Materials and Index of Agricultural Production in India from 1950-51 to 1974-75

Year	Gold Prices Bombay Int.*	Int. Primary* Prod. Prices 1963-100	Agrl production (1959-62 average = 100)
1950–51	97.28	—	76.9
1951–52	93.51	34.70	77.6
1952–53	88.00	34.72	116	
1953–54	86.09	34.75	109	88.
1954–55	89.14	35.03	112	88.4
1955–56	82.18	35.10	109	88.5
1956–57	89.61	35.18	110	92.7
1957–58	92.99	35.24	111	88.2
1958–59	96.09	35.28	105	97.0
1959–60	103.71	35.28	102	96.0
1960–61	98.52	35.30	101	101.5
1961–62	103.95	35.13	99	102.5
1962–63	100.92	35.10	98	101.1
1963–64	96.00	35.09	102	103.1
1964–65	106.84	35.11	105	111.3
1965–66	120.72	35.14	105	98.0
1966–67	130.14	35.17	106	97.8
1967–68	182.61	35.19	103	113.2
1968–69	187.14	40.76	106	114.3
1969–70	209.51	38.89	109	120.5
1970–71	215.73	36.83	116	128.8
1971–72	233.46	43.34	123	128.3
1972–73	282.43	67.25	133	118.5
1973–74	430.66	118.92	116	131.3
1974–75	605.47	167.15	231	—

*Refers to calendar years 1951–1973.

TABLE II
**Changes in Agricultural Production in Relation to Changes in
Prices of Gold in Bombay**

Year	Change in Agr. Prod.	Change in Gold Price in Succeeding Year
1951–52	+ 1.20	− 5.90
1952–53	+ 5.30	− 2.17
1953–54	+ 7.40	+ 3.54
1954–55	+ 0.44	− 7.81
1955–56	+ 0.20	+ 9.04
1956–57	+ 9.67	+ 3.77
1957–58	− 4.81	+ 3.33
1958–59	+ 9.98	+ 7.93
1959–60	− 1.09	—
1960–61	+ 5.79	+ 5.51
1961–62	+ 0.93	− 2.91
1962–63	− 1.37	− 4.88
1963–64	+ 1.98	+12.91
1964–65	+ 8.00	+12.99
1965–66	−11.99	+ 7.80
1966–67	− 0.23	—
1967–68	+15.81	+ 2.48
1968–69	+ 0.97	+11.95
1969–70	+ 5.42	+ 2.97
1970–71	+ 6.89	+ 8.22

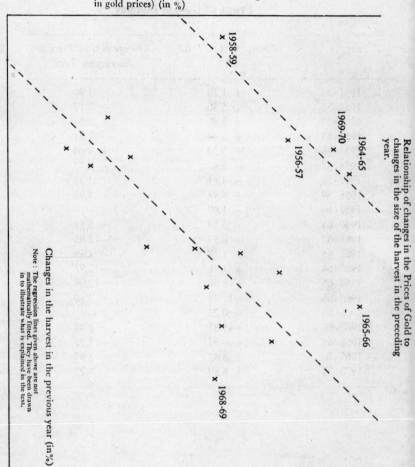

Annual changes in the average of Spot Prices of Gold in Bombay, (Years given refer to changes in gold prices) (in %)

Relationship of changes in the Prices of Gold to changes in the size of the harvest in the preceding year.

1958-59

1969-70

1964-65

1956-57

1965-66

1968-69

Changes in the harvest in the previous year (in %)

Note: The regression lines given above are not mathematically fitted. They have been drawn in to illustrate what is explained in the text.

Index